Presidents, First Ladies & First Family Trivia

George Washington through Donald Trump

Cheryl Pryor

Arlington & Amelia Publishers

ISBN-13:978-1-886541-28-3

ISBN-10:1-886541-28-0

FOR

CHELSEY MARIAH PRYOR

TABLE OF CONTENTS

Presidents & First Ladies of the United
States & Their Years In Office

Presidents

First Ladies

Children of the Presidents & First Ladies   321

Presidents & First Ladies
& Their Years In Office

Some presidents have been married more than once, but only the wives that were First Ladies are listed. Some wives however that were deceased previous to their husband's presidency are listed, as they are noted post-humously as First Ladies.

1. George Washington / Martha Dandridge Custis Washington   1789 – 1797

2. John Adams / Abigail Smith Adams 1797 – 1801

3. Thomas Jefferson / Martha Wayles Skelton Jefferson (deceased)   1801 – 1809

4. James Madison / Dolley Payne Todd Madison 1809 – 1817

5. James Monroe / Elizabeth Kortright Monroe   1817 – 1825

6. John Quincy Adams / Louisa Catherine Johnson Adams   1825 – 1829

7. Andrew Jackson / Rachel Donelson Jackson (deceased) 1829 – 1837

8. Martin Van Buren / Hannah Hoes Van Buren (deceased) 1837 – 1841

9. William Henry Harrison / Anna Tuthill Symmes Harrison   1841 – 1841

10. John Tyler / Letitia Christian Tyler (1st wife died during his presidency) Julia Gardiner Tyler (2nd wife he married during his presidency) 1841 – 1845

11. James Polk / Sarah Childress Polk   1845 – 1849

12. Zachary Taylor / Margaret "Peggy" Mackall Smith Taylor 1849 – 1850

13. Millard Fillmore / Abigail Powers Fillmore 1850 – 1853

14. Franklin Pierce / Jane Means Appleton Pierce   1853 – 1857

15. James Buchanan / Harriet Lane (niece of James Buchanan) 1857 – 1861

16. Abraham Lincoln / Mary Todd Lincoln 1861 – 1865

17. Andrew Johnson / Eliza McCardle Johnson 1865 – 1869

18. Ulysses S. Grant / Julia Dent Grant 1869 – 1877

19. Rutherford B. Hayes / Lucy Ware Webb Hayes 1877 – 1881

20. James Garfield / Lucretia Rudolph Garfield 1881 – 1881

21. Chester Arthur / Ellen Lewis Herndon Arthur 1881 – 1885

22. Grover Cleveland / Frances Folsom Cleveland 1885 – 1889

23. Benjamin Harrison / Caroline Lavinia Scott Harrison 1889 – 1893

24. Grover Cleveland / Frances Folsom Cleveland 1893 – 1897

25. William McKinley / Ida Saxton McKinley 1897 – 1901

26. Theodore Roosevelt / Edith Kermit Carow Roosevelt (2nd wife) 1901 – 1909

27. William H. Taft / Helen "Nellie" Herron Taft 1909 – 1913

28. Woodrow Wilson / Ellen Axson Wilson (1st wife- died during his presidency) Edith Bolling Galt Wilson (2nd wife – married during presidency) 1913 – 1921

29. Warren Harding / Florence Kling Harding 1921 – 1923

30. Calvin Coolidge / Grace Anna Goodhue Coolidge 1923 – 1929

31. Herbert Hoover / Lou Henry Hoover 1929 – 1933

32. Franklin D. Roosevelt / Anna "Eleanor" Roosevelt (her maiden name was also Roosevelt) Roosevelt 1933 – 1945

33. Harry Truman / Elizabeth "Bess" Virginia Wallace Truman 1945 – 1953

34. Dwight D. Eisenhower / Mamie Geneva Doud Eisenhower 1953 – 1961

35. John F. Kennedy / Jacqueline "Jackie" Lee Bouvier Kennedy 1961 – 1963

36. Lyndon B. Johnson / Claudia "Lady Bird" Taylor Johnson 1963 – 1969

37. Richard Nixon / Patricia "Pat" Ryan Nixon 1969 – 1974

38. Gerald Ford / Elizabeth "Betty" Bloomer Ford 1974 – 1977

39. Jimmy Carter / Rosalynn Smith Carter 1977 – 1981

40. Ronald Reagan / Nancy Davis Reagan (2nd wife) 1981 – 1989

41. George H.W. Bush / Barbara Pierce Bush 1989 – 1993

42. Bill Clinton / Hillary Rodham Clinton 1993 – 2001

43. George W. Bush / Laura Welch Bush 2001 – 2009

44. Barack Obama / Michelle LaVaughn Robinson Obama 2009 – 2017

45. Donald Trump / Melania Knavs Trump (3rd wife)   2017 - ?

Presidents

1

Presidential Campaigns & Elections

Answers are given on page 4.

1. Which president, while campaigning for the presidency, made the statement that he had campaigned in fifty-seven states with one state left to go?

    A. George W. Bush   *C. Jimmy Carter*

    B. Barack Obama   *D. Bill Clinton*

2. Who was the only president elected by a unanimous electoral vote?

    A. George Washington   *C. Thomas Jefferson*

    B. John Adams   *D. Franklin D. Roosevelt*

3. Who was also running on the ballot for America's first president, other than George Washington?

    A. John Adams   *C. Alexander Hamilton*

    B. Thomas Jefferson   *D. Samuel Adams*

4. Which president's campaign was not only entertaining, but shocking

and controversial where he, a billionaire businessman and real estate magnate and *not* a politician, stunned the establishment when he beat all seventeen of his primary opponents and went on to win the presidency to win against his Democratic nominee who was considered a shoo-in for the win?

A. *Abraham Lincoln*   C. *Herbert Hoover*

B. *John F. Kennedy*   D. *Donald Trump*

5. Which president helped fund his first political campaign from money he won playing poker while in the Navy?

A. *Jimmy Carter*   C. *Richard Nixon*

B. *George H.W. Bush*   D. *Dwight D. Eisenhower*

6. Which president took his oath of office privately because of turmoil over his disputed election?

A. *Rutherford B. Hayes*   C. *Andrew Jackson*

B. *James Garfield*   D. *Warren Harding*

7. When this president ran for a second term he received 525 out of 538 electoral votes and carried 49 out of 50 states – *the largest number ever won*. Who was he?

A. *George Washington*   C. *Thomas Jefferson*

B. *John F. Kennedy*   D. *Ronald Reagan*

8. Which president during his campaign threatened to "lock her up" referring to his opponent a former first lady?

A. Barack Obama   C. Donald Trump

B. George W. Bush   D. Bill Clinton

9. Which president won the Electoral College vote in one of the closest and most controversial elections in America's history? It took over a month of recounts from Florida's voters before the winner was announced. He was declared president, even though his opponent had more popular votes.

A. Donald Trump   C. Ronald Reagan

B. George W. Bush   D. Richard Nixon

10. Which president won his presidential election by 61% of the popular vote, the largest margin of victory in history?

A. Lyndon B. Johnson   C. Ronald Reagan

B. John F. Kennedy   D. Bill Clinton

11. Expecting to lose the election after the first returns came in, what president went to bed thinking he had lost the election? He ended up winning the election with the final count being 185 to 184.

A. Harry Truman   C. Warren Harding

B. John Tyler   D. Rutherford B. Hayes

12. Which president and vice-president never met until after their election?

A. Washington & Adams   C. Taylor & Filllmore

B. Harrison & Tyler   D. Garfield & Arthur

Answers

Chapter 1 – Presidential Campaigns & Elections

1. B - Barack Obama

That's right, he said fifty-seven states with one left to go.

2. A - George Washington

3. A - John Adams

4. D - Donald Trump

5. C - Richard Nixon

6. A - Rutherford B. Hayes

7. D - Ronald Reagan

8. C - Donald Trump

9. B - George W. Bush

10. A - Lyndon B. Johnson

11. D - Rutherford B. Hayes

12. C – Taylor & Fillmore

2

Before And After Their Presidential Administrations

Answers are given on pages 13 - 15.

1. Which president was a U.S. minister to the Netherlands during one presidential administration, minister to Prussia during a different administration, and ambassador to the Russian court of Czar Alexander I during yet another administration, and then off to Great Britain, all before becoming president himself?

A. John Quincy Adams

B. Thomas Jefferson

C. James Madison

D. Rutherford B. Hayes

2. Which president in the days before his presidency was a reality TV star?

A. Ronald Reagan

B. Gerald Ford

C. Donald Trump

D. George W. Bush

3. During his career in the Navy five of his seven years included submarine duty. Who was he?

A. *Richard Nixon*   C. *John F. Kennedy*

B. *George H.W. Bush*   D. *Jimmy Carter*

4. Who was the only American president to have headed two branches of government – executive and judicial?

A. *William McKinley*   C. *Woodrow Wilson*

B. *William Howard Taft*   D. *Rutherford B. Hayes*

5. Which president was an inventor, and many of his inventions can be seen at his home today which is open to visitors?

A. *Herbert Hoover*   C. *Calvin Coolidge*

B. *James Garfield*   D. *Thomas Jefferson*

6. Which president wrote nine of the ten amendments known as the Bill of Rights?

A. *Thomas Jefferson*   C. *James Monroe*

B. *James Madison*   D. *John Quincy Adams*

7. Who were the only two signers of the Declaration of Independence to become president?

A. *Adams & Jefferson*   C. *Washington & Adams*

B. *Washington & Jefferson*   D. *Jefferson & Madison*

8. He was in China during the Boxer Rebellion where he organized help

for foreigners and years later when WWI began he helped Americans who were in Europe. This humanitarian, years later would also help Belgians after the intrusion of German troops. Who was he?

A. John Quincy Adams   C. James Buchanan

B. William H. Taft   D. Herbert Hoover

9. Which president, after retirement, penned his memoirs while suffering from throat cancer so his wife would be financially stable?

A. Ulysses S. Grant   C. John Adams

B. Zachary Taylor   D. Franklin D. Roosevelt

10. As a delegate to the Constitutional Convention in 1787, which president earned the title 'Father of the Constitution'?

A. Thomas Jefferson   C. George Washington

B. James Monroe   D. James Madison

11. Which president was an actor before he was president?

A. Ronald Reagan   C. George W. Bush

B. John F. Kennedy   D. Donald Trump

12. Before he became president he was promoted to general of the army. He was the first commander since George Washington to hold that rank. Who was he?

A. Dwight D. Eisenhower   C. Ulysses S. Grant

B. Zachary Taylor   D. Andrew Jackson

13. As a five year old child his father took him to visit President Grover Cleveland who told him, "I am making a strange wish for you. It is that you may never be president of the United States." Years later, that's exactly what he became. Who was he?

    A. Franklin D. Roosevelt   C. William Taft

    B. Herbert Hoover   D. John F. Kennedy

14. School officials considered this future president a discipline problem and went so far as to write to his father urging him to keep his son home. Who was he?

    A. James Buchanan   C. Franklin D. Roosevelt

    B. Abraham Lincoln   D. Andrew Johnson

15. Before he became president he served in the navy. His boat was rammed and he swam to safety and towed an injured man by his life jacket strap with his teeth. He scratched a message on a coconut shell to insure their rescue. Who was he?

    A. George H.W. Bush   C. Richard Nixon

    B. John F. Kennedy   D. Jimmy Carter

16. Which president worked as a cattle rancher?

    A. Ronald Reagan   C. Grover Cleveland

    B. Gerald Ford   D. Theodore Roosevelt

17. He, along with the U.S. minister to France, actually approved and signed the Louisiana Purchase agreement. Who was he?

A. *Thomas Jefferson*   C. *James Monroe*

B. *James Madison*   D. *John Adams*

18. Which president worked as a fashion model previous to becoming president?

A. *George W. Bush*   C. *Barack Obama*

B. *Gerald Ford*   D. *Ronald Reagan*

19. His work after his presidency earned him more respect than his presidential years. His later works include humanitarian works such as working with Habitat For Humanity. Who was he?

A. *Jimmy Carter*   C. *George W. Bush*

B. *Richard Nixon*   D. *Herbert Hoover*

20. Which president worked as a park ranger at Yellowstone National Park feeding the bears?

A. *Ronald Reagan*   C. *Gerald Ford*

B. *Franklin D. Roosevelt*   D. *Theodore Roosevelt*

21. On an average he owned about two hundred slaves any given year. In his lifetime he freed only two of his slaves and only five more in his will. Who was he?

A. *George Washington*   C. *John Tyler*

B. *James Madison*   D. *Thomas Jefferson*

22. Which president, after he retired, went on an African safari and brought back plant samples and animals for the Smithsonian?

    A. Theodore Roosevelt   C. Ulysses S. Grant

    B. Chester Arthur   D. Grover Cleveland

23. Which president was a school teacher before he was president?

    A. Millard Fillmore   C. Andrew Johnson

    B. Lyndon B. Johnson   D. Harry Truman

24. Which president made a major contribution to the ratification of the Constitution by writing The Federalist Papers?

    A. James Madison   C. Thomas Jefferson

    B. John Adams   D. John Quincy Adams

25. An Indian chieftain, Tecumseh, began an Indian confederation to prevent settlers from coming in and taking more of their land. This future president's troops killed Tecumseh and afterward the Indians scattered, no longer causing a serious threat. Who was he?

    A. Andrew Johnson   C. Andrew Jackson

    B. Zachary Taylor   D. William Henry Harrison

26. Which president was victim to a Wall Street scam leaving him and his wife in financial ruin?

    A. Donald Trump   C. George H.W. Bush

    B. Rutherford B. Hayes   D. Ulysses S. Grant

27. When he was in the Navy, one of the jobs of this future president was cleaning the toilets. Who was he?

    A. Jimmy Carter   *C. George W. Bush*

    B. Dwight D. Eisenhower   *D. Calvin Coolidge*

28. In his college days, which president was offered professional contracts with the Green Bay Packers and the Detroit Lions but turned them both down to study law?

    A. Ronald Reagan   *C. Gerald Ford*

    B. George H.W. Bush   *D. George W. Bush*

29. At one time he had to resort to selling firewood on the street to support his family. Who was he?

    A. Abraham Lincoln   *C. John Tyler*

    B. Ulysses S. Grant   *D. Zachary Taylor*

30. He was the only five star general to become president. Who was he?

    A. George Washington   *C. Theodore Roosevelt*

    B. William Henry Harrison   *D. Dwight D. Eisenhower*

31. He studied law under Thomas Jefferson who would become his mentor. Who was he?

    A. John Quincy Adams   *C. John Tyler*

    B. James Monroe   *D. Franklin Pierce*

32. He was the author of the Declaration of Independence. Who was he?

A. Thomas Jefferson   C. James Madison

B. John Adams   D. James Monroe

33. Which former president has been accused of being involved in a "pay-to-play" scheme in which foreign governments could donate money to the president's foundation in exchange for beneficial treatment from the government influenced by the former president and former first lady who at the time was the Secretary of State?

A. Barack Obama   C. Bill Clinton

B. Richard Nixon   D. George H.W. Bush

34. Which president was also a Founding Father, a vice-president to another president, and had a son who would also become president, and was also a descendant of Puritan colonists?

A. James Madison   C. James Monroe

B. Thomas Jefferson   D. John Adams

35. Which president was an accomplished pianist who played for a White House gathering when Kennedy was president?

A. Harry Truman   C. Dwight D. Eisenhower

B. Calvin Coolidge   D. Lyndon B. Johnson

Answers

Chapter 2 ▬ Before And After Their Presidential Administrations

1. A - John Quincy Adams

2. C - Donald Trump

3. D - Jimmy Carter

4. B - William Howard Taft

5. D - Thomas Jefferson

6. B - James Madison

7. A - John Adams & Thomas Jefferson

8. D - Herbert Hoover

9. A - Ulysses S. Grant

10. D - James Madison

11. A - Ronald Reagan

While technically you could also say Donald Trump was an actor as he acted in one movie which was a flop and he also starred in a reality show, Ronald Reagan was a professional actor acting in over a dozen movies.

12. C- Ulysses S. Grant

13. A - Franklin D. Roosevelt

14. A - James Buchanan

15. B - John F. Kennedy

16. D - Theodore Roosevelt

17. C- James Monroe

He was sent to France by President Thomas Jefferson to help negotiate the sale of the Port of Orleans. Once arriving in France Monroe learned that Napoleon Bonaparte, to help finance his war in Europe, was willing to sell the entire Louisiana Territory. Not having time to seek presidential approval Monroe and Livingston (U.S. minister to France) signed the agreement themselves. This doubled the size of the U.S.

18. B - Gerald Ford

19. A - Jimmy Carter

20. C - Gerald Ford

21. D - Thomas Jefferson

* Each of these slaves were members of Sally Hemings family, a slave that he had children with that has been proved through DNA testing.*

22. A - Theodore Roosevelt

23. B - Lyndon B. Johnson

24. A - James Madison

25. D. William Henry Harrison

Tecumsch was a Shawnee leader.

26. D - Ulysses S. Grant

27. A - Jimmy Carter

28. C - Gerald Ford

29. B - Ulysses S. Grant

30. D - Dwight D. Eisenhower

He retired to a home overlooking the battlefield at Gettysburg, Pennsylvania.

31. B - James Monroe

32. A - Thomas Jefferson

33. C - Bill Clinton

34. D - John Adams

35. A - Harry Truman

3

Which President Am I

Answers are given on pages 25 - 27.

1. The terrorist bombing at the Boston Marathon occurred during my presidency. Who am I?

   A. Bill Clinton   *C. George W. Bush*

   B. Barack Obama   *D. Donald Trump*

2. His time of presidency was termed the "Era of Good Feelings." Which president was he?

   A. George Washington   *C. James Monroe*

   B. Abraham Lincoln   *D. Ronald Reagan*

3. The collapse of communism in the Soviet Union occurred while I was president. Who am I?

   A. Ronald Reagan   *C. Harry Truman*

   B. George H. W. Bush   *D. Bill Clinton*

4. I was president during the covert operation that led to the killing of

Osama bin Laden. Who am I?

   A. George H.W. Bush   *C. George W. Bush*

   B. Bill Clinton   *D. Barack Obama*

5. The spread of communism was a threat during which president's second term of office?

   A. Harry Truman   *C. Franklin D. Roosevelt*

   B. Dwight D. Eisenhower   *D. John F. Kennedy*

6. Which president could write Greek with one hand while writing Latin with the other hand at the same time?

   A. Rutherford B. Hayes   *C. Chester Arthur*

   B. James Garfield   *D. Franklin D. Roosevelt*

7. Which president believed in the power of prayer and proclaimed July 4, 1952 to be the first annual day of prayer?

   A. Abraham Lincoln   *C. Harry Truman*

   B. Woodrow Wilson   *D. Jimmy Carter*

8. Which president was the only president to resign?

   A. William Henry Harrison   *C. Grover Cleveland*

   B. Ulysses S. Grant   *D. Richard Nixon*

9. The beginning of America's worst financial crisis since the Great

Depression began during his presidency. Which president was it?

A. Franklin D. Roosevelt   C. Herbert Hoover

B. Jimmy Carter   D. George W. Bush

10. The stock market crash (of 1929) happened during whose presidency which brought about the Great Depression?

A. Herbert Hoover   C. William H. Taft

B. Andrew Johnson   D. Franklin D. Roosevelt

11. Which president served on the First Continental Congress and helped draft the Declaration of Independence? He was a vice-president and a president. He earned a master's degree at Harvard. He was proved to be a patriot. He represented the British soldiers who were on trial for the Boston Massacre; even though others resented his decision to do so, he did this because of his strong belief that every person deserves a defense.

A. George Washington   C. Thomas Jefferson

B. John Adams   D. James Monroe

12. Who was president at the time suicide bombers killed over two hundred Americans when they attacked the Marine barracks in Beirut?

A. Ronald Reagan   C. George H. W. Bush

B. George W. Bush   D. Bill Clinton

13. Whcih president introduced the Bill of Rights and the first ten Amendments to the Constitution?

A. *John Adams*   C. *Thomas Jefferson*

B. *James Madison*   D. *John Quincy Adams*

14. Which president from the moment he took the oath of office was threatened by the left of impeachment? One reason given is they stated he colluded with the Russian government to meddle with the U.S.'s presidential election, even though there has been no evidence of him having done so?

A. *Lyndon B. Johnson*   C. *Donald Trump*

B. *John F. Kennedy*   D. *Bill Clinton*

15. Which president was the only twentieth century president who did not attend college?

A. *Barack Obama*   C. *Ronald Reagan*

B. *Lyndon B. Johnson*   D. *Harry Truman*

16. Which president met with Attorney General Loretta Lynch of the Justic Department on an airport tarmac when his wife the First Lady was under investigation, causing American citizens to lose all confidence in the justice system being unbiased in the investigation?

A. *Bill Clinton*   C. *Donald Trump*

B. *John F Kennedy*   D. *George H.W. Bush*

17. Who was the first president to be assassinated?

A. *James Garfield*   C. *John F. Kennedy*

B. *Abraham Lincoln*   D. *William McKinley*

18. Which president was looked upon as a traitor because he joined the Confederacy - he was the only president to have done so?

A. John Tyler

C. Andrew Jackson

B. Zachary Taylor

D. Andrew Johnson

19. Who was president during the 9/11 terrorist attacks?

A. Barack Obama

C. Jimmy Carter

B. George W. Bush

D. Bill Clinton

20. Which president was the grandson of the 9th president and also became president himself?

A. John Quincy Adams

C. Lyndon B. Johnson

B. George H.W. Bush

D. Benjamin Harrison

21. While he was president there was no vice-president.

A. George Washington

C. Chester Arthur

B. Andrew Johnson

D. Lyndon B. Johnson

22. In the final year of his presidency the stock market plunged and the housing and banking industries were in a mess. Who was he?

A. Franklin D. Roosevelt

C. Jimmy Carter

B. George W. Bush

D. Herbert Hoover

23. Which president was a direct descendant of William Brewster, the

Pilgrim leader who arrived on the Mayflower?

A. Zachary Taylor   *C. John Adams*

B Franklin Pierce   *D. William McKinley*

24. Which president was the son of Irish immigrants?

A. John Adams   *C. Millard Fillmore*

B. Andrew Jackson   *D. John F. Kennedy*

25. Which president banished alcohol from the White House?

A. Ulysses S. Grant   *C. James Buchanan*

B. Woodrow Wilson   *D. Rutherford B. Hayes*

26. Who was president when the *'Star Spangled Banner'* became our national anthem?

A. Herbert Hoover   *C. Franklin Pierce*

B. Abraham Lincoln   *D. Chester Arthur*

27. Which president believed the president was 'a steward to the people' and that it was his place to take action for the good of the public?

A. Abraham Lincoln   *C. Theodore Roosevelt*

B. Franklin D. Roosevelt   *D. Jimmy Carter*

28. After promising no new taxes in his presidential campaign which president lost the support of many people when he did indeed raise tax

revenues?

A. George H.W. Bush

C. Barack Obama

B. Richard Nixon

D. Harry Truman

29. His second term as president began with the worst financial crisis in U.S. History.

A. Franklin D. Roosevelt

C. Herbert Hoover

B. Grover Cleveland

D. Barack Obama

30. Which two presidents were impeached by Congress, but not removed from office?

A. R. Nixon & B. Clinton

C. A. Johnson & R. Nixon

B. A. Johnson & B. Clinton

D. R. Nixon & D. Trump

31. Included in which president's library is a graffiti covered section of the Berlin Wall donated to him by the people of Berlin?

A. Franklin D. Roosevelt

C. Ronald Reagan

B. Dwight D. Eisenhower

D. Harry Truman

32. Which president spoke to the public on the radio which were called "Fireside Chats?"

A. Theodore Roosevelt

C. Warren Harding

B. Calvin Coolidge

D. Franklin D. Roosevelt

33. During his presidency the U.S. enjoyed peace and economic well-being, more so than at any other time in history. Who was he?

A. Bill Clinton

C. Barack Obama

B. Ronald Reagan

D. Richard Nixon

34. He was one of the American diplomats sent to negotiate the Treaty of Paris which ended the Revolutionary War and recognized American independence. Which president is he?

A. John Adams

C. John Quincy Adams

B. Thomas Jefferson

D. James Madison

35. Which president was originally a liberal Democrat, but ran for the presidency as a conservative Republican?

A. Barack Obama

C. Ronald Reagan

B. Benjamin Harrison

D. Abraham Lincoln

36. Which president killed a man in a duel who dishonored his wife?

A. Martin Van Buren

C. James Polk

B. James Garfield

D. Andrew Jackson

37. After being vice-president for only three months and after only meeting with the president a few times he became president himself. Do you know who he is?

A. Andrew Johnson

C. Theodore Roosevelt

B. Chester Arthur

D. Harry Truman

38. Which president was criticized for his slow response and not doing enough for the victims of Hurricane Katrina?

A. Lyndon B. Johnson

C. George W. Bush

B. Ronald Reagan

D. Barack Obama

39. Which president was fluent in seven languages?

A. John Quincy Adams

C. Woodrow Wilson

B. William H. Taft

D. Warren Harding

40. Which president when he was a child almost choked to death on a peach pit? His mother saved his life by forcing it down his throat with her fingers.

A. Rutherford B. Hayes

C. Warren Harding

B. Harry Truman

D. George W. Bush

Answers

Chapter 3 - Which President Am I

1. B - Barack Obama

2. C - James Monroe

3. B - George H.W. Bush

4. D - Barack Obama

5. A - Harry Truman

6. B - James Garfield

7. C - Harry Truman

8. D - Richard Nixon

Why did he resign? He resigned rather than face an impeachment trial over Watergate.

9. D - George W. Bush

10. A - Herbert Hoover

11. B - John Adams

12. A - Ronald Reagan

13. B - James Madison

14. C - Donald Trump

15. D - Harry Truman

16. A – Bill Clinton

17. B - Abraham Lincoln

18. A- John Tyler

19. B - George W. Bush

20. D - Benjamin Harrison

21. C - Chester Arthur

President Arthur assumed office at the death of President Garfield. Arthur requested a Senate special session. to ensure that the Senate had legal authority to convene immediately and choose a Senate president pro tempore, who would be able to assume the presidency if Arthur himself died during his administration.

22. B - George W. Bush

23. A - Zachary Taylor

24. B - Andrew Jackson

There were 17 Presidents that have all or part of their ancestry that traces back to Ireland. Three of the presidents were sons of immigrants.

25. D - Rutherford B. Hayes

26. A - Herbert Hoover

27. C - Theodore Roosevelt

28. A - George H.W. Bush

29. B - Grover Cleveland

30. B - Andrew Johnson, Bill Clinton

Richard Nixon resigned before he could be impeached, so you can't count him.

31. C - Ronald Reagan

32. D - Franklin D. Roosevelt

33. A - Bill Clinton

34. A or B - John Adams or Thomas Jefferson, either or both is correct

The Treaty of Paris negotiated between the colonies and Great Britain ended the Revolutionary War and recognized American independence. Five men had been commissioned to negotiate the treaty. These men were: John Adams, Ben Franklin, John Jay, Thomas Jefferson, and Henry Laurens. The negotiations were completed by John Adams, Ben Franklin, and John Jay. Henry Laurens had been captured en route by the British and Thomas Jefferson left the colonies too late to be a part of the negotiations.

35. C - Ronald Reagan

36. D - Andrew Jackson

37. D - Harry Truman

38. C - George W. Bush

39. A - John Quincy Adams

40. B - Harry Truman

4

Presidential Quotes

Answers are given on pages 44 - 47.

Name the president who is known to have said the statement below.

1. "Nobody cares how much you know, until they know how much you care."

   A. Theodore Roosevelt   *C. James Garfield*

   B. Donald Trump   *D. Herbert Hoover*

2. "Change will not come if we wait for some other person, or if we wait for some other time. We are the ones we've been waiting for. We are the change that we seek."

   A. Abraham Lincoln   *C. Ronald Reagan*

   B. George W. Bush   *D. Barack Obama*

3. "There are no adequate substitutes for father, mother, and children bound together in a loving commitment to nurture and protect. No

government, no matter how well-intentioned, can take the place of the family in the scheme of things."

A. Ronald Reagan   C. Gerald Ford

B. Bill Clinton   D. Harry Truman

4. "I have never been hurt by what I have not said."

A. Dwight D. Eisenhower   C. Richard Nixon

B. Calvin Coolidge   D. Ronald Reagan

5. "This is more work than in my previous life."

A. Ulysses S. Grant   C. Donald Trump

B. George W. Bush   D. Warren Harding

6. "A little rebellion now and then is a good thing, as necessary in the political world as storms in the physical."

A. Thomas Jefferson   C. Zachary Taylor

B. Warren Harding   D. John Adams

7. "In this present crisis, government is not the solution to our problems; government is the problem."

A. John Adams   C. William Henry Harrison

B. Gerald Ford   D. Ronald Reagan

8. "We Americans have no commission from God to police the world."

A. Benjamin Harrison   C. George H.W. Bush

B. Woodrow Wilson   D. Donald Trump

9. "That's the good thing about being president, I can do whatever I want."

A. George W. Bush   C. Calvin Coolidge

B. Barack Obama   D. Donald Trump

10. "It takes a great man to be a good listener."

A. Ronald Reagan   C. Abraham Lincoln

B. Herbert Hoover   D. Calvin Coolidge

11. "Speak softly, and carry a big stick."

A. Theodore Roosevelt   C. Lyndon B. Johnson

B. Herbert Hoover   D. William McKinley

12. "Trust, but verify."

A. James Polk   C. Ronald Reagan

B. James Garfield   D. George H.W. Bush

13. "We did not come to fear the future. We came here to shape it."

A. Barack Obama   C. John F. Kennedy

B. Benjamin Harrison   D. Grover Cleveland

14. "Freedom is never more than one generation away from extinction. We didn't pass it to our children in the blood stream. It must be fought for, protected, and handed on for them to do the same."

A. John Adams   *C. Ronald Reagan*

B. Thomas Jefferson   *D. John F. Kennedy*

15. "If Tyranny and Oppression came to this land, it will be in the guise of fighting a foreign enemy."

A. James Madison   *C. George H.W. Bush*

B. John Quincy Adams   *D. Franklin D. Roosevelt*

16. "There is nothing stable but Heaven and the Constitution."

A. Abraham Lincoln   *C. Thomas Jefferson*

B. James Buchanan   *D. Chester Arthur*

17. "Be courteous to all but intimate with few, and let those few be well tried before you give them your confidence; true friendship is a plant of slow growth."

A. George Washington   *C. Ronald Reagan*

B. Rutherford B. Hayes   *D. Woodrow Wilson*

18. "Do I not destroy my enemies when I make them my friends?"

A. James Madison   *C. Grover Cleveland*

B. Martin Van Buren   *D. Abraham Lincoln*

19. "When even one American who has done nothing wrong - is forced by fear to shut his mind and close his mouth – then all Americans are in peril."

    A. Thomas Jefferson   *C. Theodore Roosevelt*

    B. Harry Truman   *D. Donald Trump*

20. "Only if you have been in the deepest valley, can you ever know how magnificent it is to be on the highest mountain."

    A. Abraham Lincoln   *C. Andrew Johnson*

    B. Harry Truman   *D. Richard Nixon*

21. "The only man who makes no mistake is the man who does nothing."

    A. Zachary Taylor   *C. Theodore Roosevelt*

    B. Grover Cleveland   *D. Donald Trump*

22. "Our Constitution was made only for a moral and religious people. It is wholly inadequate to the government of any other."

    A. James Monroe   *C. Millard Fillmore*

    B. John Adams   *D. Harry Truman*

23. "Prosperity cannot be restored by raids upon the Public Treasury."

    A. Herbert Hoover   *C. Donald Trump*

    B. James Monroe   *D. Barack Obama*

24. "Those who want the government to regulate matters of the mind and spirit are like men who are so afraid of being murdered that they commit suicide to avoid assassination."

A. James Madison   *C. William H. Taft*

B. Harry Truman   *D. Herbert Hoover*

25. "Every immigrant who comes here should be required within five years to learn English or leave the country."

A. Calvin Coolidge   *C. Theodore Roosevelt*

B. Donald Trump   *D. Franklin D. Roosevelt*

26. "Let your heart feel for the afflictions and distress of everyone, and let your hand give in proportion to your purse."

A. George Washington   *C. Ronald Reagan*

B. Herbert Hoover   *D. Franklin Pierce*

27. "I am proud to be the first American president to come to Kenya – and of course; I'm the first Kenyan-American to be president of the United States."

A. James Monroe   *C. Warren Harding*

B. Andrew Jackson   *D. Barack Obama*

28. "Always give your best, never get discouraged, never be petty; always remember, others may hate you. Those who hate you don't win unless you hate them. And then you destroy yourself."

A. George W. Bush   C. John F. Kennedy

B. Richard Nixon   D. John Tyler

29. "That government is best which governs the least, because it's people discipline themselves."

A. Donald Trump   C. Thomas Jefferson

B. Ronald Reagan   D. Theodore Roosevelt

30. "Blessed are the young; for they shall inherit the national debt."

A. Herbert Hoover   C. Barack Obama

B. George W. Bush   D. Richard Nixon

31. "Four score and seven years ago our fathers brought forth on this continent a new nation, conceived in Liberty, and dedicated to the proposition that all men are created equal."

A. John F. Kennedy   C. Barack Obama

B. James Buchanan   D. Abraham Lincoln

32. "A government big enough to give you everything you want, is a government big enough to take from you everything you have."

A. Barack Obama   C. John F. Kennedy

B. Gerald Ford   D. Lyndon B. Johnson

33. "Honest conviction is my courage, the Constitution is my guide."

A. Andrew Johnson   C. James Monroe

B. Ronald Reagan   D. Richard Nixon

34. "Office holders are the agents of the people, not their masters."

A. Woodrow Wilson   C. Jimmy Carter

B. Grover Cleveland   D. James Garfield

35. During his campaign for president he repeatedly told voters: "I'll never tell a lie."

A. George H.W. Bush   C. Jimmy Carter

B. Barack Obama   D. Richard Nixon

36. "It is my conviction that the fundamental trouble with the people of the United States is that they have gotten too far away from Almighty God."

A. Ronald Reagan   C. Rutherford B. Hayes

B. James Polk   D. Warren Harding

37. "Read my lips: No new taxes."

A. Bill Clinton   C. George H.W. Bush

B. Jimmy Carter   D. Barack Obama

38. "Within the covers of the Bible are the answers for all the problems men face."

A. Ronald Reagan   C. George Washington

B. James Polk   D. Jimmy Carter

39. "Don't join the book burners. Do not think you are going to conceal thoughts by concealing evidence that they ever existed."

A. John F. Kennedy   C. Dwight D. Eisenhower

B. George H.W. Bush   D. Herbert Hoover

40. "May God save the country, for it is evident that the people will not."

A. John Adams   C. Harry Truman

B. James Buchanan   D. Millard Fillmore

41. "The Constitution preserves the advantage of being armed which Americans possess over the people of almost every other nation, where the governments are afraid to trust the people with arms."

A. James Madison   C. Bill Clinton

B. Dwight D. Eisenhower   D. John F. Kennedy

42. "The most terrifying words in the English language are: 'I'm from the government, and I'm here to help.'"

A. Donald Trump   C. Woodrow Wilson

B. Ronald Reagan   D. Andrew Johnson

43. "We have a tendency to condemn people who are different from us, to define their sins as paramount and our own sinfulness as being

insignificant."

A. Bill Clinton   C. Barack Obama

B. Donald Trump   D. Jimmy Carter

44. "Never again must America allow an arrogant, elite guard of political adolescents to by-pass the regular party organization and dictate the terms of a national election."

A. Donald Trump   C. Gerald Ford

B. Lyndon B. Johnson   D. Bill Clinton

45. "Enthusiasm for a cause warps judgment."

A. Harry Truman   C. Franklin Pierce

B. Ulysses S. Grant   D. William H. Taft

46. "Posterity! You will never know how much it cost the present generation to preserve your freedom! I hope you will make good use of it."

A. George Washington   C. Thomas Jefferson

B. John Adams   D. John Tyler

47. "The truth is that all men having power ought to be mistrusted."

A. James Madison   C. Martin Van Buren

B. John Quincy Adams   D. Abraham Lincoln

48. "Any man worth his salt will stick up for what he believes right, but it takes a slightly better man to acknowledge instantly and without reservation that he is in error."

   A. Abraham Lincoln   *C. Andrew Jackson*

   B. George Washington   *D. Woodrow Wilson*

49. "We can't help everyone, but everyone can help someone."

   A. Ronald Reagan   *C. Gerald Ford*

   B. James Madison   *D. John Tyler*

50. "We can have no 50-50 allegiance in this country. Either a man is an American and nothing else, or he is not an American at all."

   A. Franklin D. Roosevelt   *C. Donald Trump*

   B. Theodore Roosevelt   *D. Dwight D. Eisenhower*

51. "That's all a man can hope for in his lifetime – to set an example – and when he is dead, to be an inspiration for history."

   A. William McKinley   *C. John Quincy Adams*

   B. Theodore Roosevelt   *D. Woodrow Wilson*

52. "Politics makes me sick."

   A. Jimmy Carter   *C. Donald Trump*

   B. William Taft   *D. Ulysses S. Grant*

53. "The less government interferes with private pursuits, the better for general prosperity."

A. Andrew Johnson

C. Martin Van Buren

B. George W. Bush

D. Theodore Roosevelt

54. "No person was ever honored for what he received. Honor has been the reward for what he gave."

A. Lyndon B. Johnson

C. John F. Kennedy

B. Franklin D. Roosevelt

D. Calvin Coolidge

55. "A president's hardest task is not to do what is right, but to know what is right."

A. Lyndon B. Johnson

C. George Washington

B. Woodrow Wilson

D. Abraham Lincoln

56. "And so my fellow Americans, ask not what your country can do for you; ask what you can do for your country."

A. John F. Kennedy

C. Barack Obama

B. Ronald Reagan

D. Franklin D. Roosevelt

57. "I pray Heaven to bestow the best of blessing on this house," (referring to the White House) "and on all that shall hereafter inhabit it. May none but honest and wise men ever rule under this roof."

A. James Monroe

C. Abraham Lincoln

B. John Adams

D. James Buchanan

58. "Government's first duty is to protect the people, not run their lives."

    A. George W. Bush   C. Ronald Reagan

    B. Dwight D. Eisenhower   D. Thomas Jefferson

59. "No tendency is quite so strong in human nature as the desire to lay down rules of conduct for other people."

    A. William Taft   C. Donald Trump

    B. Calvin Coolidge   D. Barack Obama

60. "Those who deny freedom to others, deserve it not for themselves."

    A. Donald Trump   C. Ronald Reagan

    B. Abraham Lincoln   D. John F. Kennedy

61. "Do what you can, with what you have, where you are."

    A. Jimmy Carter   C. Zachary Taylor

    B. Theodore Roosevelt   D. Herbert Hoover

62. "It is far better to be alone, than to be in bad company."

    A. George Washington   C. Donald Trump

    B. James Garfield   D. Ronald Reagan

63. "The only thing we have to fear is fear itself."

A. Abraham Lincoln   C. Barack Obama

B. Grover Cleveland   D. Franklin D. Roosevelt

64. "Most folks are as happy as they make up their minds to be."

A. George W. Bush   C. Jimmy Carter

B. Abraham Lincoln   D. John F. Kennedy

65. "If you can't stand the heat, get out of the kitchen."

A. Calvin Coolidge   C. Ulysses S. Grant

B. Lyndon B. Johnson   D. Harry Truman

66. "If you think too much about being reelected, it is very difficult to be worth reelecting."

A. Woodrow Wilson   C. Grover Cleveland

B. Calvin Coolidge   D. Thomas Jefferson

67. "Better to remain silent and be thought a fool, than to speak out and remove all doubt."

A. Calvin Coolidge   C. Ulysses S. Grant

B. Abraham Lincoln   D. John Quincy Adams

68. "Defeat doesn't finish a man, quit does. A man is not finished when he's defeated. He's finished when he quits."

A. Martin Van Buren   C. Richard Nixon

B. Rutherford B. Hayes   D. Warren Harding

69. "America will never be destroyed from the outside. If we falter and lose our freedoms, it will be because we destroyed ourselves."

A. George H.W. Bush   C. Donald Trump

B. Abraham Lincoln   D. Franklin D. Roosevelt

70. "If you want to make enemies, try to change something."

A. Woodrow Wilson   C. Calvin Coolidge

B. Donald Trump   D. Jimmy Carter

71. "One of my proudest moments is, I didn't sell my soul for the sake of popularity."

A. Bill Clinton   C. Ulysses S. Grant

B. Barack Obama   D. George W. Bush

72. "You can put wings on a pig, but you can't make it an eagle."

A. George W. Bush   C. Bill Clinton

B. Barack Obama   D. Richard Nixon

73. "It is not strange...to mistake change for progress."

A. *Millard Fillmore*   C. *Barack Obama*

B. *Theodore Roosevelt*   D. *Donald Trump*

74. "It is easier to do a job right, than to explain why you didn't."

A. *Dwight D. Eisenhower*   C. *Harry Truman*

B. *Martin Van Buren*   D. *James Madison*

75. "We will bring the terrorists to justice; or we will bring justice to the terrorists. Either way, justice will be done."

A. *Barack Obama*   C. *George W. Bush*

B. *Donald Trump*   D. *Bill Clinton*

Answers

Chapter 4 – Presidential Quotes

1. A - Theodore Roosevelt

2. D - Barack Obama

3. C - Gerald Ford

4. B - Calvin Coolidge

5. C - Donald Trump

6. A - Thomas Jefferson

Thomas Jefferson wrote this quote in a letter on January 30, 1787, to James Madison after Shay's Rebellion. Jefferson felt that the people had a right to express their grievances against the government, even if those grievances might take the form of violent action.

7. D - Ronald Reagan

8. A - Benjamin Harrison

9. B - Barack Obama

10. D - Calvin Coolidge

11. A - Theodore Roosevelt

12. C - Ronald Reagan

13. A - Barack Obama

14. C - Ronald Reagan

15. A - James Madison

16. B - James Buchanan

17. A - George Washington

18. D - Abraham Lincoln

19. B - Harry Truman

20. D - Richard Nixon

21. C - Theodore Roosevelt

22. B - John Adams

23. A - Herbert Hoover

24. B - Harry Truman

25. C - Theodore Roosevelt

26. A - George Washington

27. D - Barack Obama

28. B - Richard Nixon

29. C - Thomas Jefferson

30. A - Herbert Hoover

31. D – Abraham Lincoln

32. B - Gerald Ford

33. A – Andrew Johnson

34. B - Grover Cleveland

35. C - Jimmy Carter

36. D - Warren Harding

37. C - George H.W. Bush

38. A - Ronald Reagan

39. C - Dwight D. Eisenhower

40. D - Millard Fillmore

41. A - James Madison

42. B - Ronald Reagan

43. D – Jimmy Carter

44. C – Gerald Ford

45. D - William H. Taft

46. B - John Adams

47. A - James Madison

48. C – Andrew Jackson

49. A - Ronald Reagan

50. B - Theodore Roosevelt

51. A – William McKinley

52. B - William Taft

53. C - Martin Van Buren

54. D -Calvin Coolidge

55. A - Lyndon B. Johnson

56. A - John F. Kennedy

57. B - John Adams

58. C - Ronald Reagan

59. A - William Taft

60. B - Abraham Lincoln

61. B - Theodore Roosevelt

62. A - George Washington

63. D - Franklin D. Roosevelt

64. B - Abraham Lincoln

65. D - Harry Truman

66. A - Woodrow Wilson

67. B - Abraham Lincoln

68. C - Richard Nixon

69. B - Abraham Lincoln

70. A - Woodrow Wilson

71. D - George W. Bush

72. C - Bill Clinton

73. A - Millard Fillmore

74. B - Martin Van Buren

75. C – George W. Bush

5

The First One To Do So

Answers are given on pages 57 - 59.

I was the first president to...

1. Who was the first president to die while in office?

    A. Abraham Lincoln

    B. William Henry Harrison

    C. William McKinley

    D. Zachary Taylor

2. Who was the first president with a physical disability?

    A. James Polk

    B. Franklin Pierce

    C. Franklin D. Roosevelt

    D. Woodrow Wilson

3. Who was the first president to have a code name with the Secret Service?

    A. Harry Truman

    B. Andrew Johnson

    C. Grover Cleveland

    D. Theodore Roosevelt

4. Who was the first president to take the oath of office in Washington, D.C.?

A. George Washington

C. James Madison

B. John Adams

D. Thomas Jefferson

5. Who was the first president to marry while in office?

A. James Buchanan

C. John Tyler

B. Woodrow Wilson

D. James Polk

6. Who was the first president to have his oath of office administered by a woman?

A. Barack Obama

C. John F. Kennedy

B. Franklin D. Roosevelt

D. Lyndon B. Johnson

7. Which sitting president was the first to visit the Western Wall in Jerusalem, one of Judaism's holiest sites?

A. William McKinley

C. William H. Taft

B. Donald Trump

D. George H.W. Bush

8. Who was the first president to travel outside the United States while president?

A. Theodore Roosevelt

C. James Monroe

B. Herbert Hoover

D. Rutherford B. Hayes

9. While he was president the first telephone was installed in the White House. Who is he?

    A. Andrew Johnson   *C. Grover Cleveland*

    B. Rutherford B. Hayes   *D. James Garfield*

10. Who was the first president to have set eyes on the Pacific Ocean?

    A. Millard Fillmore   *C. Benjamin Harrison*

    B. Ulysses S. Grant   *D. William H. Taft*

11. Who was the first president to invite an African American to dinner at the White House?

    A. Theodore Roosevelt   *C. Grover Cleveland*

    B. Warren Harding   *D. Andrew Johnson*

12. Who was the first president (first and only) to have the oath of office administered aboard Air Force One?

    A. George H.W. Bush   *C. Lyndon B. Johnson*

    B. Gerald Ford   *D. Harry Truman*

13. By the end of his presidency the nation reached from the Atlantic to the Pacific Ocean for the first time. Who is he?

    A. James Polk   *C. Martin Van Buren*

    B. Millard Fillmore   *D. James Buchanan*

14. Who was the first president to have nominated the first Jewish person to the U.S. Supreme Court?

    A. Woodrow Wilson   *C. Jimmy Carter*

    B. Calvin Coolidge   *D. Richard Nixon*

15. Which president was the first American to win the Nobel Peace Prize?

    A. Barack Obama   *C. Jimmy Carter*

    B. Theodore Roosevelt   *D. William H. Taft*

16. Who was the first president to be photographed?

    A. James Madison   *C. Zachary Taylor*

    B. Abraham Lincoln   *D. John Quincy Adams*

17. Who was the first Quaker president? *(We've had two. Can you name them both?)*

    A. Richard Nixon   *C. Herbert Hoover*

    B. James Garfield   *D. Woodrow Wilson*

18. Who was the first president to be born in the United States?

    A. Andrew Jackson   *C. Chester Arthur*

    B. Martin Van Buren   *D. John Tyler*

19. Who was the first president to visit the West Coast?

A. *James Polk*   C. *John Quincy Adams*

B. *Franklin Pierce*   D. *Rutherford B. Hayes*

20. Who was the first president who was not a politician, but a businessman when he became president?

A. *Herbert Hoover*   C. *Donald Trump*

B. *George W. Bush*   D. *Harry Truman*

21. Who was the first president to be impeached, but was acquitted by one vote?

A. *Andrew Johnson*   C. *Richard Nixon*

B. *Bill Clinton*   D. *Donald Trump*

22. Who was the first president to travel underwater in a submarine?

A. *George H.W. Bush*   C. *Jimmy Carter*

B. *Richard Nixon*   D. *Harry Truman*

23. Who was the first president to visit all fifty states?

A. *Richard Nixon*   C. *Dwight D. Eisenhower*

B. *Bill Clinton*   D. *William McKinley*

24. Who was the first president whose inauguration was streamed on the internet?

A. *Ronald Reagan*   C. *Gerald Ford*

B. *Bill Clinton*   D. *George W. Bush*

25. Who became the first unelected president?

A. *Theodore Roosevelt*   C. *Andrew Johnson*

B. *Harry Truman*   D. *Gerald Ford*

26. Which president was the first to be sworn into office outdoors in Washington?

A. *William Henry Harrison*   C. *George Washington*

B. *James Monroe*   D. *Theodore Roosevelt*

27. Which president was the first to use an armored limousine?

A. *Franklin D. Roosevelt*   C. *William H. Taft*

B. *Harry Truman*   D. *John F. Kennedy*

28. Who was the first president to name the president's home in Washington, D.C. the White House?

A. *James Monroe*   C. *James Buchanan*

B. *Theodore Roosevelt*   D. *Grover Cleveland*

29. Who was president when the first annual Thanksgiving dinner took place at the White House?

A.Thomas Jefferson

B. Abraham Lincoln

C. James Polk

D. Benjamin Harrison

30. Though a few presidents have married women who had been divorced, who are the only two presidents to have been divorced?

A. J. Madison, M Van Buren

B. H. Truman, W. Harding

C. J. Tyler, W. Wilson

D. R. Reagan, D. Trump

31. Who was the first president licensed to fly a plane?

A. Calvin Coolidge

B. George H.W. Bush

C. Dwight D. Eisenhower

D. Gerald Ford

32. Who was the first sitting president to visit China?

A. Ulysses S. Grant

B. Richard Nixon

C. William H. Taft

D. Dwight D. Eisenhower

33. Who was the first president to have electricity in the White House?

A. Benjamin Harrison

B. Theodore Roosevelt

C. James Buchanan

D. Rutherford B. Hayes

34. Who was the first African-American president?

A.Warren Harding

B. Barack Obama

C. Chester Arthur

D. Bill Clinton

35. Who was the first president to live in the White House?

    A. John Adams   *C. James Madison*

    B. Thomas Jefferson   *D. George Washington*

36. Who is the first president, and only to date, to earn a doctorate degree, PhD.?

    A. Harry Truman   *C. Barack Obama*

    B. Bill Clinton   *D. Woodrow Wilson*

37. Who was the first president to voice support for same-sex marriage?

    A. Bill Clinton   *C. Barack Obama*

    B. George W. Bush   *D. Jimmy Carter*

38. Who was the first president born in the twentieth century?

    A. Dwight D. Eisenhower   *C. George W. Bush*

    B. Gerald Ford   *D. John F. Kennedy*

39. Who was the first vice-president to succeed to the presidency after the death of his predecessor?

    A. John Adams   *C. John Tyler*

    B. Andrew Johnson   *D. Theodore Roosevelt*

40. Who won the first presidential race in which women were allowed to vote?

A. *Warren Harding*

B. *Harry Truman*

C. *Woodrow Wilson*

D. *Franklin D. Roosevelt*

Answers

Chapter 5 - The First One To Do So

1. B - William Henry Harrison

2. C - Franklin D. Roosevelt

He had polio previous to becoming president, though even throughout his presidency many people were unaware he wore braces and couldn't walk without crutches.

3. A - Harry Truman

4. D - Thomas Jefferson

5. C - John Tyler

6. D - Lyndon B. Johnson

7. B - Donald Trump

8. A - Theodore Roosevelt

9. B - Rutherford B. Hayes

Alexander Graham Bell himself installed the telephone. The phone number was #1.

10. B – Ulysses S. Grant

11. A. Theodore Roosevelt

The first African-American invited to an official function at the White House was Booker T. Washington. He was not the first black man invited to the White House however, as Abraham Lincoln had invited Frederick Douglass to the White House.

12. C - Lyndon B. Johnson

13. A - James Polk

14. A - Woodrow Wilson

15. B - Theodore Roosevelt

*He won the Nobel Peace Prize for mediating peace between Russia and Japan.

16. D - John Quincy Adams

17. C- Herbert Hoover was the first, Richard Nixon also was a Mormon

18. B - Martin Van Buren

*The previous presidents all were born prior to the Declaration of Independence so were born British subjects.

19. D - Rutherford B. Hayes

20. C - Donald Trump

*While all of the answers given were businessmen before becoming president, Donald Trump is the only one who was not involved in politics (other than donating to politicians campaigns) before becoming president.

21. A - Andrew Johnson

22. D- Harry Truman

23. A - Richard Nixon

*Dwight D. Eisenhower was the first president to serve all fifty states as it was under his administration that Hawaii and Alaska joined the Union. There have been four presidents to have visited all 50 states: Richard Nixon, George H.W. Bush, Bill Clinton, and Barack Obama.

24. B - Bill Clinton

25. D - Gerald Ford

26. B - James Monroe

27. A - Franklin D. Roosevelt

The limousine originally belonged to Al Capone, a gangster. The Secret Service needed a car to drive President Roosevelt to deliver his speech on Pearl Harbor the day after they were attacked. The Treasury Department had impounded Capone's armored car years earlier so it was available for the president's use.

28. B - Theodore Roosevelt

Prior to this time, the White House had been called the Executive Mansion or the President's House.

29. C - James Polk

30. D - Ronald Reagan, Donald Trump

31. C - Dwight D. Eisenhower

32. B - Richard Nixon

33. A - Benjamin Harrison

34. B - Barack Obama

35. A - John Adams

He moved in the White House while the paint was still wet in November, 1800.

36. D - Woodrow Wilson

37. C - Barack Obama

38. D - John F. Kennedy

39. C - John Tyler

40. A - Warren Harding

6

The One And Only President To Have Done So

Answers are given on page 63.

The only president to have....

1. Who was the only president to serve two terms not in succession?

    A. Franklin D. Roosevelt   *C. George Washington*

    B. John Adams   *D. Grover Cleveland*

2. Which president, due to not trusting the mainstream media, was the only president to have used "tweets" to communicate with the public?

    A. George W. Bush   *C. Donald Trump*

    B. Bill Clinton   *D. Barack Obama*

3. Who was the only unanimously elected president by the Electoral College?

    A. Ronald Reagan   *C. John F. Kennedy*

    B. Franklin D. Roosevelt   *D. George Washington*

4. What president became both vice-president and president without being elected to either office?

    A. George Washington   *C. Gerald Ford*

    B. Thomas Jefferson   *D. George H.W. Bush*

5. Which president was the only man to serve both as president and as chief justice?

    A. William H. Taft   *C. George Washington*

    B. Grover Cleveland   *D. Thomas Jefferson*

6. Who was the only president elected to serve more than two terms?

    A. Grover Cleveland   *C. George Washington*

    B. Franklin D. Roosevelt   *D. Abraham Lincoln*

7. Who was the only president that didn't represent a political party?

    A. Donald Trump   *C. Abraham Lincoln*

    B. Thomas Jefferson   *D. George Washington*

8. Who was the only president who had two assassination attempts against him made by women?

    A. Ronald Reagan   *C. Gerald Ford*

    B. William McKinley   *D. George H.W. Bush*

9. Who was the only president to resign?

A. Donald Trump   C. Gerald Ford

B. Ulysses S. Grant   D. Richard Nixon

10. Who was the only bachelor president in American history?

A. James Buchanan   C. Martin Van Buren

B. Thomas Jefferson   D. Andrew Jackson

11. Who was the only president to have been married in the White House?

A. Woodrow Wilson   C. William H. Taft

B. Grover Cleveland   D. Chester Arthur

12. Who was the only president to have also been the director of the CIA?

A. George H.W. Bush   C. Dwight D. Eisenhower

B. Franklin D. Roosevelt   D. Herbert Hoover

Answers

Chapter 6 - The One And Only President To Have Done So

1. D - Grover Cleveland

2. C - Donald Trump

3. D - George Washington

James Monroe, the fifth president, received every Electoral College vote except for one. A New Hampshire delegate wanted to preserve the legacy of George Washington, and that is the only reason he didn't receive all the Electoral College votes.

4. C - Gerald Ford

5. A - William Howard Taft

He was the only man in history to hold the highest position in not only the executive branch, but also the judicial branch of the government

6. B - Franklin D. Roosevelt

He was the only president to have been elected as president four times. After he served as president, the Twenty-Second Amendment was ratified in 1951 which limited the presidential office to two terms.

7. D - George Washington

8. C - Gerald Ford

9. D - Richard Nixon

10. A - James Buchanan

11. B - Grover Cleveland

12. A – George H.W. Bush

7

Do You Know Which President...

Answers are given on pages 75 - 78.

1. Which president was a peanut farmer?

    A. Lyndon B. Johnson   *C. Ronald Reagan*

    B. Andrew Johnson   *D. Jimmy Carter*

2. Which president secretly sent Iran, a country in which the United States has no diplomatic relations, $400 million *in cash* which resulted in charges by the American public of violating a U.S. practice not to pay for hostages and in doing so empowering a major source of terrorism?

    A. George H.W. Bush   *C. George W. Bush*

    B. Barack Obama   *D. Bill Clinton*

3. Which president is the only president to have had his father administer the presidential oath of office to him?

    A. George W. Bush   *C. Calvin Coolidge*

    B. Franklin D. Roosevelt   *D. John Quincy Adams*

4. Which president married his teacher?

A. *Warren Harding*   C. *Andrew Johnson*

B. *Millard Fillmore*   D. *Franklin Pierce*

5. Which two presidents died on the same day, the 50th Anniversary of the Declaration of Independence in 1826?

A. *G. Washington & T. Jefferson*   C. *J. Adams & T. Jefferson*

B. *J. Madison & J. Monroe*   D. *T. Jefferson & J. Madison*

6. Who is the only president buried in Washington?

A. *John F. Kennedy*   C. *George Washington*

B. *Woodrow Wilson*   D. *Abrahm Lincoln*

7. How were the two presidents Theodore Roosevelt and Franklin Roosevelt related?

A. *Cousins*   C. *Brothers-in-law*

B. *Brothers*   D. *Grandfather & Grandson*

8. Which was the last president who was born a British subject?

A. *Martin Van Buren*   C. *James Monroe*

B. *John Tyler*   D. *William Henry Harrison*

9. Which sitting president accused the mainstream media of reporting "fake news" when they clearly reported their biased opinions and rumors rather than the news?

A. Bill Clinton   C. Donald Trump

B. Barack Obama   D. George W. Bush

10. Who was the second president to be impeached?

A. Bill Clinton   C. Ulysses S. Grant

B. Andrew Johnson   D. Donald Trump

11. Of all the presidents, which one lived the longest?

A. Jimmy Carter   C. Ronald Reagan

B. George H.W. Bush   D. Gerald Ford

12. The tradition began of playing 'Hail to the Chief' to announce the arrival of what president, due to the fact that he was so short that no one noticed when he entered a room?

A. James Monroe   C. James Madison

B. James Polk   D. Abraham Lincoln

13. Was Abraham Lincoln a Democrat or Republican?

A. Democrat   B. Republican

14. Which vice-president was visiting his father, when in the middle of the night he was informed that the president was dead? He was sworn in to the office of the presidency by candlelight and then went back to sleep.

A. *John Adams*   C. *Calvin Coolidge*

B. *John Tyler*   D. *Millard Fillmore*

15. Who was the first president to marry while president?

A. *John Tyler*   C. *Martin Van Buren*

B. *James Buchanan*   D. *Woodrow Wilson*

16. In the presidential election of the year 2000, it was the United States Supreme Court who finally determined who the next president would be. Who did they decide won the office of the presidency?

A. *Gerald Ford*   C. *George W. Bush*

B. *Bill Clinton*   D. *George H.W. Bush*

17. Which president gave President Nixon a full pardon?

A. *George H.W. Bush*   C. *Lyndon B. Johnson*

B. *Jimmy Carter*   D. *Gerald Ford*

18. What president hated political partisanship and felt that leaders should be able to discuss important issues without being bound by party loyalty?

A. *Donald Trump*   C. *Ronald Reagan*

B. *George Washington*   D. *James Monroe*

19. Which president delivered the longest inaugural address, lasting one hour and forty minutes?

A. *John Adams*   C. *William Henry Harrison*

B. *Martin Van Buren*   D. *George Washington*

20. Which president wrote his own epitaph and never even mentioned that he had been president?

A. *Thomas Jefferson*   C. *James Monroe*

B. *Ulysses S. Grant*   D. *Dwight D. Eisenhower*

21. Courtesy has always been that a former president is never seen or heard criticizing his successors, therefore preserving the integrity of the office. Which president after leaving office not only didn't leave Washington, D.C. but was vocal about the incoming president's actions and worked behind his back to undermine his presidency?

A. *John Adams*   C. *Lyndon B. Johnson*

B. *Dwight D. Eisenhower*   D. *Barack Obama*

22. Which president never attended a single day of school?

A. *Abraham Lincoln*   C. *Zachary Taylor*

B. *Andrew Johnson*   D. *Franklin Pierce*

23. Before becoming president he was a sheriff, public executioner, and personally hung two murderers. Who was he?

A. *Andrew Johnson*   C. *Benjamin Harrison*

B. *Grover Cleveland*   D. *William H. Taft*

24. Which president talked to astronauts on the moon from the White House by using a radio-telephone?

   A. John F. Kennedy   C. Richard Nixon

   B. George H.W. Bush   D. Lyndon B. Johnson

25. Do you know which president was nominated for the Emmy Award twice?

   A. John F. Kennedy   C.Ronald Reagan

   B. Barack Obama   D. Donald Trump

26. Which president started the tradition of throwing out the first ball for the opening of baseball season?

   A. William Howard Taft   C. Calvin Coolidge

   B. George W. Bush   D. Woodrow Wilson

27. Who became president when President Nixon resigned?

   A. Lyndon B. Johnson   C. George H.W. Bush

   B. Gerald Ford   D. Jimmy Carter

28. Which president couldn't read until he was nine years old?

   A. Andrew Johnson   C. Woodrow Wilson

   B. Abraham Lincoln   D. Grover Cleveland

29. Who was the oldest man to be inaugurated as president?

A. Donald Trump

B. Ronald Reagan

C. George H.W. Bush

D. Lyndon B. Johnson

30. Which president is the only president to have a patent in his name?

A. Abraham Lincoln

B. Millard Fillmore

C. Barack Obama

D. Thomas Jefferson

31. Which president was scouted by more than one professional baseball team while still a high school student?

A. George W. Bush

B. Gerald Ford

C. Donald Trump

D. George H.W. Bush

32. Which president was the last president of the Founding Fathers?

A. George Washington

B. John Quincy Adams

C. Thomas Jefferson

D. James Monroe

33. His approval ratings dropped significantly when it was found the IRS was targeting conservative organizations and also due to the cover up of the Benghazi terrorist killings. Who was he?

A. George W. Bush

B. Lyndon B. Johnson

C. Barack Obama

D. Bill Clinton

34. During the Watergate scandal, which future president formally requested that Nixon resign from office?

A. Gerald Ford   C. Ronald Reagan

B. George H.W. Bush   D. Harry Truman

35. Which president served the shortest term of presidency?

A. William H. Harrison   C. James Garfield

B. Zachary Taylor   D. James Buchanan

36. Which president's vice-president, Richard Mentor Johnson, took a slave for his common-law wife and raised and educated their bi-racial children as free persons?

A. Martin Van Buren   C. Thomas Jefferson

B. Andrew Jackson   D. Abraham Lincoln

37. Which president described himself as 'the most athletic president to occupy the White House in years'?

A. George W. Bush   C. Gerald Ford

B. John F. Kennedy   D. Herbert Hoover

38. Which two presidents signed the Constitution?

A. G. Washington & J. Madison   C. G. Washington & J. Adams

B. T. Jefferson & J. Monroe   D. J. Adams & T. Jefferson

39. Which two presidents signed the Declaration of Independence?

A. G. Washington & T. Jefferson

B. J. Adams & T. Jefferson

C. G. Washington & J. Adams

D. J. Adams & J. Monroe

40. Which president has a star on the Hollywood Walk of Fame?

A. John F. Kennedy

B. Bill Clinton

C. Ronald Reagan

D. Donald Trump

41. Which president was the only president to elope?

A. Donald Trump

B. John Tyler

C. Woodrow Wilson

D. Abraham Lincoln

42. Which president signed into legislation for the founding of the Smithsonian Institution as an establishment dedicated to the "increase and diffusion of knowledge" ?

A. James Polk

B. James Buchanan

C. Thomas Jefferson

D. Rutherford B. Hayes

43. Which president studied nuclear physics?

A. Herbert Hoover

B. Harry Truman

C. Jimmy Carter

D. Woodrow Wilson

44. Which president's heads are depicted on Mt. Rushmore?

A. *Washington, Jefferson, Lincoln, T. Roosevelt*

B. *Washington, Jefferson, Madison, Lincoln,*

C. *Washington, Jefferson, Lincoln, F. Roosevelt*

D. *Washington, Jefferson, Lincoln, Reagan*

45. Which president hated cats and after retiring would shoot at any cats that came near his home?

A. *John Adams*   C. *Lyndon B. Johnson*

B. *Calvin Coolidge*   D. *Dwight D. Eisenhower*

46. Who was the first Republican to be elected to the Presidency?

A. *George Washington*   C. *Thomas Jefferson*

B. *Abraham Lincoln*   D. *Theodore Roosevelt*

47. In warm weather which president went skinny-dipping in the Potomac early in the morning?

A. *John Quincy Adams*   C. *George Washington*

B. *Andrew Jackson*   D. *James Polk*

48. Which president had several inventions?

A. *Abraham Lincoln*   C. *Thomas Jefferson*

B. *Theodore Roosevelt*   D. *Herbert Hoover*

49. Which president was an indentured servant who ran away?

    A. James Monroe   *C. John Tyler*

    B. Zachary Taylor   *D. Andrew Johnson*

50. Which president often made his own breakfast in the White House?

    A. Gerald Ford   *C. Woodrow Wilson*

    B. Lyndon B. Johnson   *D. George W. Bush*

Answers

Chapter 7 – Do You Know Which President

1. D - Jimmy Carter

2. B - Barack Obama

3. C - Calvin Coolidge

4. B - Millard Fillmore

He could barely read or spell at the time he married his wife. She would later teach him to write and do arithmetic.

5. C - John Adams and Thomas Jefferson

6. B - Woodrow Wilson

If you were thinking of John F. Kennedy and William H. Taft who are buried at Arlington National Cemetery, that is actually located in Virginia. Woodrow Wilson was buried at Washington Cathedral in Washington, D.C.

7. A - They were cousins.

8. D - William Henry Harrison

9. C - Donald Trump

10. A - Bill Clinton

11. D - Gerald Ford.

He lived to be 93 years old.

12. B - James Polk

Though the song was played for other presidents first, James Polk was so short it was used to announce his presence.

13. B - Republican

14. C - Calvin Coolidge

15. A - John Tyler

His first wife died while he was president. He remarried while still in office.

16. C - George W Bush

* *The United States Supreme Court resolved the dispute in the 2000 presidential election determining that George W. Bush won the presidency.*

17. D - Gerald Ford

18. B - George Washington.

He was unable to put a stop to political parties.

19. C - William Henry Harrison

The shortest inaugural address was given by George Washington which consisted of only 133 words.

20. A - Thomas Jefferson

21. D – Barack Obama

22. B - Andrew Johnson

23. B - Grover Cleveland

24. C - Richard Nixon

25. D - Donald Trump

26. A - William Howard Taft

27. B - Gerald Ford

28. C - Woodrow Wilson

29. B - Ronald Reagan

30. A - Abraham Lincoln

31. C - Donald Trump

While still a high school student he was scouted by both the Phillies and the Boston Red Sox.

32. D - James Monroe

33. C - Barack Obama

34. B - George H.W. Bush

35. A - William H. Harrison

He died thirty two days after elected. His inaugural address lasted almost two hours in which time he stood in the bad weather wearing no hat or coat. After his inaugural address he attended a round of receptions in his wet clothing and developed a chill which within days turned into a cold and then progressed into pneumonia. One month after taking office he passed away.

36. A - Martin Van Buren

37. C - Gerald Ford

38. A - George Washington & James Madison

39. B – John Adams & Thomas Jefferson

40. D - Donald Trump

41. B - John Tyler

42. A – James Polk

43. C - Jimmy Carter

44. A - George Washington, Thomas Jefferson, Abraham Lincoln, and Theodore Roosevelt

45. D - Dwight D. Eisenhower

46. B - Abraham Lincoln

47. A - John Quincy Adams

The last time he went skinny-dipping in the Potomac River he was seventy nine years old.

48. C - Thomas Jefferson

49. D - Andrew Johnson

Many children from poor families were sold into indentured servitude. When he was twelve years old, he escaped from his master, a tailor in North Carolina.

50. A - Gerald Ford

8

Achievements While President

Answers are given on pages 92 - 95.

Which president is responsible for these achievements...

1. Which president gave the Star Wars speech about the Strategic Defense Initiative, also known as SDI?

    A. John F. Kennedy   *C. George H.W. Bush*

    C. Dwight D. Eisenhower   *D. Ronald Reagan*

2. Which president was responsible for keeping the Union intact?

    A. Dwight D. Eisenhower   *C. James Buchanan*

    B. Abraham Lincoln   *D. Ulysses S. Grant*

3. Which president signed the treaty to purchase Alaska from Russia?

    A. Andrew Johnson   *C. James Buchanan*

    B. Chester Arthur   *D. Theodore Roosevelt*

4. Which president ratified Jay's Treaty?

    A. Donald Trump   *C. James Monroe*

    B. George Washington   *D. John F. Kennedy*

5. Which president's greatest achievement is considered to be the Affordable Care Act?

    A. Lyndon B. Johnson   *C. Barack Obama*

    B. Jimmy Carter   *D. Herbert Hoover*

6. Which president expanded the American boundaries to the Pacific Ocean and expanded U.S. territory by more than 1/3?

    A. James Polk   *C. Rutherford B. Hayes*

    B. William McKinley   *D. Thomas Jefferson*

7. Which president put an end to the problem of Barbary pirates by deploying warships?

    A. George Washington   *C. Andrew Jackson*

    B. James Madison   *D. Thomas Jefferson*

8. Which president brought home the P.O.W.'s from Vietnam?

    A. Lyndon B. Johnson   *C. Jimmy Carter*

    B. Richard Nixon   *D. Ronald Reagan*

9. Which president issued the Emancipation Proclamation?

A. *Abraham Lincoln*   C. *Donald Trump*

B. *Thomas Jefferson*   D. *John F. Kennedy*

10. Which president created the departments: Department of Energy and the Department of Education?

A. *Harry Truman*   C. *Jimmy Carter*

B. *John F. Kennedy*   D. *Lyndon B. Johnson*

11. Which president was responsible for deactivating more than 1,700 nuclear warheads from the former Soviet Union?

A. *Ronald Reagan*   C. *George H.W. Bush*

B. *Bill Clinton*   D. *Dwight D. Eisenhower*

12. Which president signed into law the Chinese Exclusion Act prohibiting immigration of Chinese immigrants from entering the United States?

A. *Franklin D. Roosevelt*   C. *William H. Taft*

B. *Rutherford B. Hayes*   D. *Chester Arthur*

13. Which president signed the Indian Citizenship Act? This granted citizenship to Native Americans and allowed them to retain tribal land rights.

A. *Calvin Coolidge*   C. *Andrew Jackson*

B. *Warren Harding*   D. *Theodore Roosevelt*

14. Which president helped reduce tensions with the Soviet Union when he signed the Helsinki Accords?

A. Ronald Reagan   *C. John F. Kennedy*

B. George H.W. Bush   *D. Gerald Ford*

15. Which president signed the first federal child welfare program ?

A. Lyndon B. Johnson   *C. Warren Harding*

B. Ronald Reagan   *D. John F. Kennedy*

16. Which president founded the Environmental Protection Agency?

A. Theodore Roosevelt   *C. George W. Bush*

B. Richard Nixon   *D. Barack Obama*

17. Which president signed the Civil Rights Act of 1875 that extended the rights of emancipated slaves?

A. Ulysses S. Grant   *C. Abraham Lincoln*

B. Andrew Johnson   *D. Benjamin Harrison*

18.   Which president visited both China and the Soviet Union to reduce tensions between these countries and the United States? These visits helped establish diplomatic relations?

A. Richard Nixon   *C. Ulysses S. Grant*

B. George H.W. Bush   *D. Jimmy Carter*

19. Which president established federal protection for national parks, forests, and national monuments?

   A. Barack Obama   C. Herbert Hoover

   B. Chester Arthur   D. Theodore Roosevelt

20. Which president signed the Civil Rights Acts of 1964 and 1968?

   A. John F. Kennedy   C. Lyndon B. Johnson

   B. Jimmy Carter   D. Richard Nixon

21. Which president, on his third day in office, signed an executive action withdrawing the U.S. from the Trans-Pacific Partnership?

   A. John F. Kennedy   C. Woodrow Wilson

   B. Donald Trump   D. Dwight D. Eisenhower

22. Which president established the Family and Medical Leave Act?

   A. Barack Obama   C. John F. Kennedy

   B. George W. Bush   D. Bill Clinton

23. Which president negotiated the Nuclear Test – Ban treaty?

   A. John F. Kennedy   C. Ronald Reagan

   B. Harry Truman   D. Dwight D. Eisenhower

24. Which president led the U.S. from isolationism to a victory over Nazi Germany and their allies during WWII?

A. William H. Taft   *C. Woodrow Wilson*

B. Franklin D. Roosevelt   *D. Herbert Hoover*

25. Which president had some of his greatest achievements in the area of conservation?

A. Gerald Ford   *C. Theodore Roosevelt*

B. John Tyler   *D. Bill Clinton*

26. Which president created programs to tackle poverty such as: Head Start, food stamps, Medicare, and Medicaid?

A. Lyndon B. Johnson   *C. Harry Truman*

B. Franklin D. Roosevelt   *D. Herbert Hoover*

27. Which president signed the Nineteenth Amendment granting women the right to vote?

A. James Garfield   *C. Benjamin Harrison*

B. William H. Taft   *D. Woodrow Wilson*

28. Which president ended the draft?

A. Richard Nixon   *C. Lyndon B. Johnson*

B. Dwight D. Eisenhower   *D. Jimmy Carter*

29. Which president signed peace treaties with Germany and Austria after WWI?

A. *Woodrow Wilson*   C. *Warren Harding*

B. *William McKinley*   D. *Calvin Coolidge*

30. Which president significantly lowered tax rates for nearly all U.S. tax payers?

A. *Barack Obama*   C. *Donald Trump*

B. *George W. Bush*   D. *Ronald Reagan*

31. Which president was responsible for nuclear weapons cuts?

A. *Ronald Reagan*   C. *John F. Kennedy*

B. *Harry Truman*   D. *Dwight D. Eisenhower*

32. After the assassination of a Republican president, his Democrat vice-president became president. Who was he?

A. *Andrew Johnson*   C. *Abraham Lincoln*

B. *Ulysses S. Grant*   D. *Grover Cleveland*

33. Which president signed The Missouri Compromise?

A. *Thomas Jefferson*   C. *James Madison*

B. *John Quincy Adams*   D. *James Monroe*

34. Which president signed the Paris Peace Accords ending U.S. involvement in the Vietnam War?

A. *Lyndon B. Johnson*   C. *Richard Nixon*

B. *John F. Kennedy*   D. *Gerald Ford*

35. Which president issued the doctrine that would contain communism?

A. *Ronald Reagan*   C. *Dwight D. Eisenhower*

B. *Harry Truman*   D. *George W. Bush*

36. As a conservationist, which president preserved approximately two hundred million acres for wildlife refuges, national forests, and reserves – which was five times the amount of land all his predecessors combined preserved?

A. *Andrew Jackson*   C. *Grover Cleveland*

B. *Chester Arthur*   D. *Theodore Roosevelt*

37. Which president fulfilled every single one of his campaign promises while serving only one term of office?

A. *John Adams*   C. *James Polk*

B. *John Quincy Adams*   D. *James Buchanan*

38. Which president kept America at peace, even though he was faced with major Cold War issues every year he was in office?

A. *Dwight D. Eisenhower*   C. *George H.W. Bush*

B. *Ronald Reagan*   D. *Bill Clinton*

39. Which president prevented nuclear Armageddon?

A. Barack Obama   C. Jimmy Carter

B. John F. Kennedy   D. Harry Truman

40. Which president was responsible for the Monroe Doctrine?

A. James Monroe   C. John Quincy Adams

B. Thomas Jefferson   D. James Madison

41. Who was president when the new treaty the Gadsden Purchase *(land the U.S. purchased via a treaty that consists of present-day southern Arizona and southwestern New Mexico)* was signed?

A. William McKinley   C. Franklin Pierce

B. James Polk   D. James Buchanan

42. Which president drastically reduced unemployment from 25% - 2%?

A. Bill Clinton   C. Donald Trump

B. John F. Kennedy   D. Franklin D. Roosevelt

43. Which president used atomic bombs on Hiroshima and Nagasaki forcing Japan to surrender and ending the war?

A. Dwight D. Eisenhower   C. Franklin D. Roosevelt

B. Harry Truman   D. Calvin Coolidge

44. Who was president when the Louisiana Purchase came about?

A. James Madison   C. Thomas Jefferson

B. James Monroe   D. John Quincy Adams

45. Which president balanced the budget – not just once; but three times?

A. Dwight D. Eisenhower   C. Bill Clinton

B. Jimmy Carter   D. Barack Obama

46. Which president promoted public works such as the Hoover Dam?

A. Franklin D. Roosevelt   C. Calvin Coolidge

B. Herbert Hoover   D. Theodore Roosevelt

47. With the Oregon Treaty of 1846, this president acquired a substantial amount of land for the U.S. from the British without having to go to war to do so. Who was he?

A. James Polk   C. William H. Harrison

B. Millard Fillmore   D. James Buchanan

48. Which president established the Peace Corps?

A. Lyndon B. Johnson   C. George W. Bush

B. Jimmy Carter   D. John F. Kennedy

49. Who was president when the Treaty of Ghent was signed by British and American representatives ending the War of 1812?

A. *Thomas Jefferson*   C. *James Madison*

B. *John Quincy Adams*   D. *Martin Van Buren*

50. Which president oversaw desegregation peacefully of the schools in the South?

A. *Lyndon B. Johnson*   C. *Jimmy Carter*

B. *Richard Nixon*   D. *John F. Kennedy*

51. Which president established the Open Door policy with China?

A. *William McKinley*   C. *Richard Nixon*

B. *William H. Taft*   D. *Theodore Roosevelt*

52. Which president announced in a speech the end of U.S. involvement in the Vietnam War, leaving one final scene to be finished – the evacuation of Americans in Saigon?

A. *Lyndon B. Johnson*   C. *Richard Nixon*

B. *Gerald Ford*   D. *Jimmy Carter*

53. Which president created the interstate highway system?

A. *Franklin D. Roosevelt*   C. *Jimmy Carter*

B. *Lyndon B. Johnson*   D. *Dwight D. Eisenhower*

54. Which president recognized the state of Israel when it declared itself a nation?

A. George H.W. Bush　　　　　C. Harry Truman

B. Barack Obama　　　　　　　D. Richard Nixon

55. Which president established Social Security?

A. Thomas Jefferson　　　　　C. Herbert Hoover

B. William H. Taft　　　　　　D. Franklin D. Roosevelt

56. Which president was responsible for eliminating Osama bin Laden?

A. George W Bush　　　　　　C. Bill Clinton

B. Barack Obama　　　　　　　D. George H.W. Bush

57. Which president lowered the voting age from twenty-one years to eighteen years?

A. Richard Nixon　　　　　　　C. Lyndon B. Johnson

B. John F. Kennedy　　　　　　D. Dwight D. Eisenhower

58. Who was president when America's territory grew by more than one-third extending out west, which caused a major fight between the northern and southern states over slavery?

A. James Buchanan　　　　　　C. James Polk

B. Andrew Johnson　　　　　　D. Abraham Lincoln

59. Which president presided over meetings at Camp David with Egypt's president and Israel's prime minister? The result of these meetings ended the state of war between the two nations for which this president was

awarded the Nobel Peace Prize.

    A. Barack Obama   *C. Donald Trump*

    B. John F. Kennedy   *D. Jimmy Carter*

60. Which president established the Department of Homeland Security?

    A. Barack Obama   *C. Ronald Reagan*

    B. George W. Bush   *D. Bill Clinton*

Answers

Chapter 8 - Achievements While President

1. D - Ronald Reagan

2. B - Abraham Lincoln

3. A - Andrew Johnson

It is considered his most important foreign policy action.

4. B - George Washington

5. C - Barack Obama

Obamacare or The Affordable Care Act while considered Obama's greatest achievement many will argue that fact considering it was promised that people who were presently uninsured would now be insured; this was not found to be true as the poor still couldn't afford the premiums and still found themselves uninsured, deductibles and premiums soared, the promise of being able to keep your own insurance or doctor were not true, increased America's debt problems, and became a deterrant to new doctors entering the field. The Affordable Care Act appeared to have brought on more problems than it solved – so was this an achievement or a failure?

6. A - James Polk

7. D - Thomas Jefferson

8. B - Richard Nixon

9. A - Abraham Lincoln

10. C - Jimmy Carter

11. B - Bill Clinton

12. D - Chester Arthur

13. A - Calvin Coolidge

14. D - Gerald Ford

15. C - Warren Harding

16. B - Richard Nixon

17. A - Ulysses S. Grant

18. A - Richard Nixon

19. D - Theodore Roosevelt

20. C - Lyndon B. Johnson

21. B - Donald Trump

22. D - Bill Clinton

23. A - John F. Kennedy

24. B - Franklin D. Roosevelt

25. C - Theodore Roosevelt

26. A - Lyndon B. Johnson

27. D - Woodrow Wilson

28. A - Richard Nixon

29. C - Warren Harding

30. B - George W. Bush

31. A - Ronald Reagan

32. A - Andrew Johnson

33. D - James Monroe

34. C - Richard Nixon

35. B - Harry Truman

36. D - Theodore Roosevelt

37. C - James Polk

He acquired California from Mexico, settled the Oregon dispute, lowered tariffs, established a sub-treasury, and accomplished it all in one term and then retired from office.

38. A - Dwight D. Eisenhower

39. B - John F. Kennedy

40. A - James Monroe

If you thought this was just too easy so it must be a trick question it was not. If you guessed C – John Quincy Adams, go ahead and give yourself credit as it was J.Q. Adams who not only worded the declaration which became a cornerstone of American foreign policy, but Adams also helped shape the doctrine.

41. C - Franklin Pierce

42. D - Franklin D. Roosevelt

43. B - Harry Truman

While some may argue that this was an achievement, it was a decision that was not easily made, and was successful in bringing an end to the war.

44. C - Thomas Jefferson

45. A - Dwight D. Eisenhower

46. B - Herbert Hoover

47. A - James Polk

This added full control of what is the current states of Washington, Oregon, Idaho, and a portion of what is now the states of Montana and Wyoming.

48. D - John F. Kennedy

49. C- James Madison

The Peace Treaty of Ghent ended the War of 1812.

50. B - Richard Nixon

51. A - William McKinley

52. B - Gerald Ford

53. D - Dwight D. Eisenhower

54. C - Harry Truman

55. D - Franklin D. Roosevelt

56. B - Barack Obama

57. A - Richard Nixon

58. C - James Polk

59. D - Jimmy Carter

60. B - George W. Bush

9

Failures & Embarrasments Of The Presidents

Answers are given on pages 108 - 110.

1. Which president's biggest failure during his first days as president was his failure to repeal and replace The Affordable Care Act in his first 100 days as promised during his campaign?

A. Barack Obama

C. George W. Bush

B. Donald Trump

D. Bill Clinton

2. Who was president during the Bay of Pigs Invasion?

A. Barack Obama

C. George H.W. Bush

B. Dwight D. Eisenhower

D. John F. Kennedy

3. Who was president when the number of people having to turn to food stamps was at a record high?

A. George W. Bush

C. Jimmy Carter

B. Gerald Ford

D. Barack Obama

4. Which president failed to defuse the Cold War?

    A. Dwight D. Eisenhower   *C. Ronald Reagan*

    B. Bill Clinton   *D. George H.W. Bush*

5. Which president's policy of communist containment is what started the Cold War?

    A. Franklin D. Roosevelt   *C. Harry Truman*

    B. Herbert Hoover   *D. John F. Kennedy*

6. Which president fought for gun control, but his legislation requiring background checks on all guns purchased and a ban on assault weapons wasn't approved through Congress?

    A. Bill Clinton   *C. Donald Trump*

    B. Barack Obama   *D. Jimmy Carter*

7. Who was president during the "space race" with the Russians which cost American taxpayers $50 billion?

    A. John F. Kennedy   *C. Ronald Reagan*

    B. Richard Nixon   *D. George H.W. Bush*

8. Which president failed to heal the nation after the Civil War?

    A. Abraham Lincoln   *C. Ulysses S. Grant*

    B. James Buchanan   *D. Andrew Johnson*

9. The Depression worsened during which president's administration?

    A. Franklin D. Roosevelt   *C. Harry Truman*

    B. Herbert Hoover   *D. Barack Obama*

10. Which president's medical reform was to ensure *"everyone"* was insured; but not only did that not happen, but this insurance plan came at too high an expense for taxpayers?

    A. Donald Trump   *C. Franklin D. Roosevelt*

    B. Lyndon B. Johnson   *D. Barack Obama*

11. The White House knew about the plans for Rwandan genocide and did nothing to stop it. Who was president at the time?

    A. Barack Obama   *C. Bill Clinton*

    B. George H.W. Bush   *D. Jimmy Carter*

12. Which president vetoed every equal rights bill that would help African-Americans?

    A. Andrew Johnson   *C. Ulysses S. Grant*

    B. Warren Harding   *D. Donald Trump*

13. This president justified the War of Iraq by claiming they had weapons of mass destruction. Who was he?

    A. George H.W. Bush   *C. Bill Clinton*

    B. Barack Obama   *D. George W. Bush*

14. Racial divisions worsened during his presidency, instead of healing like people expected. Who was he?

    A. Franklin D. Roosevelt   *C. Barack Obama*

    B. Lyndon B. Johnson   *D. Donald Trump*

15. Which president helped establish the League of Nations, and then failed to join the U.S. as a part?

    A. Woodrow Wilson   *C. Franklin D. Roosevelt*

    B. John F. Kennedy   *D. Harry Truman*

16. Which president fired over one thousand postmasters in the South who weren't sympathetic to his policies? He fired so many that the Tenure of Office Act was passed prohibiting the president from firing any confirmed appointees without having the Senate's approval.

    A. Abraham Lincoln   *C. Andrew Johnson*

    B. Jimmy Carter   *D. Zachary Taylor*

17. Which president failed to free the American hostages in Iran? A failed rescue attempt led his reputation to be inept and ineffective. Who was he?

    A. Lyndon B. Johnson   *C. George H.W. Bush*

    B. Jimmy Carter   *D. Richard Nixon*

18. Who was president when Prohibition, the banning of manufacture, sale, and transporting of alcohol went into effect? This president vetoed the National Prohibition Act, but his veto was overridden by Congress.

A. *Woodrow Wilson*   C. *William H. Taft*

B. *Rutherford B. Hayes*   D. *Grover Cleveland*

19. Sex scandals, including but not limited to the actress Marilyn Monroe, left this president with a bad reputation as a womanizer? Who was he?

A. *Bill Clinton*   C. *Warren Harding*

B. *Richard Nixon*   D. *John F. Kennedy*

20. Which president ended the Persian Gulf War without deposing Iraq's dictator, Saddam Hussein?

A. *George H.W. Bush*   C. *Jimmy Carter*

B. *Bill Clinton*   D. *George W. Bush*

21. Who was president when the War of 1812 occurred? Some considered this war a second war for independence, however the United States suffered many costly defeats including the capture and burning of the nation's capital which included the Executive Mansion or White House.

A. *Thomas Jefferson*   C. *James Madison*

B. *John Quincy Adams*   D. *James Monroe*

22. Who was president when the housing market crashed, and it was the beginning of the recession?

A. *George W. Bush*   C. *Herbert Hoover*

B. *Barack Obama*   D. *Theodore Roosevelt*

23. Which president's stimulus did little to stimulate the economy?

A. John F. Kennedy   C. Barack Obama

B. Franklin D. Roosevelt   D. Grover Cleveland

24. Who was president during the rise of McCarthyism?

A. John F. Kennedy   C. Calvin Coolidge

B. Harry Truman   D. Dwight D. Eisenhower

25. Which president failed to turn over documents subpoenaed by Congressional committees and claimed immunity from civil lawsuits claiming presidential immunity?

A. Bill Clinton   C. Richard Nixon

B. Barack Obama   D. Donald Trump

26. Which president was responsible for the passing of the Sherman Silver Purchase Act which depleted the gold supply?

A. Grover Cleveland   C. Andrew Johnson

B. William H. Taft   D. Benjamin Harrison

27. Who was president during the hostage crisis in Iran?

A. Ronald Reagan   C. Jimmy Carter

B. George W. Bush   D. Gerald Ford

28. Which president's 'War On Poverty' had no clear plan on how to go

about fixing the problem and was more talk than action?

    A. Andrew Jackson   *C. Herbert Hoover*

    B. James Buchanan   *D. Lyndon B. Johnson*

29. Who was president during "The Plame Leak" which identified a covert operative in the CIA?

    A. George W. Bush   *C. Barack Obama*

    B. George H.W. Bush   *D. Bill Clinton*

30. In June of 1950, the Korean War began when soldiers from the North Korean People's Army crossed the 38th parallel, the boundary between Soviet backed Democratic People's Republic of Korea to the north and pro-Western Republic of Korea to the south. This invasion was the first military action of the Cold War. America came to the defense of South Korea considering this a war against communism. What president ordered our troops into action to join in to aid South Korea as a "police action"? The fighting ended in July of 1953 when an armistice was signed, however no peace treaty was ever signed and the two Koreas are, *technically* at least, still at war.

    A. Dwight D. Eisenhower   *C. Harry Truman*

    B. Calvin Coolidge   *D. Franklin D. Roosevelt*

31. Which president, and his administration, was involved with the cover up of their involvement of the scandal of Watergate?

    A. Bill Clinton   *C. Gerald Ford*

    B. Richard Nixon   *D. George H.W. Bush*

32. Who was president when the 'The Brownsville Incident' occurred, whose action to the incident has remained a matter of controversy and an embarrassment to the army?

A. Theodore Roosevelt   C. Barack Obama

B. George W. Bush   D. Grover Cleveland

33. Which president is associated with 'The Monica Lewinsky Scandal'?

A. John F. Kennedy   C. James Buchanan

B. Lyndon B. Johnson   D. Bill Clinton

34. Which president relocated Japanese-Americans into internment camps?

A. Abraham Lincoln   C. Franklin D. Roosevelt

B. Zachary Taylor   D. Dwight D. Eisenhower

35. The 'Teapot Dome Scandal' occurred during which president's administration?

A. Franklin D. Roosevelt   C. William H. Taft

B. Warren Harding   D. Grover Cleveland

36. Which president failed to defuse the Cold War and it became even more of a threat at the time he left the presidency than when he began it eight years earlier?

A. Dwight D. Eisenhower   C. John F. Kennedy

B. Jimmy Carter   D. George H.W. Bush

37. Which president gave up on his fight against slavery, deciding to fight only battles he could win?

A. James Buchanan

C. Andrew Johnson

B. Ulysses S. Grant

D. Thomas Jefferson

38. Which president was accused by the succeeding administration of removing all the W's from the computer keyboards in the White House?

A. Barack Obama

C. Gerald Ford

B. Bill Clinton

D. Jimmy Carter

39. What president had problems within his White House staff with leaks, often on a daily basis?

A. Donald Trump

C. John Tyler

B. George W. Bush

D. Lyndon B. Johnson

40. Which president's administration failed at one of it's main objectives which was energy? This president believed it imperative that the U.S. not rely on foreign oil. The result with his fight against foreign oil caused long lines at the gas stations and driving up oil prices. Who was he?

A. Lyndon B. Johnson

C. Jimmy Carter

B. George H.W. Bush

D. Barack Obama

41. Which president received illegal campaign contributions by Indonesians which was called 'Indogate', which gave the impression American foreign policy was up for sale?

A. Barack Obama   C. Donald Trump

B. Bill Clinton   D. George W. Bush

42. Who was president during the Iran-Contra Affair?

A. John F. Kennedy   C. George H.W. Bush

B. Dwight D. Eisenhower   D. Ronald Reagan

43. Inconsistent on social issues, what president opposed discrimination against Chinese immigrants, but failed to support womens' right to vote, equality for African-American voting rights, or the rights of American Indians to preserve their culture?

A. Grover Cleveland   C. Franklin D. Roosevelt

B. Andrew Johnson   D. Harry Truman

44. What president promised to ask Great Britain to give Ireland their independence, but failed to do so?

A. John F. Kennedy   C. Woodrow Wilson

B. William McKinley   D. Calvin Coolidge

45. Which president turned Lincoln's historic bedroom into a means of receiving large donations or basically rented out Lincoln's room for the right price?

A. Bill Clinton   C. Barack Obama

B. Donald Trump   D. John F. Kennedy

46. Which president brought in his daughter and son-in-law as senior advisors to work with him in the White House which the American public considered nepotism?

   A. Andrew Johnson   *C. Rutherford B. Hayes*

   B. Franklin D. Roosevelt   *D. Donald Trump*

47. Which president's Embargo Act, which restricted trade, ended up hurting Americans more than Britain or France who it was originally intended to hurt?

   A. John Adams   *C. John Quincy Adams*

   B. Thomas Jefferson   *D. James Madison*

48. Which president failed to deal with the issue of slavery, instead leaving the matter for the states and territories to decide for themselves?

   A. James Buchanan   *C. Abraham Lincoln*

   B. Ulysses S. Grant   *D. James Garfield*

49. The Depression didn't end until the start of WWII. Who was president during the time of the Great Depression?

   A. Theodore Roosevelt   *C. Franklin D. Roosevelt*

   B. George W. Bush   *D. Warren Harding*

50. Which president tied up four runways at Los Angeles International Airport, one of the busiest airports in the nation, for nearly an hour while Air Force One's engines were running, just so the president could get his hair trimmed?

A. John F. Kennedy   *C. Barack Obama*

B. Donald Trump   *D. Bill Clinton*

Answers

Chapter 9 – Failures & Embarrasments of the Presidents

1. B - Donald Trump

2. D - John F. Kennedy

3. D - Barack Obama

4. A - Dwight D. Eisenhower

5. C - Harry Truman

6. B - Barack Obama

7. A - John F. Kennedy

8. D - Andrew Johnson

9. B - Herbert Hoover

10. D -Barack Obama

11. C - Bill Clinton

12. A - Andrew Johnson

13. D - George W. Bush

14. C - Barack Obama

15. A - Woodrow Wilson

16. C - Andrew Johnson

17. B - Jimmy Carter

18. A - Woodrow Wilson

19. D - John F. Kennedy

20. A - George H.W. Bush

21. C - James Madison

22. A - George W. Bush

23. C - Barack Obama

24. B - Harry Truman

25. A - Bill Clinton

26. D - Benjamin Harrison

27. C - Jimmy Carter

28. D - Lyndon B. Johnson

29. A - George W. Bush

30. C - Harry Truman

31. B - Richard Nixon

32. A - Theodore Roosevelt

33. D - Bill Clinton

34. C - Franklin D. Roosevelt

35. B - Warren Harding

36. A - Dwight D. Eisenhower

37. D - Thomas Jefferson

38. B – Bill Clinton

Obviously those W's were relevant with the new president being George W. Bush.

39. A – Donald Trump

40. C - Jimmy Carter

41. B - Bill Clinton

42. D - Ronald Reagan

43. A - Grover Cleveland

44. C - Woodrow Wilson

45. A - Bill Clinton

46. D - Donald Trump

Not only does this scream of nepotism but is also unethical. While in the early days of the presidents many presidential sons worked closely by their father's sides in the White House and received esteemed appointments, but such signs of nepotism hasn't been seen in the White House since the days of John F. Kennedy when he hired his own brother as attorney general and his brother-in-law Sergent Shriver also served in his administration. In 1967 the Federal Anti-Nepotism Statute, known as Section 3110, was passed.

President Trump gets around this by stating that they are "unpaid" advisors. While it is true that it has been proven that the president can't trust many of those even on his own staff and most likely feels he can trust his own family members, many consider Ivanka and Jared Kushner to have their own agendas and the American public didn't vote for a Trump dynasty.

47. B -Thomas Jefferson

48. A - James Buchanan

49. C - Franklin D. Roosevelt

50. D – Bill Clinton

His 2nd controversy that occurred at an airport; the other being his meeting with Loretta Lynch while First Lady Hillary Clinton was under investigation.

10

Memorable Works by the Presidents

Answers are given on pages 117 - 118.

1. Which president signed legislation establishing Yellowstone National Park, the nation's first national park?

    A. Ulysses S. Grant   *C. Theodore Roosevelt*

    B. Chester Arthur   *D. Benjamin Harrison*

2. Which president announced a plan to develop and build space based weapons to protect American soil against Soviet nuclear missiles?

    A. John F. Kennedy   *C. Dwight D. Eisenhower*

    B. George H.W. Bush   *D. Ronald Reagan*

3. Which president introduced the program Medicare?

    A. Herbert Hoover   *C. Lyndon B. Johnson*

    B. Franklin D. Roosevelt   *D. Harry Truman*

4. Which president supported the Lewis and Clark Expedition?

A. *James Madison*   C. *John Quincy Adams*

B. *James Monroe*   D. *Thomas Jefferson*

5. Which president gained popularity when he stood up to Khrushchev who people considered a Soviet bully?

A. *John F. Kennedy*   C. *Ronald Reagan*

B. *Richard Nixon*   D. *Lyndon B. Johnson*

6. Which president declared war on global terrorism?

A. *Donald Trump*   C. *George W. Bush*

B. *Barack Obama*   D. *Bill Clinton*

7. Which president fought to have the Panama Canal built?

A. *Theodore Roosevelt*   C. *Dwight D. Eisenhower*

B. *Grover Cleveland*   D. *William H. Taft*

8. Which president set the precedent for a limit of two terms as president?

A. *Franklin D. Roosevelt*   C. *Abraham Lincoln*

B. *Thomas Jefferson*   D. *George Washington*

9. Which president created the Federal Reserve?

A. William McKinley   C. Harry Truman

B. Woodrow Wilson   D. William H. Taft

10. Which president vetoed the most bills?

A. Grover Cleveland   C. William H. Taft

B. Barack Obama   D. Franklin D. Roosevelt

11. One of this president's main objectives was to focus on Reconstruction. Who was he?

A. Abraham Lincoln   C. Ulysses S. Grant

B. Andrew Johnson   D. James Garfield

12. Which president appointed more women to federal posts than any other president?

A. Harry Truman   C. Woodrow Wilson

B. Franklin D. Roosevelt   D. John F. Kennedy

13. Which president worked at alleviating poverty and creating a 'Great Society' for all Americans?

A. John F. Kennedy   C. Thomas Jefferson

B. Herbert Hoover   D. Lyndon B. Johnson

14. On his last day in office which president signed a bill making Florida the 27th state?

A. *John Tyler*   C. *James Polk*

B. *Andrew Johnson*   D. *Grover Cleveland*

15. Which president was the driving force between the alliance between the U.S., Great Britain, and the Soviet Union which brought about the United Nations?

A. *Harry Truman*   C. *Woodrow Wilson*

B. *Dwight D. Eisenhower*   D. *Franklin D. Roosevelt*

16. Which president appointed Sandra Day O'Connor as the first woman in the U.S. Supreme Court?

A. *Jimmy Carter*   C. *George H.W. Bush*

B. *Ronald Reagan*   D. *Richard Nixon*

17. During whose presidency did his Secretary of State, William Seward, negotiate with Russia for the purchase of Alaska?

A. *Andrew Jackson*   C. *Andrew Johnson*

B. *Martin Van Buren*   D. *James Polk*

18. Same sex marriage was passed during which president's administration?

A. *Barack Obama*   C. *Bill Clinton*

B. *George W. Bush*   D. *Ronald Reagan*

19. Which president launched the Space Race?

A. *Dwight D. Eisenhower*   C. *John F. Kennedy*

B. *Richard Nixon*   D. *Ronald Reagan*

20. Which president signed into law a bill recognizing squatter's rights to occupy public lands?

A. *Grover Cleveland*   C. *Millard Fillmore*

B. *John Tyler*   D. *William H. Harrison*

21. Who was president at the time Congress first successfully overrode a president on a bill that the president had vetoed?

A. *Barack Obama*   C. *Warren Harding*

B. *Bill Clinton*   D. *John Tyler*

22. Who was president when the Erie Canal was completed?

A. *John Quincy Adams*   C. *Ulysses S. Grant*

B. *Martin Van Buren*   D. *Grover Cleveland*

23. Lawmakers overrode which president's veto to enact a law which allowed victims of international terrorist attacks to sue foreign governments. ?

A. *Barack Obama*   C. *Bill Clinton*

B. *George W. Bush*   D. *George H.W. Bush*

24. Which president fought hard against special favors to any economic

groups? He stated the reason for this was that, "Federal Aid encourages the expectation of paternal care on the part of the government and weakens the sturdiness of our national character"?

A. Ronald Reagan

C. Grover Cleveland

B. Thomas Jefferson

D. Calvin Coolidge

25. Which president took up the cause of the Clean Power Plan which was aimed at reducing greenhouse gas emissions, which he considered an important move against climate change?

A. George W. Bush

C. Jimmy Carter

B. Barack Obama

D. Bill Clinton

Answers

Chapter 10 - Memorable Works by the Presidents

1. A - Ulysses S. Grant

2. D - Ronald Reagan

3. C - Lyndon B. Johnson

4. D - Thomas Jefferson

5. B - Richard Nixon

6. C - George W. Bush

7. A - Theodore Roosevelt

8. D - George Washington

9. B - Woodrow Wilson

10. D – Franklin D. Roosevelt

11. C - Ulysses S. Grant

12. B - Franklin D. Roosevelt

13. D - Lyndon B. Johnson

14. A - John Tyler

15. D - Franklin D. Roosevelt

16. B - Ronald Reagan

17. C - Andrew Johnson

Alaska was purchased from Russia for $7 million. At the time critics called it 'Seward's Folly' thinking the purchase was a mistake.

18. A - Barack Obama

19. C – John F. Kennedy

20. B - John Tyler

People who settled on and improved unsurveyed public land were entitled to first purchase rights.

21. D – John Tyler

The first successful congressional override occurred on March 3, 1845, when Congress overrode President John Tyler's veto.

22. A - John Quincy Adams

23. A. Barack Obama

24. C - Grover Cleveland

25. B - Barack Obama

11

Dirty Acts Of Presidents Revealed

Answers are given on pages 131 – 135.

1. Which president had extramarital affairs and left behind love letters to a mistress which were considered crude to the point of being vulgar and are now available to see at the Library of Congress?

    A. John F. Kennedy   *C. Warren Harding*

    B. Donald Trump   *D. Bill Clinton*

2. Who was president during the cover-up of the attack on the American consulate in Benghazi where four U.S. nationals were killed in the attack?

    A. Bill Clinton   *C. George W. Bush*

    B. Barack Obama   *D. Richard Nixon*

3. Which president was accused of leaving his dog behind after a family vacation and then sent a Navy destroyer, at tax payers expense, to rescue the dog?

    A. Franklin D. Roosevelt   *C. Warren Harding*

    B. Calvin Coolidge   *D. George H.W. Bush*

4. Which president had the scandal of being accused of agreeing with McCarthyism during his term of office due to his silence on the matter?

  A. John F. Kennedy   C. Calvin Coolidge

  B. Harry Truman   D. Dwight D. Eisenhower

5. Which president ordered American forces to occupy the Philippines where a brutal war broke out against the Philippine Republic? This decision was radically opposed by American citizens to the point that they offered   to purchase the Philippines to give them their independence.

  A. William McKinley   C. William H. Taft

  B. Theodore Roosevelt   D. Chester Arthur

6. Which president in his bachelor days was accused of rape, impregnating a woman, and then having her baby kidnapped and adopted without her consent?

  A. James Polk   C. Bill Clinton

  B. Andrew Johnson   D. Grover Cleveland

7. Which president's administration was considered to be the most corrupt with two major scandals, The Whiskey Ring Scandal and the Credit Mobilier Scandal occuring during his presidency?

  A. Warren Harding   C. Ulysses S. Grant

  B. Andrew Johnson   D. Rutherford B. Hayes

8. Which president had several mistresses, even leaving one of them half

of his $3 million estate?

    A. John F. Kennedy   *C. John Quincy Adams*

    B. Franklin D. Roosevelt   *D. Lyndon B. Johnson*

9. Which president drank alcohol in the White House, which at that time was a violation of the Eighteenth Amendment?

    A. Warren Harding   *C. Rutherford B. Hayes*

    B. Grover Cleveland   *D. Calvin Coolidge*

10. Congress was a constant thorn in his side during his entire presidency due to the fact that he was the first vice-president to become president after the death of his predecessor. Congress did not want him in office and they made it as difficult for him as possible. In retaliation, the president counteracted by vetoing several pieces of legislation. Which president was this?

    A. John Tyler   *C. Andrew Johnson*

    B. Chester Arthur   *D. Lyndon B. Johnson*

11. During his presidency the IRS was used to illegally abuse and target his political opponents and when exposed federal investigations and congressional oversight were obstructed and protected.. Who was this president?

    A. Donald Trump   *C. Barack Obama*

    B. Bill Clinton   *D. George H.W. Bush*

12. Which president's reputation and respect suffered due to his ties with members of organized crime and his womanizing ways?

A. *Lyndon B. Johnson*   C. *Bill Clinton*

B. *John F. Kennedy*   D. *Franklin D. Roosevelt*

13. Which president had an affair with his wife's social secretary?

A. *John F. Kennedy*   C. *Bill Clinton*

B. *Jimmy Carter*   D. *Franklin D. Roosevelt*

14. Which president was accused of having illegitimate children with one of his slaves, which just years ago was confirmed by DNA testing?

A. *John Tyler*   C. *Thomas Jefferson*

B. *George Washington*   D. *Willaim H. Harrison*

15. The scandal of the Monica Lewinsky affair was at first denied by this president. This president was impeached for perjury and obstruction of justice, but remained in office. Who was he?

A. *Richard Nixon*   C. *Barack Obama*

B. *John F. Kennedy*   D. *Bill Clinton*

16. How many U.S. presidents are known to have smoked marijuana?

A. *5*   C. *3*

B. *11*   D. *7*

17. Which president was married to a woman who was already married to another man?

A. *Andrew Jackson*   C. *Barack Obama*

B. *Donald Trump*   D. *James Buchanan*

18. Which president was known to have romantic trysts with his mistress in the closet in the presidential office and had an illegitimate daughter with her that he refused to ever lay eyes on?

A. *Lyndon B. Johnson*   C. *Donald Trump*

B. *Warren Harding*   D. *Bill Clinton*

19. Which president gave former President Nixon an unconditional pardon for his involvement in Watergate, which not only did he state before he took office that he wouldn't do but both political parties were adamantly opposed to?

A. *John F. Kennedy*   C. *George H.W. Bush*

B. *Jimmy Carter*   D. *Gerald Ford*

20. Which president, along with his brother, was having an affair with the actress Marilyn Monroe who was found dead after having threatened to come forward about the president's infidelities?

A. *John F. Kennedy*   C. *Lyndon B. Johnson*

B. *Bill Clinton*   D. *Donald Trump*

21. Which of our presidents left office in disgrace over the Watergate Scandal?

A. *Ronald Reagan*   C. *Bill Clinton*

B. *Jimmy Carter*   D. *Richard Nixon*

22. Which president's reputation suffered after his death when the Teapot Dome Scandal was uncovered, even though he himself wasn't involved in any illegal doings?

A. Ulysses S. Grant   *C. Franklin D. Roosevelt*

B. Warren Harding   *D. Grover Cleveland*

23. Which president was accused of sexual misconduct and rape? He was confronted by his accusers when his own wife, a former First Lady, was herself running for the presidency.

A. Grover Cleveland   *C. Bill Clinton*

B. Donald Trump   *D. Franklin D. Roosevelt*

24. Which president sent his mistress a ticket to his inauguration?

A. John F. Kennedy   *C. Lyndon B. Johnson*

B. Franklin D. Roosevelt   *D. Bill Clinton*

25. Which president, after the end of his administration, refused 'to go away' from the public eye and leave presidential business to the sitting president?

A. John Adams   *C. Jimmy Carter*

B. Bill Clinton   *D. Barack Obama*

26. Which president was involved in the Star Route Scandal, a scheme where postal officials received bribes in exchange for giving postal delivery contracts to southern areas?

A. James Garfield

C. Andrew Johnson

B. Jimmy Carter

D. John Tyler

27. Who was president during the Iran-Contra Scandal, where money obtained from selling arms to Iran was secretly passed on to the revolutionary Contras in Nicaragua?

A. Jimmy Carter

C. Gerald Ford

B. Ronald Reagan

D. George H.W. Bush

28. Which president's administration was involved with speculation in the gold market driving up the price of gold which adversely affected those who had invested in gold?

A. Martin Van Buren

C. Benjamin Harrison

B. Chester Arthur

D. Ulysses S. Grant

29. Which president surprisingly was corruption free as a president, yet in his days before the presidency he had been tossed out of other political offices due to corruption?

A. Chester Arthur

C. Warren Harding

B. Ulysses S. Grant

D. Theodore Roosevelt

30. Which president was involved in the Watergate scandal, which is considered to be the most notorious presidential scandal to date?

A. Gerald Ford

C. Richard Nixon

B. Harry Truman

D. Jimmy Carter

31. Which president was accused by the mainstream media, with no evidence to collaborate their accusations, that the president colluded with Russia during the presidential election?

    A. Bill Clinton   *C. John F. Kennedy*

    B. Donald Trump   *D. George W. Bush*

32. Which president was condemned for his handling of the Great Depression and to further blacken his name was responsible for turning Army troops out to break up a protest of WWI veterans who had assembled in Washington to demand more pay that they had been previously promised?

    A. Franklin D. Roosevelt   *C. Harry Truman*

    B. Andrew Johnson   *D. Herbert Hoover*

33. Which president was accused of accepting "gifts" even going so far as to fill his retirement home with gifts he had received while president?

    A. Dwight D. Eisenhower   *C. Lyndon B. Johnson*

    B. Bill Clinton   *D. Abraham Lincoln*

34. Which former president has been accused by 'the right' of undermining the work of the sitting president and running a shadow government?

    A. George H.W. Bush   *C. John Adams*

    B. Barack Obama   *D. Bill Clinton*

35. Which president has been accused of fathering a black son whose

mother was a prostitute?

A. Warren Harding

C. Grover Cleveland

B. Andrew Johnson

D. Bill Clinton

36. Which president was discovered to have spied on the incoming president and leaked information, both during his presidential campaign and after he ws elected, along with spying on American citizens and political opponents?

A. Barack Obama

C. Bill Clinton

B. Donald Trump

D. Richard Nixon

37. Which president lied during his campaign when he said, 'Read my lips: No new taxes,' and then did indeed raise taxes?

A. Ronald Reagan

C. George H.W. Bush

B. Bill Clinton

D. Donald Trump

38. Which president had an on-going battle with the press, both during the elections and during his presidency, and called them "fake news"?

A. Barack Obama

C. Bill Clinton

B. Donald Trump

D. Jimmy Carter

39. Which president was responsible for a *significantly* high number of lethal drone strikes which also killed hundreds of innocent civilians? These drone strikes began on his third day of office and will remain a part of his legacy.

A. Bill Clinton   C. Donald Trump

B. George W. Bush   D. Barack Obama

40. Which president has had to deal with leaks within his own office and those who work closely to him?

A. George W. Bush   C. Richard Nixon

B. Donald Trump   D. Ronald Reagan

41. Which president had to live with the controversy of his decision to buy the Panama Canal from the French, a decision that was adamantly opposed by Congress, and then organized a revolution overthrowing the government of Panama?

A. Franklin D. Roosevelt   C. Theodore Roosevelt

B. William McKinley   D. James Garfield

42. Who was president when the Department of Justice told the FBI director to 'stand down' in his investigation of a former First Lady who was at the time running for the presidency? This appeared to have the backing of the president, considering the fact that when interviewed the president stated before the investigation was completed that there had been no crime committed.

A. Donald Trump   C. John F. Kennedy

B. Barack Obama   D. Andrew Johnson

43. Which president's vice president had to resign due to criminal charges, and then the president himself also had to resign at a later date?

A. *Richard Nixon*   C. *Andrew Johnson*

B. *James Garfield*   D. *Warren Harding*

44. Which president leaves behind a path of destruction with stories of murder of those who have crossed the president and first lady?

A. *Donald Trump*   C. *Zachary Taylor*

B. *Herbert Hoover*   D. *Bill Clinton*

45. Which president, after leaving office, was discovered to have lied to the American people about America's actions during the Vietnam War?

A. *John F. Kennedy*   C. *Dwight D. Eisenhower*

B. *Lyndon B. Johnson*   D. *Richard Nixon*

46. Which president has been married three times, and his young children learned of their father's extra-maritial affair in the tabloid headlines?

A. *John F. Kennedy*   C. *Donald Trump*

B. *John Tyler*   D. *Franklin D. Roosevelt*

47. Which president appeared weak in his actions when 52 American hostages were taken in Tehran and failed to secure their release during his presidency?

A. *Ronald Reagan*   C. *Jimmy Carter*

B. *Gerald Ford*   D. *Barack Obama*

48. Which former president has been accused of being involved in a "pay-to-play" scheme in which foreign governments could donate money to the president's foundation in exchange for beneficial treatment from the government influenced by the former president and former first lady who at the time was the Secretary of State with plans to run for the presidency?

A. Bill Clinton

C. Barack Obama

B. George W. Bush

D. Jimmy Carter

49. Which president fired the FBI director, some believing the reason to be due to the FBI's investigation of the president?

A. Barack Obama

C. Harry Truman

B. Woodrow Wilson

D. Donald Trump

50. Which president in a poker game lost a set of White House china dating from the days of Benjamin Harrison?

A. Richard Nixon

C. Warren Harding

B. Ulysses S. Grant

D. Grover Cleveland

Answers

Chapter 11 - Dirty Acts Of Presidents Revealed

1. C - Warren Harding

The letters were written before he became president but he was making blackmail payments at the expense of American taxpayers to the recipient of the letters while president.

2. B - Barack Obama

3. A - Franklin D. Roosevelt

4. D – Dwight D. Eisenhower

5. A - William McKinley

6. D - Grover Cleveland

7. C – Ulysses S. Grant

8. B - Franklin D. Roosevelt

9. A - Warren Harding

10. A - John Tyler

11. C - Barack Obama

12. B - John F. Kennedy

13. D - Franklin D. Roosevelt

When his wife discovered the affair she gave him an ultimatum – stop seeing the other woman or she would divorce him. He agreed to stop seeing the woman, but continued seeing her for the rest of his life. She was even by his side when he died.

14. C - Thomas Jefferson

It was rumored for over two hundred years that Thomas Jefferson had illegitimate children with his slave Sally Hemings. DNA tests were done and after careful study and consideration of all the facts presented, The Thomas Jefferson Foundation Research Committee concluded that there was a "high probability that Thomas Jefferson was the father of Eston Hemings, and that he was likely the father of all six of her children."

*Other presidents also accused of having had children with their slaves.

William H. Harrison *also had children with one of his slaves.*

John Tyler *also was rumored to have at least one child with a slave, but has not been proven one way or the other.*

Grover Cleveland. *There are two stories about this: One is that the mother of his illegitimate child threatened to go to the authorities due to Grover raping her which resulted in the child. He threatened her life and had her placed in a mental asylum, where she was later let go after it was determined she wasn't crazy, but instead had a politician out to destroy her to cover up his own actions. The other story was she was a mistress that he had a consensual affair with and the child was a result of this affair. He did have her committed to a mental asylum where she was soon released when it was found that she had no mental health problems. The child was snatched and given up for adoption without the mother's consent.*

Warren Harding *had an illegitimate child with a mistress.*

Only Thomas Jefferson's and Warren Harding's illegitimate children have been proven through DNA testing. The other presidents are rumors that have not been substantiated.

More detailed information on the legitimate & illegitimate children of the presidents and the stories of their lives can be found in **'Children of the Presidents,' by Cheryl Pryor.*

15. D - Bill Clinton

*It later came out that Monica Lewinsky wasn't the only one that pointed the finger at him about his sexual activities.

16. B - Eleven. There could have been more as many farmers grew hemp back in the early days of the U.S. Some presidents have been accused,

and some have admitted to, taking other illegal drugs also.

The presidents known to have smoked are:

George Washington – *He made notes in his diary about growing hemp and about it's use for smoking.*

Thomas Jefferson

James Madison

James Monroe – *He smoked hashish up until his death.*

Andrew Jackson – *He was known to have smoked with his troops.*

Zachary Taylor - *He was known to have smoked with his troops.*

Franklin Pierce - *He was known to have smoked with his troops during the Mexican-American War.*

John F. Kennedy – *He smoked using his back pain as the reason and once after smoking a few joints stated, "Suppose the Russians did something now."*

Bill Clinton – *He said he didn't inhale, but a college mate of his said he didn't have to inhale, he loved his pot brownies.*

George W. Bush – *He wouldn't admit to it when asked by a reporter, as he said he didn't want young children to follow in his footsteps.*

Barack Obama – *He has admitted to drug use during his younger days and in college.*

17. A - Andrew Jackson

Neither he nor his wife were aware at the time of their marriage that her divorce had not gone through. Both Jackson and his wife were under the impression the divorce had been finalized before they were married.

18. B - Warren Harding

DNA findings proved that he was indeed the father of the child even though throughout his lifetime he denied it.

19. D - Gerald Ford

20. A – John F. Kennedy

Official reports state Marilyn Monroe's death as suicide, but there have always been rumors that the Kennedys had something to do with her death to protect their image.

21. D - Richard Nixon

22. B - Warren Harding

23. C – Bill Clinton

24. B - Franklin D. Roosevelt

25. D – Barack Obama

26. A - James Garfield

27. B - Ronald Reagan

28. D - Ulysses S. Grant

29. A - Chester Arthur

30. C - Richard Nixon

31. B - Donald Trump

32. D – Herbert Hoover

33. A - Dwight D. Eisenhower

Gifts received while president don't actually belong to the president but is considered property of the United States and after their presidency goes to a Presidencial Library or can be purchased at the value of the item.

** *If you said B – Bill Clinton, he also "helped himself" to gifts received while president which he had to return once the White House discovered they had been taken by the former president and first lady.*

34. B – Barack Obama

35. D - Bill Clinton

To date this has not been proved or disproved as the president refuses to have DNA testing done.

36. A - Barack Obama

37. C – George H.W. Bush

38. B – Donald Trump

39. D – Barack Obama

40. B - Donald Trump

41. C - Theodore Roosevelt

His daughter Ethel years after her father's death supported the proposed revision of the Panama Canal Treaty

42. B - Barack Obama

43. A - Richard Nixon

44. D - Bill Clinton

45. B - Lyndon B. Johnson

46. C – Donald Trump

47. C - Jimmy Carter

48. A - Bill Clinton

49. D - Donald Trump

50. C - Warren Harding

12

War Hawks and Warmongers

Answers are given on pages 147 - 149.

1. How many future presidents fought in the Revolutionary War?

    A. 2   *C. 4*

    B. 3   *D. 7*

2. Which president was famous for the Battle of Tippecanoe?

    A. Zachary Taylor   *C. Dwight D. Eisenhower*

    B. William Henry Harrison   *D. Ulysses S. Grant*

3. Which president, when just a young boy, watched the Battle of Bunker Hill that was fought near his family farm?

    A. James Madison   *C. Franklin Pierce*

    B. James Garfield   *D. John Quincy Adams*

4. What future president was a part of the Rough Riders during the Spanish-American War?

A. *Grover Cleveland*   C. *Theodore Roosevelt*

B. *Chester Arthur*   D. *Abraham Lincoln*

5. Who was president when the U.S. invaded Panama and overthrew the dictator Noriega?

A. *Ronald Reagan*   C. *Theodore Roosevelt*

B. *George H.W. Bush*   D. *Dwight D. Eisenhower*

6. Which future president was Supreme Allied Commander of WWII?

A. *Dwight D. Eisenhower*   C. *George Washington*

B. *William McKinley*   D. *Harry Truman*

7. During the Mexican War, what future president barely escaped injury as a shot tore through his sleeve and another passed through the front of his coat taking off a button?

A. *Andrew Jackson*   C. *John Tyler*

B. *William H. Harrison*   D. *Zachary Taylor*

8. Which president was responsible for ending the Korean War?

A. *Franklin D. Roosevelt*   C. *John F. Kennedy*

B. *Dwight D. Eisenhower*   D. *Richard Nixon*

9. Which president was responsible for U.S. invading Iraq after convincing the American public that Iraq was in possession of weapons of mass destruction?

A. *George H.W. Bush*   C. *Bill Clinton*

B. *Barack Obama*   D. *George W. Bush*

10. Which president was responsible for the use of the atomic bomb against Japan to put an end to WWII?

A. *Harry Truman*   C. *Dwight D. Eisenhower*

B. *Franklin D. Roosevelt*   D. *Herbert Hoover*

11. Who was the last Civil War general to become president?

A. *Ulysses S. Grant*   C. *Zachary Taylor*

B. *Benjamin Harrison*   D. *William McKinley*

12. Which president had served in the army for four decades which included the War of 1812, Black Hawk War, and the second Seminole Wars?

A. *Abraham Lincoln*   C. *James Madison*

B. *William H. Harrison*   D. *Zachary Taylor*

13. In the War of 1812, which future president became a hero when he defeated the British at New Orleans?

A. *Andrew Jackson*   C. *Zachary Taylor*

B. *John Tyler*   D. *James Madison*

14. Which future president had opposed the use of the atomic bomb against Japan?

A. Harry Truman   C. Dwight D. Eisenhower

B. Franklin D. Roosevelt   D. John F. Kennedy

15. When this president took office, the war in Vietnam was costing Americans $60 – $80 million dollars a day and were losing the lives of approximately three hundred American soldiers a week. This president's main concern when he took office was to solve this issue. Who was he?

A. John F. Kennedy   C. Gerald Ford

B. Richard Nixon   D. Lyndon B. Johnson

16. What future president survived four plane crashes during WWII?

A. Dwight D. Eisenhower   C. George H.W. Bush

B. Ronald Reagan   D. Gerald Ford

17. Confederate General Robert E. Lee surrendered to this future president at Appomattox Court House in Virginia putting an end to the Civil War. Who was he?

A. Zachary Taylor   C. Abraham Lincoln

B. Andrew Johnson   D. Ulysses S. Grant

18. Which president stated detainees of terrorists were not protected by the Geneva Convention, and as a result many of the detainees were tortured?

A. Barack Obama   C. George H.W. Bush

B. Bill Clinton   D. George W. Bush

19. What president along with his Secretary of State are considered the "founding fathers" of ISIS, the world's most brutal terrorist organization, by supporting the Syrian organization which was dominated by al Qaeda which morphed into what we today call ISIS?

A. Donald Trump

C. Bill Clinton

B. Barack Obama

D. George H.W. Bush

20. What future president was wounded during the American Revolutionary War?

A. James Monroe

C. George Washington

B. John Adams

D. Andrew Jackson

21. Can you name the four presidents who fought or served in the Revolutionary War?

A. G. Washington, J. Adams, J. Monroe, & A. Jackson

B. G. Washington, J. Madison, T. Jefferson, & A. Jackson

C. G. Washington, J. Madison, J. Monroe, & A. Jackson

D. G. Washington, J. Adams, J. Monroe, J. Quincy Adams

22. Which president won a Nobel Peace Prize for mediating the Russo-Japanese War?

A. Jimmy Carter

C. Richard Nixon

B. Franklin D. Roosevelt

D. Theodore Roosevelt

23. The Treaty of Versailles, which brought an end to WWI, was drafted

by the Big Four powers – those of the United States, Great Britain, France, and Italy. What U.S. president helped draft this treaty?

A. Woodrow Wilson   C. Theodore Roosevelt

B. Harry Truman   D. William H. Taft

24. What president received the Distinguished Flying Cross for bravery?

A. George W. Bush   C. Dwight D. Eisenhower

B. George H.W. Bush   D. Jimmy Carter

25. Who was president during the days when the world was on the brink of nuclear annihilation known as the Cuban Missile Crisis?

A. Woodrow Wilson   C. Herbert Hoover

B. Calvin Coolidge   D. John F. Kennedy

26. Which future president led the invasion known in history as D-Day?

A. Franklin D. Roosevelt   C. Dwight D. Eisenhower

B. John F. Kennedy   D. George H.W. Bush

27. How many presidents fought or served in the Civil War?

A. 2   C. 5

B. 4   D. 8

28. Who was president when the United States invaded Afghanistan to overthrow the Taliban government?

A. George H.W. Bush   C. Barack Obama

B. George W. Bush   D. Ronald Reagan

29. Which president led the U.S. into the Korean War?

A. Harry Truman   C. Calvin Coolidge

B. Dwight D. Eisenhower   D. Warren Harding

30. What future president, on Christmas night in the year 1776, led his men across the Delaware River and attacked the Hessian mercenaries?

A. George Washington   C. James Monroe

B. Andrew Jackson   D. James Madison

31. Which president led the nation into war with Spain over Cuban independence?

A. Theodore Roosevelt   C. William McKinley

B. Benjamin Harrison   D. Woodrow Wilson

32. A few weeks after he left the office of the presidency, Confederates fired on Ft. Sumter which was the beginning of the Civil War. Who was the president who had just left office?

A. James Buchanan   C. Franklin Pierce

B. Zachary Taylor   D. Abraham Lincoln

33. What future president was in the Navy and in a torpedo boat when it was rammed by a Japanese warship? This future president led the

survivors to a nearby island where they were later rescued.

A. Richard Nixon   C. John F. Kennedy

B. George H.W. Bush   D. Jimmy Carter

34. Who was president when British troops set fire to the White House and the Capitol?

A. James Monroe   C. Thomas Jefferson

B. James Madison   D. John Adams

35. Which future president was with George Washington and his troops at Valley Forge during the harsh winter of 1777 – 1778?

A. John Adams   C. Andrew Jackson

B. William H. Harrison   D. James Monroe

36. Which future president sent troops to China to help put an end to the Boxer Rebellion, an uprising against foreign intervention in China?

A. Herbert Hoover   C. William H. Taft

B. William McKinley   D. Benjamin Harrison

37. During WWII this future president's plane was hit and on fire, but he continued on and successfully bombed his target before ejecting out of his plane. He was rescued in the water by an American submarine. Who was he?

A. George H.W. Bush   C. Bill Clinton

B. John F. Kennedy   D. George W. Bush

38. Which future president was appointed Commander-in-Chief of the Colonials against Great Britain?

    A. Dwight D. Eisenhower   *C. Ulysses S. Grant*

    B. William H. Harrison   *D. George Washington*

39. Which president was a general and a hero in the Mexican-American War and the War of 1812?

    A. James Polk   *C. Zachary Taylor*

    B. Theodore Roosevelt   *D. Andrew Jackson*

40. At the beginning of WWI what president declared America neutral, but by 1917 he asked Congress to declare war when Germany sunk American ships and ignored U.S. neutrality? Who was he?

    A. Woodrow Wilson   *C. Franklin D. Roosevelt*

    B. William H. Taft   *D. Calvin Coolidge*

41. What future president fought in the Revolutionary War when he was a teenager?

    A. Thomas Jefferson   *C. James Madison*

    B. James Monroe   *D. Andrew Jackson*

42. What future president commanded the Union Army during the Civil War?

    A. Abraham Lincoln   *C. Ulysses S. Grant*

    B. Franklin Pierce   *D. Benjamin Harrison*

43. Which president created an air lift to get supplies to the people of Berlin when the Russians blockaded western areas of Berlin?

A. Harry Truman

C. Herbert Hoover

B. Calvin Coolidge

D. Warren Harding

44. In 1863, what president reshaped the cause of the war from keeping the union intact to abolishing slavery?

A. Ulysses S. Grant

C. Zachary Taylor

B. James Polk

D. Abraham Lincoln

45. The day after Pearl Harbor was bombed by the Japanese, which president declared war on Japan?

A. Theodore Roosevelt

C. Herbert Hoover

B. Harry Truman

D. Franklin D. Roosevelt

46. What future president had winter quarters in the year 1777 at Valley Forge during the Revolutionary War?

A. James Madison

C. Andrew Jackson

B. George Washington

D. James Monroe

47. Who was the only president who had been a prisoner of war?

A. George Washington

C. Andrew Jackson

B. Ulysses S. Grant

D. John F. Kennedy

48. Which future president enlisted in the Black Hawk War and seeing no action, after leaving the military made the joke that the only blood he lost in the war was to mosquitoes?

A. Zachary Taylor

C. Benjamin Harrison

B. Abraham Lincoln

D. Millard Fillmore

49. Which president declared war which was known as Operation Desert Storm or the Persian Gulf War?

A. George H.W. Bush

C. Ronald Reagan

B. Dwight D. Eisenhower

D. George W. Bush

50. What future president served as a military aide to General Douglas MacArthur?

A. John F. Kennedy

C. George H.W. Bush

B. Theodore Roosevelt

D. Dwight D. Eisenhower

Answers

Chapter 12 - War Hawks and Warmongers

1. C – Four

2. B - William H. Harrison

3. D - John Quincy Adams

4. C - Theodore Roosevelt

5. B - George H.W. Bush

6. A - Dwight D. Eisenhower

7. D - Zachary Taylor

8. B - Dwight D. Eisenhower

9. D - George W. Bush

10. A - Harry Truman

11. B - Benjamin Harrison

12. D - Zachary Taylor

13. A - Andrew Jackson

14. C - Dwight D. Eisenhower

15. B - Richard Nixon

16. C - George H.W. Bush

17. D - Ulysses S. Grant

18. D - George W. Bush

19. B - Barack Obama

Secretary of State Hillary Clinton was equally responsible.

20. A - James Monroe

21.C - George Washington, James Madison, James Monroe, and Andrew Jackson

22. D - Theodore Roosevelt

23. A - Woodrow Wilson

24. B - George H.W. Bush

25. D - John F. Kennedy

26. C - Dwight D. Eisenhower

27. D - 8

Andrew Johnson, Ulysses S. Grant, Rutherford B. Hayes, James Garfield, Chester Arthur, Benjamin Harrison, William McKinley, and Millard Fillmore

28. B - George W. Bush

29. A - Harry Truman

30. A - George Washington

31. C - William McKinley

The end result was U.S. possession over Puerto Rico, Guam, and the Philippines.

32. A - James Buchanan

33. C - John F. Kennedy

34. B - James Madison

35. D - James Monroe

36. B - William McKinley

37. A - George H.W. Bush

38. D - George Washington

39. C - Zachary Taylor

40. A - Woodrow Wilson

41. B - James Monroe

42. C - Ulysses S. Grant

43. A - Harry Truman

44. D - Abraham Lincoln

45. D - Franklin D. Roosevelt

President Roosevelt actually stated his reason on why we should declare war before a joint session of Congress and then declared war on Japan.

46. B - George Washington

47. C - Andrew Jackson

He was taken prisoner by British soldiers when they invaded the Carolinas. While prisoner he refused to shine an officer's boots, the officer then hit Jackson across the face with his saber leaving a scar.

48. B - Abraham Lincoln

49. A - George H.W. Bush

50. D - Dwight D. Eisenhower

13

Fun Facts About The Presidents

Answers are given on pages 159 - 161.

1. Which president was ambidextrous (could write with either hand)?

   A. Richard Nixon   C. Harry Truman

   B. John Quincy Adams   D. James Garfield

2. Which president, at the age of fifteen, ran away from home?

   A. Andrew Johnson   C. Abraham Lincoln

   B. Lyndon B. Johnson   D. Zachary Taylor

3. Which president was blind in one eye from a boxing match he was in?

   A. Lyndon B. Johnson   C. Gerald Ford

   B. Grover Cleveland   D. Theodore Roosevelt

4. Who is the only president in the twentieth century to not have a college degree?

A. *Harry Truman*   C. *Barack Obama*

B. *Lyndon B. Johnson*   D. *Donald Trump*

5. Which president had a job as a Yellowstone Park Ranger?

A. *Theodore Roosevelt*   C. *Gerald Ford*

B. *Grover Cleveland*   D. *Benjamin Harrison*

6. What president measured at 6'4"?

A. *Donald Trump*   C. *Lyndon B. Johnson*

B. *Abraham Lincoln*   D. *Thomas Jefferson*

7. Which president was a skilled chef?

A. *George H.W. Bush*   C. *Calvin Coolidge*

B. *William McKinley*   D. *Dwight D. Eisenhower*

8. Which two presidents were married to foreign born First Ladies?

A. *J. Adams & J.F. Kennedy*   C. *J. Monroe & D. Trump*

B. *W. McKinley & M. Van Buren*   D. *J.Q. Adams & D. Trump*

9. Which president stated he had seen a UFO?

A. *George W. Bush*   C. *Jimmy Carter*

B. *Dwight D. Eisenhower*   D. *Ronald Reagan*

10. What president played the saxophone?

    A. Gerald Ford   *C. Warren Harding*

    B. Bill Clinton   *D. James Buchanan*

11. Which president had a photographic memory?

    A. Theodore Roosevelt   *C. John F. Kennedy*

    B. Donald Trump   *D. Richard Nixon*

12. Which president was a mimic, and loved to tell dialect jokes in English, Irish, and Scottish accents?

    A. Woodrow Wilson   *C. Theodore Roosevelt*

    B. Lyndon B. Johnson   *D. George W. Bush*

13. What president loved to paint for relaxation? He couldn't draw, so someone else would sketch the picture and he would paint it.

    A. Woodrow Wilson   *C. Dwight D. Eisenhower*

    B. George W. Bush   *D. William H. Taft*

14. Which president had a son that was an actor and played on a soap opera?

    A. Ronald Reagan   *C. John F. Kennedy*

    B. George H.W. Bush   *D. Gerald Ford*

15. What president collected comic books?

A. George W. Bush   C. Bill Clinton

B. Barack Obama   D. Donald Trump

16. Which president painted his golf balls black in the winter so he could see them in the snow?

    A. Woodrow Wilson   C. Dwight D. Eisenhower

    B. George H.W. Bush   D. Barack Obama

17. Who was the only bachelor to be president in American history?

    A. Thomas Jefferson   C. James Buchanan

    B. Martin Van Buren   D. John Tyler

18. What president was captain of Yale University's baseball team?

    A. George W. Bush   C. Ronald Reagan

    B. Gerald Ford   D. George H.W. Bush

19. Which president could read English, Latin, French, and Greek?

    A. Donald Trump   C. Harry Truman

    B. Thomas Jefferson   D. James Madison

20. It's a well-known fact that many of our presidents have loved to play golf, but can you name which president actually owned seventeen golf courses at the time of his presidency?

A. *George H.W. Bush*   C. *Donald Trump*

B. *Dwight D. Eisenhower*   D. *John F. Kennedy*

21. As a child, which president was too sickly to go to school?

A. *Theodore Roosevelt*   C. *Andrew Jackson*

B. *James Polk*   D. *James Monroe*

22. Which president was one of, if not "the most", accomplished athletes ever to become president?

A. *Donald Trump*   C. *George H.W. Bush*

B. *Gerald Ford*   D. *Theodore Roosevelt*

23. Who was the only president to weigh under one hundred pounds?

A. *William H. Taft*   C. *James Madison*

B. *Millard Fillmore*   D. *Franklin Pierce*

24. Which president, receiving his wings at the age of nineteen, was the nation's youngest commissioned pilot?

A. *George W. Bush*   C. *Dwight D. Eisenhower*

B. *Jimmy Carter*   D. *George H.W. Bush*

25. Which president smoked twenty cigars a day?

A. Ulysses S. Grant   C. William H. Harrison

B. Zachary Taylor   D. Franklin D. Roosevelt

26. Which president is the only president whose first language was not English?

A. Rutherford B. Hayes   C. Ulysses S. Grant

B. Martin Van Buren   D. James Monroe

27. Who was the only president to earn a doctorate?

A. Woodrow Wilson   C. Harry Truman

B. Bill Clinton   D. Calvin Coolidge

28. Which president was a stamp collector and even made suggestions on designs of new commemorative stamps?

A. Ronald Reagan   C. George Washington

B. Franklin D. Roosevelt   D. William McKinley

29. During his college days, which president was Most Valuable Player and was offered a football career by the Green Bay Packers and the Detroit Lions?

A. George H.W. Bush   C. Gerald Ford

B. William H. Taft   D. Theodore Roosevelt

30. Which president gave up horseback riding and instead took up riding a mechanical horse?

A. *Calvin Coolidge*   C. *Lyndon B. Johnson*

B. *George W. Bush*   D. *Grover Cleveland*

31. Which president was an ordained minister?

A. *Richard Nixon*   C. *Rutherford B. Hayes*

B. *James Madison*   D. *James Garfield*

32. Many former presidents have been interviewed on late night talk shows and asked about aliens and Area 51. Which president admitted when the 50th anniversary of the alleged UFO crash in Roswell was coming up, he had his aides look into if there were aliens at Area 51?

A. *Dwight D. Eisenhower*   C. *George W. Bush*

B. *Jimmy Carter*   D. *Bill Clinton*

33. Which president never voted until he was sixty-two years of age?

A. *Donald Trump*   C. *Thomas Jefferson*

B. *Ulysses S. Grant*   D. *Zachary Taylor*

34. Who is the only president to have been a professional actor?

A. *Gerald Ford*   C. *Warren Harding*

B. *Ronald Reagan*   D. *Donald Trump*

35. At one time which president was an owner of the Texas Rangers baseball team?

A. Gerald Ford   C. George H.W. Bush

B. Lyndon B. Johnson   D. George W. Bush

36. Which future president had the job of scrubbing toilets while in the navy?

A. Jimmy Carter   C. George W. Bush

B. Richard Nixon   D. Lyndon B. Johnson

37. Who was president at the time that Charles Lindbergh made his historic flight across the Atlantic Ocean?

A. Warren Harding   C. Theodore Roosevelt

B. Calvin Coolidge   D. Harry Truman

38. Which president was the teddy bear named after?

A. George Washington   C. Theodore Roosevelt

B. Thomas Jefferson   D. William H. Taft

39. Which president, while in college took part in football, track, captain of the swim team, drama, and was student council president?

A. George W. Bush   C. Grover Cleveland

B. Franklin D. Roosevelt   D. Ronald Reagan

40. Which president worked as a fashion model?

A. Gerald Ford

C. John F. Kennedy

B. Ronald Reagan

D. Bill Clinton

Answers

Chapter 13 - Fun Facts About The Presidents

1. D - James Garfield

2. B - Lyndon B. Johnson

3. D - Theodore Roosevelt

4. A - Harry Truman

5. C - Gerald Ford

6. B - Abraham Lincoln

7. D - Dwight D. Eisenhower

8. D - John Quincy Adams & Donald Trump

9. C - Jimmy Carter

10. B - Bill Clinton

11. A - Theodore Roosevelt

12. A - Woodrow Wilson

13. C - Dwight D. Eisenhower

14. D - Gerald Ford

15. B - Barack Obama

16. A - Woodrow Wilson

17. C - James Buchanan

Grover Cleveland was a bachelor when he was elected but was married during his first administration.

18. D - George H.W. Bush

19. B - Thomas Jefferson

20. C - Donald Trump

21. A - Theodore Roosevelt

22. B - Gerald Ford

Each of the presidents listed were exceptional athletes.

23. C - James Madison

He was 5'4 and weighed ninety-eight pounds.

24. D - George H.W. Bush

25. A - Ulysses S. Grant

26. B – Martin Van Buren

His first language was Dutch.

27. A - Woodrow Wilson

28. B - Franklin D. Roosevelt

29. C - Gerald Ford

30. A - Calvin Coolidge

31. D - James Garfield

32. D - Bill Clinton

33. C - Zachary Taylor

34. B - Ronald Reagan

His first wife, Jane Wyman, who he was divorced from was a well-known actress also. His second wife, First Lady Nancy Reagan, was a lesser known actress.

35. D - George W. Bush

36. A - Jimmy Carter

37. B - Calvin Coolidge

38. C - Theodore Roosevelt

The teddy bear was named after him when a cartoon was put out showing Theodore Roosevelt saving the life of a bear cub while hunting.

39. D - Ronald Reagan

40. A -Gerald Ford

During his days at Yale he had invested in a modeling agency. He posed for ski-wear ads.

14

Illness, Accidents, and Deaths Of The Presidents

Answers are given on pages 169 - 170.

1. Of the first five presidents, how many of them died on the 4th of July?

    A. 1   C. 4

    B. 3   D. 2

2. Which president suffered a stroke while president and unbeknowst to the American public was incapacitated and it was actually the First Lady who was acting as the president?

    A. James Garfield   C. Woodrow Wilson

    B. Franklin D. Roosevelt   D. Warren Harding

3. You could actually say this president's lengthy inaugural address is what killed him, since he stood in the outdoors with no hat or coat and ended up with pneumonia and died. Who was he?

    A. William H. Harrison   C. Zachary Taylor

    B. William McKinley   D. John Tyler

4. Who succeeded to the presidency after President Lincoln was assassinated?

A. Andrew Johnson

C. James Buchanan

B. Ulysses S. Grant

D. Franklin Pierce

5. Which of our presidents was in a wheelchair as a result of polio?

A. Martin Van Buren

C. Chester Arthur

B. Franklin D. Roosevelt

D. Willaim H. Taft

6. Which president died from a heart attack while in office?

A. Woodrow Wilson

C. William H. Harrison

B. Zachary Taylor

D. Warren Harding

7. Which president was assassinated after only a few months in office?

A. James Garfield

C. William McKinley

B. Abraham Lincoln

D. John F. Kennedy

8. Which president was shot and hit twice by Lee Harvey Oswald as the president was driving by in a motorcade?

A. William McKinley

C. John F. Kennedy

B. James Garfield

D. Franklin D. Roosevelt

9. Which president had a secret operation due to cancer aboard a yacht in order to keep it a secret from the American public?

A. Grover Cleveland   C. Theodore Roosevelt

B. Rutherford B. Hayes   D. Herbert Hoover

10. Which president in his last days as he was dying was offered stimulants to keep him alive until July 4th, so he could join three other former presidents to have died on that historic date?

A. James Monroe   C. Thomas Jefferson

B. James Madison   D. John Adams

11. Which president survived an assassination attempt in the 1912 election, when the metal case for his glasses in his pocket stopped a bullet from going through to his heart?

A. William McKinley   C. Rutherford B. Hayes

B. William H. Taft   D. Theodore Roosevelt

12. Which president was buried at Washington National Cathedral, the only president buried in the nation's capital?

A. Harry Truman   C. Woodrow Wilson

B. John F. Kennedy   D. Chester Arthur

13. After which president was shot did Alexander Graham Bell attempt to find the bullet still inside the President by using a metal detector Bell had designed?

A. James Garfield   C. William McKinley

B. Abraham Lincoln   D. Theodore Roosevelt

14. Which two presidents died on July 4, 1826 – the 50th anniversary of the adoption of the Declaration of Independence?

A. G. Washington & T. Jefferson

B. J. Adams & T. Jefferson

C. J. Adams & J. Monroe

D. J. Adams & J. Madison

15. Over 50 years after his death, the American public is still not buying the story they were told that there was a single shooter in the assassination of which president?

A. Abraham Lincoln

B. James Garfield

C. Zachary Taylor

D. John F. Kennedy

16. Which president during his youth was saved from drowning?

A. Ulysses S. Grant

B. Abraham Lincoln

C. George Washington

D. Donald Trump

17. After which president's sudden death was the First Lady suspected of poisioning him?

A. Zachary Taylor

B. William H. Harrison

C. Warren Harding

D. Franklin D. Roosevelt

18. Which president was shot on his way to make a speech? He insisted on giving his speech before going to the hospital. The bullet was never removed.

A. Theodore Roosevelt

B. Chester Arthur

C. James Garfield

D. Millard Fillmore

19. Which sitting president was "assassinated" in a Shakespeare's '*Julius Caesar*' play where the part of Caesar was made over to represent the president and was depicted as being brutally stabbed to death on stage?

A. James Madison

C. Barack Obama

B. Donald Trump

D. Herbert Hoover

20. Which president had two assassination attempts made on his life, both by women?

A. Ronald Reagan

C. George H.W. Bush

B. Bill Clinton

D. Gerald Ford

21. Which president requested that at his death his body be wrapped in an American flag with his head resting on a copy of the Constitution?

A. James Madison

C. Andrew Johnson

B. James Monroe

D. Abraham Lincoln

22. There was a failed assassination attempt on which president's life in the form of a car bomb in Kuwait?

A. George W. Bush

C. Ronald Reagan

B. Richard Nixon

D. George H.W. Bush

23. Which president, just two months after his inauguration, survived an assassination attempt?

A. James Garfield

C. Jimmy Carter

B. Ronald Reagan

D. George H.W. Bush

24. Who was the first president to have his funeral broadcast on the radio?

A. Willaim McKinley

C. William H. Taft

B. Abraham Lincoln

D. Woodrow Wilson

25. Who was the first president to have an assassination attempt made on his life, but was saved because the gun did not fire properly?

A. Andrew Jackson

C. John Quincy Adams

B. James Buchanan

D. Martin Van Buren

26. As a teen, what president underwent major surgery and was given only brandy as a sedative?

A. James Polk

C. William H. Harrison

B. John Tyler

D. Ulysses S. Grant

27. Which president, just a year after becoming president, learned he had a fatal kidney disease?

A. James Polk

C. Benjamin Harrison

B. Chester Arthur

D. Warren Harding

28. It was revealed after which president's retirement that he had Alzheimers. Who was he?

A. George W. Bush

C. Bill Clinton

B. Ronald Reagan

D. Jimmy Carter

29. How many presidents have been assassinated?

    A. 6   *C. 3*

    B. 5   *D. 4*

30. After an assassination attempt was made on this president's life, on the way to surgery to remove the bullet he jokingly said, "I forgot to duck." Who is he?

    A. George W. Bush   *C. Ronald Reagan*

    B. Barack Obama   *D. Calvin Coolidge*

Answers

Chapter 14 - Illness, Accidents, and Deaths Of The Presidents

1. B - 3

John Adams and Thomas Jefferson both died on July 4th, 1826 and James Monroe died on July 4th, 1831.

2. C - Woodrow Wilson

3. A - William H. Harrison

4. A - Andrew Johnson

5. B - Franklin D. Roosevelt

6. D - Warren Harding

It is believed he died of a heart attack though some suspected the First Lady of poisioning the president. No autopsy was preformed at her request.

7. A - James Garfield

8. C - John F. Kennedy

Though still to this day, many question the fact of who actually shot and killed the president making this one of the longest, ongoing conspiracy theories in American history.

9. A - Grover Cleveland

10. B - James Madison

He refused.

11. D - Theodore Roosevelt

12. C - Woodrow Wilson

While Arlington National Cemetery is just across the Potomac River, it lies in the state of Virginia.

13. A - James Garfield

Unfortunately, he was unsuccessful in locating the bullet and the president died from infection and internal hemorrhaging.

14. B - John Adams and Thomas Jefferson

15. D - John F. Kennedy

16. A - Ulysses S. Grant

17. C - Warren Harding

18. A - Theodore Roosevelt

19. B - Donald Trump

20. D - Gerald Ford

21. C - Andrew Johnson

22. D - George H.W. Bush

23. B - Ronald Reagan

24. C - William H. Taft

25. A - Andrew Jackson

26. A - James Polk

27. B - Chester Arthur

28. B - Ronald Reagan

29. D - 4

Abraham Lincoln, James Garfield, William McKinley, and John F. Kennedy

30. C - Ronald Reagan

First Ladies

15

Before Becoming First Lady

Answers are given on pages 179 - 180.

1. While in Paris this future First Lady used her popularity to save the life of the wife of the Marquis de Lafayette who was imprisoned and was being held under a death sentence for treason.

   A. Abigail Adams   C. Martha Washington

   B. Dolley Madison   D. Elizabeth Monroe

2. Which future First Lady was walking with her maid and infant son when the baby was ripped out of her arms? The thief took the child and ran.

   A. Harriet Lane   C. Jane Pierce

   B. Florence Harding   D. Louisa Adams

3. While living in China her husband was a consulting engineer to the Chinese government. The Empress Dowager Cixi declared war on all foreigners, what has become known as the Boxer Rebellion. This future First Lady patrolled her garden with a .38 pistol. She rode her bike in town until the day a bullet blew out one of her tires. She was fearless and refused to leave the country as long as her husband was still there.

A. *Lou Hoover*   C. *Barbara Bush*

B. *Julia Grant*   D. *Martha Jefferson*

4. She lived in France with her husband during the French Revolution.

A. *Abigail Adams*   C. *Elizabeth Monroe*

B. *Dolley Madison*   D. *Mary Todd Lincoln*

5. She and her husband had been invited to attend the theater with the Lincolns the night President Lincoln was shot.

A. *Eliza Johnson*   C. *Nellie Taft*

B. *Julia Grant*   D. *Martha Washington*

6. She carried much of the burden at home caring for the family farm and their children while her husband was often away busy with work from his law practice, as an active member of the Revolution, and a part of the Continental Congress.

A. *Abigail Adams*   C. *George Washington*

B. *Rachel Jackson*   D. *Dolley Madison*

7. She joined her husband at his winter encampments during the Revolutionary War.

A. *Dolley Madison*   C. *Elizabeth Monroe*

B. *Abigail Adams*   D. *Martha Washington*

8. She died from a heart attack three months before her husband's

inauguration.

A. Eleanor Roosevelt

C. Jane Pierce

B. Rachel Jackson

D. Letitia Tyler

9. Growing up she had the reputation of a tomboy. One neighbor boy said about her, "She was the first girl I ever knew who could whistle through her teeth and bat a ball as far as any boy could."

A. Barbara Bush

C. Bess Truman

B. Melania Trump

D. Mary Todd Lincoln

10. During the early years as newlyweds they lived in exotic places such as: China, Egypt, Europe, Ceylon, Burma, Japan, Australia, and Siberia.

A. Melania Trump

C. Jackie Kennedy

B. Nellie Taft

D. Lou Hoover

11. Both her and her husband came from poverty. She was the 1st First Lady to come from a lower-economic class.

A. Abigail Fillmore

C. Pat Nixon

B. Melania Trump

D. Hillary Clinton

12. She was a part of the impeachment inquiry staff advising the House of Judiciary Committee during President Nixon's impeachment trial.

A. Michelle Obama

C. Betty Ford

B. Hillary Clinton

D. Lady Bird Johnson

13. When she met her future husband, the future president, she was a wealthy widow who owned over 7,000 acres of land and 300 slaves.

A. Dolley Madison

C. Elizabeth Monroe

B. Martha Washington

D. Abigail Adams

14. Her first job was as a photographer for a newspaper where she took pictures of people she met on the street asking them questions on issues of the day. Some of the people and events she photographed on the job were Richard Nixon, Dwight D. Eisenhower's first inauguration, and the coronation of Queen Elizabeth II.

A. Pat Nixon

C. Lady Bird Johnson

B. Grace Coolidge

D. Jackie Kennedy

15. Her husband owned a newspaper. When she married him she took over the circulation department and was even known to spank the newsboys when they needed it.

A. Florence Harding

C. Frances Cleveland

B. Ida McKinley

D. Bess Truman

16. She led fund raising efforts for the Lewis & Clark Expedition.

A. Abigail Adams

C. Dolley Madison

B. Julia Grant

D. Eleanor Roosevelt

17. She was an orphan by the age of eighteen where she grew up on a farm. In her early teens after her mother's death, she cleaned and cooked for the family and farm workers. When her father was deathly ill she

cared for him while also working as a janitor and bookkeeper to pay his medical bills, all while caring for the house and farm chores while under the age of eighteen.

A. *Rosalynn Carter*   C. *Nancy Reagan*

B. *Pat Nixon*   D. *Michelle Obama*

18. She was decorated by King Albert I for help in coordinating food and financial aid in neutral Belgium during WWI.

A. *Lou Hoover*   C. *Eleanor Roosevelt*

B. *Grace Coolidge*   D. *Frances Cleveland*

19. Which First Lady was formerly a model beginning her modeling career at the age of sixteen, has a jewelry and skin care line, a philanthropist, married to a billionaire, but her priority was always her role as a mother and wife?

A. *Betty Ford*   C. *Melania Trump*

B. *Jackie Kennedy*   D. *Grace Coolidge*

20. She became friends with Napoleon Bonaparte's family when her husband was U.S. Minister to France.

A. *Abigail Adams*   C. *Julia Grant*

B. *Hannah Van Buren*   D. *Elizabeth Monroe*

21. Her husband called her "*his little Rebel wife*" as during the Civil War her loyalties were with the South. Her husband was a Union Army Quartermaster General and Inspector General of State Troops.

A. *Ellen Arthur*   C. *Mary Todd Lincoln*

B. *Peggy Taylor*   D. *Frances Cleveland*

22. She was a lawyer, city administrator, and community outreach worker before becoming First Lady.

A. *Hillary Clinton*   C. *Betty Ford*

B. *Michelle Obama*   D. *Eleanor Roosevelt*

23. She was a teacher at a school for the deaf.

A. *Lucy Hayes*   C. *Grace Coolidge*

B. *Nellie Taft*   D. *Lady Bird Johnson*

24. She was pretty and a great athlete. She played as a third baseman, she was a tennis player, and an ice skater.

A. *Bess Truman*   C. *Betty Ford*

B. *Grace Coolidge*   D. *Laura Bush*

25. This First Lady's first husband was an heir to one of the greatest fortunes in colonial Virginia, which she inherited after his death.

A. *Dolley Madison*   C. *Eliza Johnson*

B. *Hannah Van Buren*   D. *Martha Washington*

Answers

Chapter 15 — Before Becoming First Lady

1. D - Elizabeth Monroe, wife of James Monroe

Lafayette was the French revolutionary leader who came to the aid of the colonies during the American Revolutionary War.

2. D - Louisa Adams, wife of John Quincy Adams

Louisa and her maid went door to door at different houses banging on the doors until the thief came out and returned the baby.

3. A - Lou Hoover, wife of Herbert Hoover

4. C - Elizabeth Monroe, wife of James Monroe

5. B - Julia Grant, wife of Ulysses S. Grant

6. A - Abigail Adams, wife of John Adams

7. D - Martha Washington, wife of George Washington

8. B - Rachel Jackson, wife of Andrew Jackson

9. C- Bess Truman, wife of Harry Truman

10. D - Lou Hoover, wife of Herbert Hoover

11. A - Abigail Fillmore, wife of Millard Fillmore

12. B - Hillary Clinton, wife of Bill Clinton

She was fired by her boss giving the reason, "She was a liar. She was an unethical, dishonest lawyer, she conspired to violate the Constitution, the rules of the House, the rules of the Committee, and the rules of confidentiality."

13. B - Martha Washington, wife of George Washington

14. D - Jacqueline Kennedy, wife of John F. Kennedy

15. A - Florence Harding, wife of Warren Harding

16. C - Dolley Madison, wife of James Madison

17. B - Pat Nixon, wife of Richard Nixon

18. A - Lou Hoover, wife of Herbert Hoover

19. C - Melania Trump, wife of Donald Trump

20. D - Elizabeth Monroe, wife of James Monroe

21. A - Ellen Arthur, wife of Chester Arthur

22. B - Michelle Obama, wife of Barack Obama

23. C - Grace Coolidge, wife of Calvin Coolidge

24. A - Bess Truman, wife of Harry Truman

25. D - Martha Washington, wife of George Washington

16

Political Life

Answers are given on page 184.

1. Reporters called her "a diplomat in high heels."

A. Eleanor Roosevelt

B. Michelle Obama

C. Pat Nixon

D. Mamie Eisenhower

2. Even though her husband was cold and indifferent to her feelings, thoughts, and illnesses; for him she endured cold winters in Russia, eight years of separation from two of her sons, and a six week coach ride across a Europe at war where she had to save her own life by convincing French troops she was Napoleon's sister.

A. Elizabeth Monroe

B. Louisa Adams

C. Lou Hoover

D. Abigail Fillmore

3. While a student at Wellesley College, she was president of the Young Republicans Club and organized a student strike after the assassination of Dr. Martin Luther King Jr.

A. Jackie Kennedy

B. Hillary Clinton

C. Ida McKinley

D. Betty Ford

4. Which First Lady faced "the firing squad" from the press during her husband's presidential campaign? She sued *The Daily Mail* after they published false and defamatory statements about her being involved in an escort service and a nude photo of the prospective First Lady from her younger days was released by *The New York Post* by an opponent of her husbands?

A. Melania Trump

C. Hillary Clinton

B. Jackie Kennedy

D. Laura Bush

5. When she met her future husband he was a delegate in the Continental Congress. He was forty-three years old, had never married, and was seventeen years older than her.

A. Martha Washington

C. Elizabeth Monroe

B.Abigail Adams

D. Dolley Madison

6. She performed the social duties of a political wife, though she was unhappy doing so and avoided them whenever possible. She blamed her husband's political friends for his excessive drinking and blamed the tragedies and even the death of their first child on his life in politics.

A. Jane Pierce

C. Julia Grant

B. Lucy Hayes

D. Laura Bush

7. She regretted marrying into a political family and strongly disliked living in the White House.

A. Laura Bush

C. Louisa Adams

B. Eleanor Roosevelt

D. Michelle Obama

8. Unusual for the times of the 19th century, she was deeply involved in her husband's career and had substantial influence in politics.

A. Sarah Polk

C. Florence Harding

B. Eleanor Roosevelt

D. Michelle Obama

9. When she joined her husband in Washington, D.C. after he became Vice President, she became the most popular woman in the capital.

A. Edith Roosevelt

C. Julia Grant

B. Eliza Johnson

D. Grace Coolidge

10. She is most remembered by her active role in American politics.

A. Martha Washington

C. Jane Pierce

B. Eleanor Roosevelt

D. Mary Todd Lincoln

Answers

Chapter 16 — Political Life

1. C - Pat Nixon, wife of Richard Nixon

2. B - Louisa Adams, wife of John Quincy Adams

3. B - Hillary Clinton, wife of Bill Clinton

Yes, she used to be a Republican. Hard to believe; isn't it?

4. A - Melania Trump, wife of Donald Trump

5. D - Dolley Madison, wife of James Madison

6. A - Jane Pierce, wife of Franklin Pierce

7. C - Louisa Adams, wife of John Quincy Adams

8. A - Sarah Polk, wife of James Polk

9. D - Grace Coolidge, wife of Calvin Coolidge

10. B - Eleanor Roosevelt, wife of Franklin D. Roosevelt

17

Romance With A Future President

Answers are given on pages 189 - 190.

1. The future President proposed to her on their first date. Who was the bride-to-be?

    A. Julia Grant   *C. Laura Bush*

    B. Lady Bird Johnson   *D. Hillary Clinton*

2. The future First Lady and future President lived across the street from each other. She could see him standing in the window in his long underwear shaving while wearing a derby hat on the back of his head to hold his hair down. Who was she?

    A. Grace Coolidge   *C. Frances Cleveland*

    B. Edith Wilson   *D. Mamie Eisenhower*

3. This First Lady and President had an active sex life and once broke the bed in the White House.

    A. Jackie Kennedy   *C. Bess Truman*

    B. Nellie Taft   *D. Hillary Clinton*

4. Her identity as to who would be the bride about to marry a sitting President was left concealed until just a week before the wedding. Who was she?

A. Frances Cleveland

C. Edith Wilson

C. Harriet Lane

D. Rachel Jackson

5. She received her proposal of marriage by telegram which read, "Going to China via San Francisco. Will you go with me?"

A. Barbara Bush

C. Louisa Adams

B. Mamie Eisenhower

D. Lou Hoover

6. He proposed to her on Valentine's Day and gave her his West Point ring to seal the deal. Who was she?

A. Julie Grant

C. Mamie Eisenhower

B. Peggy Taylor

D. Edith Roosevelt

7. Which First Lady's wedding gown cost $200,000 and her engagement ring has a net worth of $1.5 million?

A. Hillary Clinton

C. Jackie Kennedy

B. Melania Trump

D. Nancy Reagan

8. Which First Lady celebrated her 25th wedding anniversary by repeating her vows at a White House ceremony?

A. Nellie Taft

C. Laura Bush

B. Lucy Hayes

D. Nancy Reagan

9. She was married at the age of sixteen – younger than any other First Lady.

A. Eliza Johnson   *C. Rachel Jackson*

B. Martha Washington   *D. Dolley Madison*

10. Her husband, a future President, came from a political family; and when he proposed she accepted on the condition she would never have to give a political speech.

A. Eleanor Roosevelt   *C. Laura Bush*

B. Lyndon B. Johnson   *D. Pat Nixon*

11. Her future husband's mother was overbearing and manipulative. She made them keep their engagement a secret for a year.

A. Louisa Adams   *C. Laura Bush*

B. Mary Todd Lincoln   *D. Eleanor Roosevelt*

12. In place of a romantic proposal her future husband simply declared, "I am going to be married to you." Which First Lady received this un-romantic proposal?

A. Grace Coolidge   *C. Hillary Clinton*

B. Lady Bird Johnson   *D. Laura Bush*

13. She had a job as an "inquiring photographer" for a newspaper in Washington, D.C. when she met the young senator, who would one day become President and her husband; he had the reputation of being the most eligible bachelor in the capital. So, who was the woman who

"caught" the most eligible bachelor?

A. Pat Nixon

C. Florence Harding

B. Jackie Kennedy

D. Betty Ford

14. John Philip Sousa who was to play for the President's wedding was offered money from a reporter to let him pose as a member of his band so he could crash the wedding. Needless to say, Sousa turned him down. Who was the bride?

A. Lucy Hayes

C. Frances Cleveland

B. Edith Wilson

D. Caroline Harrison

15. She married her husband seven weeks after their first date.

A. Lady Bird Johnson

C. Laura Bush

B. Mamie Eisenhower

D. Peggy Taylor

Answers

Chapter 17 — Romance With A Future President

1. B - Lady Bird Johnson, wife of Lyndon B. Johnson

2. A - Grace Coolidge, wife of Calvin Coolidge

3. C - Bess (& Harry Truman)

4. A - Frances Cleveland, wife of Grover Cleveland

5. D - Lou Hoover, wife of Herbert Hoover

He was in Australia at the time he sent the telegram. Three months later he would arrive in San Francisco. They married two weeks later and left the next day for China.

6. C - Mamie Eisenhower, wife of Dwight D. Eisenhower

7. B - Melania Trump, wife of Donald Trump

8. B - Lucy Hayes, wife of Rutherford B. Hayes

If you came up with A - Helen Taft give yourself credit as the Tafts also celebrated their silver wedding anniversary at a garden party at the White House.

9. A - Eliza Johnson, wife of Andrew Johnson

10. C - Laura Bush, wife of George W. Bush

11. D - Eleanor Roosevelt, wife of Franklin D. Roosevelt

12. A - Grace Coolidge, wife of Calvin Coolidge

13. B - Jackie Kennedy, wife of John F. Kennedy

14. C - Frances Cleveland, wife of Grover Cleveland

15. A - Lady Bird Johnson, wife of Lyndon B. Johnson

18

Who Am I

Answers are given on pages 200 - 202.

1. Who was the First Lady when Neil Armstrong walked on the moon?

   A. Jackie Kennedy

   B. Pat Nixon

   C. Lady Bird Johnson

   D. Mamie Eisenhower

2. She danced to disco music at informal White House events.

   A. Betty Ford

   B. Lady Bird Johnson

   C. Pat Nixon

   D. Barbara Bush

3. She was the youngest First Lady in American history.

   A. Jackie Kennedy

   B. Ellen Arthur

   C. Frances Cleveland

   D. Louisa Adams

4. I was wife of one President, grandmother to another President, yet I never set foot in the White House. Who am I?

A. Anna Harrison   C. Martha Washington

B. Caroline Harrison   D. Eliza Johnson

5. I was the last of the First Ladies born in the 18th century. Who am I?

A. Louisa Adams   C. Dolley Madison

B. Sarah Polk   D. Abigail Fillmore

6. I was First Lady when Charles Lindbergh made his historic solo nonstop flight across the Atlantic in 1927. Who am I?

A. Nellie Taft   C. Frances Cleveland

B. Grace Coolidge   D. Bess Truman

7. She is one of the most accomplished First Ladies as a lawyer, First Lady, Senator, presidential candidate, and Secretary of State.

A. Michelle Obama   C. Hillary Clinton

B. Lady Bird Johnson   D. Lou Hoover

8. She traveled to all fifty states and over seventy-five countries.

A. Laura Bush   C. Michelle Obama

B. Hillary Clinton   D. Mamie Eisenhower

9. With her sense of humor and down-to-earth personality, she became one of the most popular 20th century First Ladies.

A. Jackie Kennedy

B. Pat Nixon

C. Lou Hoover

D. Barbara Bush

10. Which First Lady had poker parties in the White House library where liquor was served, even though the Eighteenth Amendment made it illegal to do so?

A. Lou Hoover

B. Florence Harding

C. Dolley Madison

D. Ida McKinley

11. This First Lady surprised the Chinese when they took her to a commune and she told them how she raised pigs on a farm when she was a young girl.

A. Julia Grant

B. Lady Bird Johnson

C. Pat Nixon

D. Melania Trump

12. Which First Lady was under investigation by the FBI for having a private server in her home with classified information on it?

A. Hillary Clinton

B. Michelle Obama

C. Barbara Bush

D. Pat Nixon

13. Which First Lady was not only First Lady; but the wife of a Civil War General?

A. Martha Washington

B. Peggy Taylor

C. Elizabeth Monroe

D. Julia Grant

14. Which First Lady learned to make noodles from Chinese chefs in a Beijing restaurant?

   A. Pat Nixon   C. Julia Grant

   B. Laura Bush   D. Michelle Obama

15. Which First Lady is fluent in six languages?

   A. Louisa Adams   C. Harriet Lane

   B. Melania Trump   D. Jackie Kennedy

16. Which First Lady was head of (D.A.R.) Daughters of the American Revolution?

   A. Caroline Harrison   C. Dolley Madison

   B. Frances Cleveland   D. Sarah Polk

17. Which First Lady was the wife of the second President and the mother of the sixth President?

   A. Louisa Adams   C. Barbara Bush

   B. Anna Harrison   D. Abigail Adams

18. Which two First Ladies were breast cancer survivors?

   A. B. Ford & L. Bush   C. R. Carter & J. Kennedy

   B. B. Ford & N. Reagan   D. P. Nixon & N. Reagan

19. Which First Lady on her visit to China gave a speech where she

chastised the Chinese for their sterilization of women and their encouragement of abortions to uphold the "one child" policy?

    A. Michelle Obama   C. Hillary Clinton

    B. Barbara Bush   D. Pat Nixon

20. As the First Lady she encouraged volunteerism, the spirit of people helping people.

    A. Pat Nixon   C. Mary Todd Lincoln

    B. Eleanor Roosevelt   D. Lou Hoover

21. She was a former teacher and librarian.

    A. Rachel Jackson   C. Laura Bush

    B. Sarah Polk   D. Grace Coolidge

22. She was an accomplished pianist, music teacher, and enjoyed painting.

    A. Lucy Hayes   C. Grace Coolidge

    B. Frances Cleveland   D. Caroline Harrison

23. Her husband was President, she had a son who was President, and another son who also ran for the presidency.

    A. Lady Bird Johnson   C. Laura Bush

    B. Barbara Bush   D. Anna Harrison

24. She often was criticized for her lavish, extravagant, and extensive travels abroad when the nation was suffering from hard economic times.

    A. *Jackie Kennedy*   C. *Melania Trump*

    B. *Florence Harding*   D. *Michelle Obama*

25. In 2008, she ran unsuccessfully for the Democratic presidential nomination. She ran again in the 2016 presidential race and lost again.

    A. *Nancy Reagan*   C. *Hillary Clinton*

    B. *Michelle Obama*   D. *Rosalynn Carter*

26. She studied modern dance and was a fashion model.

    A. *Betty Ford*   C. *Jackie Kennedy*

    B. *Eleanor Roosevelt*   D. *Melania Trump*

27. She had receptions on Saturdays so working women could attend. She remembered White House servants' birthdays. She played with the children at the Colored Orphans Christmas Party. She dedicated a home for factory girls. She had a ready smile and was loved by all.

    A. *Frances Cleveland*   C. *Barbara Bush*

    B. *Dolley Madison*   D. *Lucy Hayes*

28. She wrote plays, one titled *"Suspicion or Persecuted Innocence"* about the strengths of women. Who was she?

    A. *Jane Pierce*   C. *Louisa Adams*

    B. *Harriet Lane*   D. *Ida McKinley*

29. She was the longest serving First Lady.

A. Martha Washington   C. Mary Todd Lincoln

B. Eleanor Roosevelt   D. Edith Roosevelt

30. While the country was suffering hardships from an economic depression, this First Lady and the President paid out of their own pockets when they entertained in the White House.

A. Lou Hoover   C. Michelle Obama

B. Eleanor Roosevelt   D. Laura Bush

31. On the Larry King Live show, which First Lady spoke in support of legalizing same-sex marriage and keeping abortion legal?

A. Betty Ford   C. Barbara Bush

B. Hillary Clinton   D. Laura Bush

32. After the Watergate scandal Americans demanded more openness and honesty by the residences of the White House. This First Lady was very open with her thoughts and opinions, sometimes making Congress and the President cringe at her directness and views that sometimes didn't coincide with that of the President.

A. Pat Nixon   C. Nancy Reagan

B. Betty Ford   D. Barbara Bush

33. She is the First Lady most noted for her love of nature and the importance she put on conserving the environment.

A. Edith Roosevelt   C. Grace Coolidge

B. Lou Hoover   D. Lady Bird Johnson

34. Her husband the President was impeached, but the Senate failed to convict and he remained in office. (2 possible answers). Who was the First Lady?

A. Eliza Johnson   C. Hillary Clinton

B. Melania Trump   D. Jane Pierce

35. Who is the only woman to not only be the First Lady, but also the wife of the Chief Justice of the U.S. Supreme Court?

A. Eleanor Roosevelt   C. Jackie Kennedy

B. Nellie Taft   D. Eliza Johnson

36. She traveled with the President to the People's Republic of China and to the summit meeting in the Soviet Union.

A. Laura Bush   C. Michelle Obama

B. Lou Hoover   D. Pat Nixon

37. She was one of the most outspoken First Ladies in the White House.

A. Jackie Kennedy   C. Hillary Clinton

B. Eleanor Roosevelt   D. Michelle Obama

38. Which two First Ladies were foreign born?

A. Melania Trump   C. Louisa Adams

B. Ida McKinley   D. Lucretia Garfield

39. There was a twenty-seven year age difference with her and the President.

A. Frances Cleveland   C. Dolley Madison

B. Melania Trump   D. Edith Roosevelt

40. She established the collection of china from past presidential administrations.

A. Jackie Kennedy   C. Caroline Harrison

B. Abigail Fillmore   D. Hannah Van Buren

Answers

Chapter 18 — Who Am I

1. B - Pat Nixon, wife of Richard Nixon

2. A - Betty Ford, wife of Gerald Ford

3. C - Frances Cleveland, wife of Grover Cleveland

4. A - Anna Harrison, wife of William H. Harrison

5. D - Abigail Fillmore, wife of Millard Fillmore

6. B - Grace Coolidge, wife of Calvin Coolidge

7. C - Hillary Clinton, wife of Bill Clinton

8. A - Laura Bush, wife of George W. Bush

9. D - Barbara Bush, wife of George H.W. Bush

10. B - Florence Harding, wife of Warren Harding

11. C - Pat Nixon, wife of Richard Nixon

12. A – Hillary Clinton, wife of Bill Clinton

13. D - Julia Grant, wife of Ulysses S. Grant

14. B - Laura Bush, wife of George W. Bush

15. B - Melania Trump, wife of Donald Trump

*Melania Trum speaks English, Slovenian, French, Italian, German, and Serbo-Croatian

*Another First Lady with the gift of speaking many languages was Lou Hoover who spoke five languages and is the only First Lady to have spoken an Asian language.

16. A - Caroline Harrison, wife of Benjamin Harrison

17. D - Abigail Adams, wife of John Adams

18. B - Betty Ford, wife of Gerald Ford & Nancy Reagan, wife of Ronald Reagan

19. C - Hillary Clinton, wife of Bill Clinton

20. A - Pat Nixon, wife of Richard Nixon

21. C - Laura Bush, wife of George W. Bush

22. D - Caroline Harrison, wife of Benjamin Harrison

23. B - Barbara Bush, wife of George H.W. Bush

24. D - Michelle Obama, wife of Barack Obama

25. C - Hillary Clinton, wife of Bill Clinton

26. A - Betty Ford, wife of Gerald Ford

27. A - Frances Cleveland, wife of Grover Cleveland

28. C - Louisa Adams, wife of John Quincy Adams

29. B - Eleanor Roosevelt, wife of Franklin D. Roosevelt

30. A - Lou Hoover, wife of Herbert Hoover

31. D - Laura Bush, wife of George W. Bush

32. B - Betty Ford, wife of Gerald Ford

33. D - Lady Bird Johnson, wife of Lyndon B. Johnson

34. A - Eliza Johnson, wife of Andrew Johnson *or* C - Hillary Clinton, wife of Bill Clinton would be correct

35. B - Nellie Taft, wife of William H. Taft

36. D - Pat Nixon, wife of Richard Nixon

37. B - Eleanor Roosevelt, wife of Franklin D. Roosevelt

38. A – Melania Trump, wife of Donald Trump **&** C - Louisa Adams, wife of John Quincy Adams

39. A - Frances Cleveland, wife of Grover Cleveland

*A close second, *First Lady Melania Trump is 25 years younger than President Trump*

40. C - Caroline Harrison, wife of Benjamin Harrison

19

Quotes Of The First Ladies

Answers are given on pages 211 - 212.

1. "It is one of my sources of happiness never to desire a knowledge of other people's business." Can you name the First Lady who said this?

    A. Martha Washington   *C. Dolley Madison*

    B. Melania Trump   *D. Laura Bush*

2. "You can get so anesthetized by your own pain or your own problem, that you don't quite fully share the hell of someone close to you."

    A. Eleanor Roosevelt   *C. Betty Ford*

    B. Lady Bird Johnson   *D. Bess Truman*

3. "You may not give a hoot about baseball, but to me it is my very life."

    A. Bess Truman   *C. Laura Bush*

    B. Hillary Clinton   *D. Grace Coolidge*

4. "Maybe it is the media that has us divided."

A. Melania Trump   C. Laura Bush

B. Pat Nixon   D. Rosalynn Carter

5. "No one can make you feel inferior without your consent."

A. Barbara Bush   C. Lady Bird Johnson

B. Grace Coolidge   D. Eleanor Roosevelt

6. "I am determined to be cheerful and happy in whatever situation I may find myself. For I have learned that the greater part of our misery or unhappiness is determined not by our circumstances but by our disposition."

A. Betty Ford   C. Mamie Eisenhower

B. Martha Washington   D. Louisa Adams

7. "Do what you can to show you care about other people, and you will make our world a better place."

A. Rosalynn Carter   C. Eleanor Roosevelt

B. Lucy Hayes   D. Nellie Taft

8. "If particular care and attention is not paid to the ladies, we are determined to foment a rebellion and will not hold ourselves bound by any laws in which we have no voice, or representation."

A. Hillary Clinton   C. Michelle Obama

B. Abigail Adams   D. Lou Hoover

9. "I suppose I could have stayed home and baked cookies and had teas."

A. Michelle Obama

C. Pat Nixon

B. Laura Bush

D. Hillary Clinton

10. "At the end of your life, you will never regret not having passed one more test, not winning one more verdict, or not closing one more deal. You will regret time not spent with a husband, a friend, a child, or a parent."

A. Grace Coolidge

C. Barbara Bush

B. Betty Ford

D. Lou Hoover

11. "It's always been my feeling that God lends you your children until they're about eighteen years old. If you haven't made your points with them by then, it's too late."

A. Michelle Obama

C. Jackie Kennedy

B. Betty Ford

D. Bess Truman

12. In her autobiography and from a letter of her first day at the White House as First Lady she wrote: "This was I and yet not I, this was the wife of the President of the United States and she took precedence over me; my personal likes and dislikes must be subordinated to the consideration of those things which were required of her."

A. Grace Coolidge

C. Hillary Clinton

B. Bess Truman

D. Florence Harding

13. "My opinion is that the more languages you speak, better it is, but

when you come to America, you speak English."

  A. Eleanor Roosevelt   C. Frances Cleveland

  B. Melania Trump   D. Lou Hoover

14. "I am fond of only what comes from the heart."

  A. Laura Bush   C. Lucy Hayes

  B. Rosalynn Carter   D. Martha Washington

15. This future First Lady upset many Americans when she made this statement in a speech while campaigning for her husband. "For the first time in my adult lifetime, I am proud of my country."

  A. Hillary Clinton   C. Michelle Obama

  B. Florence Harding   D. Frances Cleveland

16. "If you bungle raising your children, I don't think whatever else you do well matters very much."

  A. Betty Ford   C. Jackie Kennedy

  B. Nancy Reagan   D. Edith Roosevelt

17. "And now, I must leave this house or the retreating army will make me a prisoner in it by filling up the road I am directed to take."

  A. Dolley Madison   C. Martha Washington

  B. Elizabeth Monroe   D. Abigail Adams

18. "Children are apt to live up to what you believe of them."

   A. Hillary Clinton   C. Rosalynn Carter

   B. Lady Bird Johnson   D. Betty Ford

19. "Do what you feel in your heart to be right - for you'll be criticized anyway. You'll be damned if you do, and damned if you don't."

   A. Mary Todd Lincoln   C. Lucy Hayes

   B. Lou Hoover   D. Eleanor Roosevelt

20. "Being First Lady is the hardest unpaid job in the world."

   A. Pat Nixon   C. Melania Trump

   B. Hillary Clinton   D. Bess Truman

21. "Never lose sight of the fact that the most important yardstick of your success will be how you treat other people – your family, friends, and coworkers, and even strangers you meet along the way."

   A. Mamie Eisenhower   C. Barbara Bush

   B. Rosalynn Carter   D. Betty Ford

22. "A woman is like a tea bag – you can't tell how strong she is until you put her in hot water."

   A. Michelle Obama   C. Lady Bird Johnson

   B. Eleanor Roosevelt   D. Mamie Eisenhower

23. "The First Lady is an unpaid public servant elected by one person – her husband."

    A. Bess Truman   *C. Grace Coolidge*

    B. Laura Bush   *D. Lady Bird Johnson*

24. "I am not the one who is elected. I have nothing to say to the public."

    A. Melania Trump   *C. Bess Truman*

    B. Pat Nixon   *D. Nancy Reagan*

25. "History does not long entrust the care of freedom to the weak or the timid."

    A. Mamie Eisenhower   *C. Peggy Taylor*

    B. Dolley Madison   *D. Mamie Eisenhower*

26. "If I want to knock a story off the front page, I just change my hairstyle."

    A. Nancy Reagan   *C. Pat Nixon*

    B. Hillary Clinton   *D. Barbara Bush*

27. "I think it is important to give a child room to make mistakes in order to learn. Mistakes build wings so later in life they can fly and go on their own. Let them fall once in awhile."

    A. Melania Trump   *C. Jackie Kennedy*

    B. Lady Bird Johnson   *D. Betty Ford*

28. "I have always tried my best to do what I thought was the right thing at the time."

    A. Laura Bush   *C. Eleanor Roosevelt*

    B. Lady Bird Johnson   *D. Pat Nixon*

29. This First Lady said this in reference to the White House. "I really believe the Clevelands and ourselves were about the only families who were really happy here."

    A. Edith Roosevelt   *C. Mary Todd Lincoln*

    B. Martha Washington   *D. Lucretia Garfield*

30. "The one who is not in trouble, will have to help the one who is in trouble."

    A. Anna Harrison   *C. Lou Hoover*

    B. Rosalynn Carter   *D. Ida McKinley*

31. "I am a big believer that eventually everything comes back to you. You get back what you give out."

    A. Nancy Reagan   *C. Melania Trump*

    B. Laura Bush   *D. Rosalynn Carter*

32. "I don't have a nanny. I have a chef, and I have my assistant, and that's it. I do it myself. You know, those hours with your child are really important ones, even if it's just the two of you, being quiet in the car together."

A. *Bess Truman*   C. *Jackie Kennedy*

B. *Melania Trump*   D. *Hillary Clinton*

33. "Good grief, we're getting offended by everything these days! People can't say anything without offending somebody."

A. *Hillary Clinton*   C. *Betty Ford*

B. *Michelle Obama*   D. *Barbara Bush*

34. "Great minds discuss ideas; average minds discuss events; small minds discuss people."

A. *Dolley Madison*   C. *Eleanor Roosevelt*

B. *Grace Coolidge*   D. *Rosalynn Carter*

35. "You should never view your challenges as a disadvantage. Instead, it's important for you to understand that your experience facing and overcoming adversity is actually one of your biggest advantages."

A. *Eleanor Roosevelt*   C. *Mamie Eisenhower*

B. *Rosalynn Carter*   D. *Michelle Obama*

Answers

Chapter 19 — Quotes Of The First Ladies

1. C - Dolley Madison, wife of James Madison

2. B - Lady Bird Johnson, wife of Lyndon B. Johnson

3. D - Grace Coolidge, wife of Calvin Coolidge

4. C - Laura Bush, wife of George W. Bush

5. D - Eleanor Roosevelt, wife of Franklin D. Roosevelt

6. B - Martha Washington, wife of George Washington

7. A - Rosalynn Carter, wife of Jimmy Carter

8. B - Abigail Adams, wife of John Adams

9. D - Hillary Clinton, wife of Bill Clinton

10. C - Barbara Bush, wife of George W. Bush

11. B - Betty Ford, wife of Gerald Ford

12. A - Grace Coolidge, wife of Calvin Coolidge

13. B - Melania Trump, wife of Donald Trump

14. D - Martha Washington, wife of George Washington

15. C - Michelle Obama, wife of Barack Obama

16. C - Jackie Kennedy, wife of John F. Kennedy

17. A - Dolley Madison, wife of James Madison

She was referring to the White House during the War of 1812.

18. B - Lady Bird Johnson, wife of Lyndon B. Johnson

19. D - Eleanor Roosevelt, wife of Franklin D. Roosevelt

20. A - Pat Nixon, wife of Richard Nixon

21. C - Barbara Bush, wife of George H.W. Bush

22. B - Eleanor Roosevelt, wife of Franklin D. Roosevelt

23. D - Lady Bird Johnson, wife of Lyndon B. Johnson

24. C - Bess Truman, wife of Harry Truman

25. A - Mamie Eisenhower, wife of Dwight D. Eisenhower

26. B - Hillary Clinton, wife of Bill Clinton

27. A - Melania Trump, wife of Donald Trump

28. D - Pat Nixon, wife of Richard Nixon

29. A - Edith Roosevelt, wife of Theodore Roosevelt

30. C - Lou Hoover, wife of Herbert Hoover

31. A - Nancy Reagan, wife of Ronald Reagan

32. B - Melania Trump, wife of Donald Trump

33. A - Hillary Clinton, wife of Bill Clinton

34. C - Eleanor Roosevelt, wife of Franklin D. Roosevelt

35. D - Michelle Obama, wife of Barack Obama

20

The First President's Wife To Do So

Some of these events took place before or after their time in the White House.

Answers are given on pages 226 - 229.

1. She was the 1st First Lady to visit a combat zone.

   A. *Lady Bird Johnson*   C. *Pat Nixon*

   B. *Hillary Clinton*   D. *Mamie Eisenhower*

2. She was the 1st First Lady of the 21st century.

   A. *Laura Bush*   C. *Hillary Clinton*

   B. *Betty Ford*   D. *Michelle Obama*

3. She was the 1st First Lady to marry a sitting president.

   A. *Julia Tyler*   C. *Ellen Arthur*

   B. *Hannah Van Buren*   D. *Edith Wilson*

4. She was the 1st First Lady to vote.

    A. Grace Coolidge   *C. Ida McKinley*

    B. Edith Wilson   *D. Florence Harding*

5. Which First Lady began the tradition of having a Christmas tree at the White House?

    A. Caroline Harrison   *C. Martha Washington*

    B. Sarah Polk   *D. Lucretia Garfield*

6. She was the 1st First Lady to to become a widow while a current First Lady.

    A. Elizabeth Monroe   *C. Peggy Taylor*

    B. Anna Harrison   *D. Mary Todd Lincoln*

7. Which First Lady along with the President found the White House an uncomfortable place to live and rented a house outside Washington, D.C. using the White House for official functions only?

    A. Martha Washington   *C. Frances Cleveland*

    B. Jane Pierce   *D. Bess Truman*

8. She was the 1st First Lady to give the President's weekly radio address speaking out against the oppression of women and children of Afghanistan.

    A. Hillary Clinton   *C. Michelle Obama*

    B. Nancy Reagan   *D. Laura Bush*

9. Which First Lady presided at the first inaugural ball in Washington when her husband became President?

A. Dolley Madison   C. Elizabeth Monroe

B. Letitia Tyler   D. Jane Pierce

10. She was the 1st First Lady to live in the White House?

A. Martha Washington   C. Abigail Adams

B. Dolley Madison   D. Louisa Adams

11. She was the first and the only First Lady to marry in the White House. The wedding was held in the Blue Room of the White House.

A. Frances Cleveland   C. Edith Wilson

B. Anna Harrison   D. Sarah Polk

12. She was the first woman who would become First Lady that graduated from college.

A. Lou Hoover   C. Lady Bird Johnson

B. Lucy Hayes   D. Jackie Kennedy

13. She was the 1st First Lady to smoke cigarettes.

A. Dolley Madison   C. Pat Nixon

B. Jackie Kennedy   D. Nellie Taft

14. She was the 1st First Lady to make a foreign policy trip.

A. Eleanor Roosevelt   C. Rosalynn Carter

B. Edith Wilson   D. Pat Nixon

15. Which First Lady was buried beside her husband at Arlington National Cemetery? They were the first presidential couple to be buried there.

A. Nellie Taft   C. Edith Wilson

B. Jackie Kennedy   D. Eleanor Roosevelt

16. Which First Lady was wife to the nation's first Republican president?

A. Hannah Van Buren   C. Dolley Madison

B. Mary Todd Lincoln   D. Abigail Fillmore

17. Which First Lady was a history enthusiast and was the first President General of DAR (Daughters of the American Revolution)?

A. Elizabeth Monroe   C. Caroline Harrison

B. Frances Cleveland   D. Grace Coolidge

18. She was the 1st First Lady to travel to China at the time her husband was the incumbent president.

A. Julia Grant   C. Lou Hoover

B. Barbara Bush   D. Pat Nixon

19. She was the 1st First Lady to occupy the family quarters at the White House.

A. Edith Roosevelt   C. Mary Todd Lincoln

B. Dolley Madison   D. Abigail Adams

20. She was the second foreign born First Lady, but the *first* First Lady for whom English was not a first language.

A. Elizabeth Monroe   C. Louisa Adams

B. Hannah Van Buren   D. Melania Trump

21. She was the 1st First Lady to hold her own press conference.

A. Florence Harding   C. Jackie Kennedy

B. Eleanor Roosevelt   D. Hillary Clinton

22. Which First Lady was the first that was a strong advocate of women's rights?

A. Abigail Adams   C. Edith Wilson

B. Laura Bush   D. Betty Ford

23. During which First Lady's eulogy did the acting President, President Zachary Taylor, first use the term First Lady?

A. Martha Washington   C. Elizabeth Monroe

B. Dolley Madison   D. Abigail Adams

24. She was the 1st First Lady to see her husband sworn into office aboard Air Force One. She is also the only one to have done so.

A. Jackie Kennedy   C. Lady Bird Johnson

B. Mamie Eisenhower   D. Bess Truman

25. Which First Lady was the first to receive permanent protection from the Secret Service?

A. Betty Ford   C. Jackie Kennedy

B. Lady Bird Johnson   D. Edith Wilson

26. Which First Lady, along with the incumbent President, was the first to visit the west coast?

A. Lucy Hayes   C. Peggy Taylor

B. Julia Grant   D. Caroline Harrison

27. She was the 1st African-American First Lady.

A. Lou Hoover   C. Florence Harding

B. Michelle Obama   D. Elizabeth Monroe

28. She was the 1st First Lady to have published memoirs.

A. Frances Cleveland   C. Julia Grant

B. Eleanor Roosevelt   D. Jackie Kennedy

29. She was the 1st First Lady to graduate from college. The college was Wesleyan Female Seminary in Cincinnati, Ohio.

A. Lucy Hayes   C. Lady Bird Johnson

B. Nellie Taft   D. Ellen Wilson

30. She was the 1st First Lady to make a campaign promise of her own –
that she would make the welfare of the nation's mentally ill her priority.

A. Betty Ford   C. Eleanor Roosevelt

B. Rosalynn Carter   D. Lady Bird Johnson

31. Which First Lady was one of the first women to attend congressional
debates.

A. Grace Coolidge   C. Florence Harding

B. Nellie Taft   D. Louisa Adams

32. Who was the first woman and First Lady to have her likeness printed
on currency and on a U.S. postage stamp?

A. Dolley Madison   C. Martha Washington

B. Eleanor Roosevelt   D. Abigail Adams

33. She was the 1st First Lady to ride with the President during the
inauguration parade.

A. Nellie Taft   C. Florence Harding

B. Nancy Reagan   D. Mamie Eisenhower

34. She was the 1st First Lady to appear on the covers of *Vogue* and

Harper's Bazaar and to be featured in several magazines, all *before* becoming the First Lady.

A. Jackie Kennedy

C. Grace Coolidge

B. Melania Trump

D. Betty Ford

35. She was the first woman in America to earn a degree in geology.

A. Lou Hoover

C. Florence Harding

B. Lady Bird Johnson

D. Nellie Taft

36. Who was First Lady when the first Easter Egg Roll took place at the White House?

A. Lucretia Garfield

C. Frances Cleveland

B. Jackie Kennedy

D. Lucy Hayes

37. She was the 1st First Lady, and to date the only First Lady, to be buried in Washington National Cathedral?

A. Mary Todd Lincoln

C. Edith Wilson

B. Jackie Kennedy

D. Bess Truman

38. She was the 1st First Lady to hold the Bible at her husband's inauguration.

A. Grace Coolidge

C. Mamie Eisenhower

B. Lady Bird Johnson

D. Jackie Kennedy

39. This First Lady and President were the first to light the community Christmas tree.

A. Nellie Taft   *C. Ida McKinley*

B. Florence Harding   *D. Grace Coolidge*

40. She was the 1st presidential widow to remarry.

A. Frances Cleveland   *C. Jackie Kennedy*

B. Anna Harrison   *D. Lucretia Garfield*

41. She was the 1st First Lady to receive a formal education. Martha Washington's granddaughter was one of her classmates.

A. Dolley Madison   *C. Anna Harrison*

B. Elizabeth Monroe   *D. Sarah Polk*

42. Which First Lady was the first to have her name brought up at the Democratic National Convention, making her the 1st First Lady to be recognized in a political arena?

A. Frances Cleveland   *C. Mary Todd Lincoln*

B. Eleanor Roosevelt   *D. Lucy Hayes*

43. She was the 1st First Lady to be elected to the U.S. Senate.

A. Nellie Taft   *C. Ellen Wilson*

B. Hillary Clinton   *D. Florence Harding*

44. She was the 1st incumbent First Lady to visit a foreign country. Not only that, she did so without the accompaniment of her husband.

A. Frances Cleveland

C. Ida McKinley

B. Nellie Grant

D. Mamie Eisenhower

45. She was the 1st First Lady to write a commercially published book on her memoirs, *'Recollections of Full Years.'*

A. Nellie Taft

C. Eleanor Roosevelt

B. Lady Bird Johnson

D. Jackie Kennedy

46. She was the 1st First Lady to fly in an airplane.

A. Elizabeth Monroe

C. Nellie Taft

B. Mamie Eisenhower

D. Florence Harding

47. She was the 1st First Lady whose death led Congress to adjourn in mourning.

A. Dolley Madison

C. Martha Washington

B. Louisa Adams

D. Eleanor Roosevelt

48. Which First Lady not only experienced flying with Amelia Earhart, but was the 1st and only First Lady to take over controls of the plane while flying with her?

A. Nancy Reagan

C. Eleanor Roosevelt

B. Lady Bird Johnson

D. Hillary Clinton

49. She was the 1st First Lady to wear pants in public.

A. Betty Ford

B. Rosalynn Carter

C. Pat Nixon

D. Eleanor Roosevelt

50. She was the 1st First Lady to give birth while First Lady.

A. Jackie Kennedy

B. Louisa Adams

C. Frances Cleveland

D. Nellie Taft

51. She was the 1st First Lady to use sign language.

A. Eleanor Roosevelt

B. Ida McKinley

C. Hannah Van Buren

D. Grace Coolidge

52. Hers was the first likeness to go on campaign buttons of the wives of the candidates.

A. Ida McKinley

B. Rachel Jackson

C. Frances Cleveland

D. Lucretia Garfield

53. She was the 1st First Lady elected to a public office and appointed to serve in a President's Cabinet.

A. Florence Harding

B. Hillary Clinton

C. Grace Coolidge

D. Eleanor Roosevelt

54. Although she was the 1st First Lady, that term wasn't actually used until well into the 19th century. Who was she?

A. Martha Washington   C. Abigail Adams

B. Dolley Madison   D. Elizabeth Monroe

55. She is the 1st First Lady who was born and raised in a communist country.

A. Louisa Adams   C. Melania Trump

B. Hannah Van Buren   D. Ida Mckinley

56. She was the 1st First Lady to live in the White House with electricity – even though she was afraid to use it.

A. Caroline Harrison   C. Grace Coolidge

B. Frances Cleveland   D. Edith Roosevelt

57. Not only was this First Lady the 1st First Lady to respond to a telegraph message (sent by inventor Samuel Morse), but she was the 1st American to do so.

A. Edith Roosevelt   C. Mary Todd Lincoln

B. Dolley Madison   D. Julia Grant

58. She was the 1st First Lady to run for president – not once, but twice; and lost both times.

A. Michelle Obama   C. Lucy Hayes

B. Florence Harding   D. Hillary Clinton

59. She was the 1st First Lady to travel abroad alone.

    A. Lucretia Garfield   *C. Mary Todd Lincoln*

    B. Eleanor Roosevelt   *D. Edith Wilson*

60. She was the 1st First Lady to tweet?

    A. Michelle Obama   *C. Melania Trump*

    B. Hillary Clinton   *D. Laura Bush*

Answers

1. C - Pat Nixon, wife of Richard Nixon

2. A - Laura Bush, wife of George W. Bush

3. A - Julia Tyler, second wife of John Tyler

4. D - Florence Harding, wife of Warren Harding

5. A – Caroline Harrison, wife of Benjamin Harrison

6. B - Anna Harrison, wife of William H. Harrison

7. C - Frances Cleveland, wife of Grover Cleveland

8. D - Laura Bush, wife of George W. Bush

9. A - Dolley Madison, wife of James Madison

10. C - Abigail Adams, wife of John Adams

11. A - Frances Cleveland, wife of Grover Cleveland

12. B - Lucy Hayes, wife of Rutherford B. Hayes

13. D - Nellie Taft, wife of William H. Taft

14. C - Rosalynn Carter, wife of Jimmy Carter

15. A - Nellie Taft, wife of William H. Taft

16. B - Mary Todd Lincoln, wife of Abraham Lincoln

17. C - Caroline Harrison, wife of Benjamin Harrison

18. D - Pat Nixon, wife of Richard Nixon

19. A - Edith Roosevelt, wife of Theodore Roosevelt

Prior to this time, what is now the Family Quarters were used for offices.

20. D - Melania Trump, wife of Donald Trump

21. B - Eleanor Roosevelt, wife of Franklin D. Roosevelt

22. A - Abigail Adams, wife of John Adams

23. B - Dolley Madison, wife of James Madison

24. C - Lady Bird Johnson, wife of Lyndon B. Johnson

25. D - Edith Wilson, second wife of Woodrow Wilson

26. A - Lucy Hayes, wife of Rutherford B. Hayes

27. B - Michelle Obama, wife of Barack Obama

28. C - Julia Grant, wife of Ulysses S. Grant

The memoirs weren't published until almost 75 years after her death.

29. A - Lucy Hayes, wife of Rutherford B. Hayes

30. B - Rosalynn Carter, wife of Jimmy Carter

31. D - Louisa Adams, wife of John Quincy Adams

32. C - Martha Washington, wife of George Washington

33. A - Nellie Taft, wife of William H. Taft

34. B - Melania Trump, wife of Donald Trump

35. A - Lou Hoover, wife of Herbert Hoover

36. D - Lucy Hayes, wife of Rutherford B. Hayes

37. C - Edith Wilson, second wife of Woodrow Wilson

38. B - Lady Bird Johnson, wife of Lyndon B. Johnson

39. D - Grace Coolidge, wife of Calvin Coolidge

Not only was this the first Christmas tree on the White House grounds to be lit up by electric lights, 2,500 in all, but it was also the first national Christmas tree on the White house grounds.

40. A - Frances Cleveland, wife of Grover Cleveland

41. C - Anna Harrison, wife of William H. Harrison

42. A – Frances Cleveland, wife of Grover Cleveland

43. B - Hillary Clinton, wife of Bill Clinton

44. C - Ida McKinley, wife of William McKinley

45. A - Nellie Taft, wife of William H. Taft

46. D – Florence Harding, wife of Warren Harding

47. B - Louisa Adams, wife of John Quincy Adams

48. C – Eleanor Roosevelt, wife of Franklin D. Roosevelt

49. C - Pat Nixon, wife of Richard Nixon

50. C - Frances Cleveland, wife of Grover Cleveland

51. D - Grace Coolidge, wife of Calvin Coolidge

52. A - Ida McKinley, wife of William McKinley

53. B - Hillary Clinton, wife of Bill Clinton

54. A - Martha Washington, wife of George Washington

55. C - Melania Trump, wife of Donald Trump

She was born and raised in Novo Mesto, Slovenia (then part of communist Yugoslavia)

56. A - Caroline Harrison, wife of Benjaimin Harrison

57. B – Dolley Madison, wife of James Madison

58. D - Hillary Clinton, wife of Bill Clinton

59. B - Eleanor Roosevelt, wife of Franklin D. Roosevelt

60. A - Michelle Obama, wife of Barack Obama

21

Life In The White House

Answers are given on pages 235 - 236.

1. Which First Lady was one of the most difficult to please – and no doubt about it, she was "the boss."

A. Hillary Clinton

C. Michelle Obama

D. Mamie Eisenhower

D. Nancy Reagan

2. Which First Lady while promoting healthy eating, with the help of some students, planted a garden on the lawn of the White House?

A. Laura Bush

C. Rosalynn Carter

B. Michelle Obama

D. Lady Bird Johnson

3. Many of the First Ladies redecorated the White House in some fashion or another, but which First Lady insisted it be restored? She said, "Every boy who comes here should see things that develop his sense of history." She brought in artwork and items that had been owned by past Presidents and played a part in American history.

A. Grace Coolidge

C. Jackie Kennedy

B. Nellie Taft

D. Rosalynn Carter

4. Which First Lady when discovering they had to pay their own food bills asked to be served leftovers?

    A. Pat Nixon   *C. Bess Truman*

    B. Nancy Reagan   *D. Rosalynn Carter*

5. The White House staff and others who worked around the President described him as a bully. Who was the First Lady that would whistle and walk away turning a blind eye to his many escapades?

    A. Hillary Clinton   *C. Jackie Kennedy*

    B. Lady Bird Johnson   *D. Jimmy Carter*

6. During her husband's presidential term, she hosted weekly parties that were frequented by her husband's colleagues including all political parties and the society of Washington. These parties were called squeezes or drawing rooms. Which First Lady was the hostess for these events?

    A. Dolley Madison   *C. Elizabeth Monroe*

    B. Anna Harrison   *D. Jane Pierce*

7. Which First Lady would shock the White House staff with her and the president cursing and yelling at each other?

    A. Michelle Obama   *C. Hillary Clinton*

    B. Barbara Bush   *D. Mamie Eisenhower*

8. Which First Lady did not immediately move into the White House after her husband's inauguration?

A. Nancy Reagan   C. Frances Cleveland

B. Melania Trump   D. Mamie Eisenhower

9. Which First Lady had beehives at the White House?

A. Grace Coolidge   C. Michelle Obama

B. Lady Bird Johnson   D. Eleanor Roosevelt

10. True or False. The President and First Lady are responsible for paying for their own personal food and drink expenses and the expenses of their guests.

True   ·   False

11. What First Lady spent $400,000 on redecorating the White House before moving in, an astonishingly high amount?

A. Nancy Reagan   C. Jackie Kennedy

B. Hillary Clinton   D. Barbara Bush

12. Which First Lady collected coupons from the newspaper?

A. Mamie Eisenhower   C. Bess Truman

B. Melania Trump   D. Rosalynn Carter

13. Which First Lady was one of the most popular hostesses of the White House, including people of various backgrounds so they could circulate with diplomats, politicians and even the president himself?

A. *Dolley Madison*   C. *Nancy Reagan*

B. *Grace Coolidge*   D. *Rosalynn Carter*

14. Being a Christian, which First Lady banned dancing and hard liquor at official receptions?

A. *Lucy Hayes*   C. *Sarah Polk*

B. *Grace Coolidge*   D. *Hillary Clinton*

15. It wasn't unusual for this First Lady to invite the staff to sit and join her for a cup of tea. She treated the staff with kindness and respect.

A. *Florence Harding*   C. *Edith Wilson*

B. *Betty Ford*   D. *Michelle Obama*

16. She ran the White House in a frugal manner by serving inexpensive meals and didn't serve hard liquor.

A. *Rosalynn Carter*   C. *Eleanor Roosevelt*

B. *Laura Bush*   D. *Lou Hoover*

17. Many of the friends invited to the White House by which First Family didn't pass their background checks and were labeled as "*Do not admits;*" but because they were invited by the President or First Lady the Secret Service were ordered to admit them, even though Secret Service agents would be placed on the floors where they were visiting to keep an eye on them?

A. Ladey Bird Johnson   C. Eleanor Roosevelt

B. Florence Harding   D. Hillary Clinton

18. Which First Lady lived in the White House for twelve years?

A. Frances Cleveland   C. Edith Roosevelt

B. Eleanor Roosevelt   D. Martha Washington

19. Which First Lady considered the days in the White House as "the happiest period of her life"?

A. Julia Grant   C. Mary Todd Lincoln

B. Hillary Clinton   D. Peggy Taylor

20. Which First Lady opened the White House to many people with disabilities? Helen Keller was one of her favorite guests.

A. Florence Harding   C. Edith Roosevelt

B. Grace Coolidge   D. Nellie Taft

Answers

Chapter 21 — Life In The White House

1. D - Nancy Reagan, wife of Ronald Reagan

2. B - Michelle Obama, wife of Barack Obama

3. C - Jackie Kennedy, wife of John F. Kennedy

4. D - Rosalynn Carter, wife of Jimmy Carter

5. B - Lady Bird Johnson, wife of Lyndon B. Johnson

6. A - Dolley Madison, wife of James Madison

7. C - Hillary Clinton, wife of Bill Clinton

8. B - Melania Trump, wife of Donald Trump

*It was 4 ½ months after the inauguration before the First Lady and their son Barron moved into the White House, waiting until after the end of Barron's school year before making the move.

9. C – Michelle Obama, wife of Barack Obama

*Charlie Brandt, who donated the original beehive to the White House, is now the White House's official beekeeper tending a hive of approximately 70,000 bees and supplying the White House chef with honey.

10. True

11. B - Hillary Clinton, wife of Bill Clinton

12. A - Mamie Eisenhower, wife of Dwight D. Eisenhower

13. A – Dolley Madison, wife of James Madison

14. C - Sarah Polk, wife of James Polk

15. B - Betty Ford, wife of Gerald Ford

16. A - Rosalynn Carter, wife of Jimmy Carter

17. D - Hillary Clinton, wife of Bill Clinton

18. B - Eleanor Roosevelt, wife of Franklin D. Roosevelt

19. A - Julia Grant, wife of Ulysses S. Grant

20. B - Grace Coolidge, wife of Calvin Coolidge

22

Extended First Family Members

Answers are given on page 240.

1. Which First Lady's father was a Loyalist during the Revolutionary War and her husband was a Founding Father?

    A. Elizabeth Monroe   *C. Dolley Madison*

    B. Abigail Adams   *D. Martha Washington*

2. Her father took her on camping trips. She learned to preserve specimens with the skill of a taxidermist and she loved discovering and learning about rocks, minerals, and mining.

    A. Lady Bird Johnson   *C. Lou Hoover*

    B. Laura Bush   *D. Bess Truman*

3. When she was only four years old her father, a Continental Army officer, dressed up as a British soldier and brought his daughter through British-occupied New York by horseback to the home of her grandparents. Her mother had died when she was a toddler and her grandparents would care for her while her father was off to fight in the war. She lived with her grandparents until she was an adolescent. Which First Lady was this?

A. *Dolley Madison*   C. *Abigail Fillmore*

B. *Eliza Johnson*   D. *Anna Harrison*

4. Documentation indicated this First Lady's parents weren't officially married at the time of her birth, which would make her the only First Lady born out of wedlock.

A. *Rosalynn Carter*   C. *Pat Nixon*

B. *Louisa Adams*   D. *Florence Harding*

5. Which First Lady's father had been treated several times for alcoholism? Her mother died at the age of twenty-nine from diphtheria. A young brother died from scarlet fever. Her father ended up dying from a seizure that was a result of a suicide attempt. She was left in the care of a grandmother in a home with two unmarried aunts and two uncles. It wasn't a happy childhood.

A. *Eleanor Roosevelt*   C. *Rosalynn Carter*

B. *Betty Ford*   D. *Mary Todd Lincoln*

6. Which First Lady's sister married a nephew of George Washington?

A. *Elizabeth Monroe*   C. *Sarah Polk*

B. *Letitia Tyler*   D. *Dolley Madison*

7. Which First Lady's father didn't show up to walk his daughter down the aisle for her wedding, because he was passed out drunk in his hotel room?

A. *Eleanor Roosevelt*   C. *Jackie Kennedy*

B. *Nancy Reagan*   D. *Bess Truman*

8. Which First Lady's father was a descendant of President Franklin Pierce?

A. *Ida McKinley*   C. *Michelle Obama*

B. *Barbara Bush*   D. *Edith Wilson*

9. Which First Lady's mother-in-law didn't approve of her as a bride for her son; as she felt that him marrying a British woman would hurt his political ambitions?

A. *Louisa Adams*   C. *Elizabeth Monroe*

B. *Hannah Van Buren*   D. *Ida McKinley*

10. Which First Lady was related to Thomas Jefferson, Martha Washington, and Letitia Tyler from her mother's side and from her father's side was related to Pocahontas?

A. *Florence Harding*   C. *Mary Todd Lincoln*

B. *Edith Wilson*   D. *Edith Roosevelt*

Answers

Chapter 22 - Extended First Family Members

1. A - Elizabeth Monroe, wife of James Monroe

2. C - Lou Hoover, wife of Herbert Hoover

3. D - Anna Harrison, wife of William Henry Harrison & grandmother of Benjamin Harrison

4. B - Louisa Adams, wife of John Quincy Adams

5. A - Eleanor Roosevelt, wife of Franklin D. Roosevelt

6. D - Dolley Madison, wife of James Madison

7. C - Jackie Kennedy, wife of John F. Kennedy

8. B - Barbara Bush, wife of George H.W. Bush

9. A - Louisa Adams, wife of John Quincy Adams

She never did get along with her mother-in-law Abigail Adams, but she got along with her father-in-law John Adams.

10. B - Edith Wilson, second wife of Woodrow Wilson

23

Do You Know...

Answers are given on pages 253 - 256.

1. Which First Lady, one who preferred to stay out of the limelight and in the background, served as an active member of the Police Athletic League, an Honorary Chairwoman for The Boy's Club, and served as a Goodwill Ambassador for the American Red Cross?

A. Betty Ford   C. Melania Trump

B. Bess Truman   D. Grace Coolidge

2. Which First Lady held séances in the White House?

A. Mary Todd Lincoln   C. Nancy Reagan

B. Jane Pierce   D. Ida McKinley

3. Which First Lady and President spent Thanksgiving of 1990 in Saudi Arabia to visit the thousands of American troops serving in Operation Desert Shield?

A. Laura Bush   C. Pat Nixon

B. Barbara Bush   D. Nancy Reagan

4. Which First Lady was considered "down-to-earth" and still went to her old beauty shop where she paid $3.00 for a weekly manicure, shampoo, and set; even though she was driven there in a limousine?

A. Bess Truman   *C. Pat Nixon*

B. Mamie Eisenhower   *D. Betty Ford*

5. How many living (current and former) First Ladies are alive today?

A. 3   *C. 5*

B. 4   *D. 6*

6. Which First Lady and President took a westward journey riding a rail line and horse-drawn wagons traveling through dangerous territory inhabited by Apache Indians and outlaw cowboys? They were the first President and First Lady to travel out west.

A. Lucy Hayes   *C. Lucretia Garfield*

B. Frances Cleveland   *D. Peggy Taylor*

7. While her husband was the incumbent President, the market crashed and the First Lady was bombarded with requests from those in need asking for help.

A. Grace Coolidge   *C. Lou Hoover*

B. Julia Grant   *D. Eleanor Roosevelt*

8. A statement made by a President's Press Secretary says a lot about this First Lady's character. He was quoted in McCall's magazine, "She is a lady unchanged by the White House and determined to remain always

what she is." Which First Lady is this statement attributed to?

A. Laura Bush

B. Bess Truman

C. Betty Ford

D. Nellie Taft

9. Which two First Ladies had the role of First Lady during the 18th century?

A. D. Madison & E. Monroe

B. D. Madison & E. Monroe

C. A. Adams & D. Madison

D. M. Washington & A. Adams

10. She was one of the most out-spoken women in the White House.

A. Eleanor Roosevelt

B. Abigail Adams

C. Florence Harding

D. Mary Todd Lincoln

11. Which First Lady is mainly remembered for her extensive correspondence with her husband and her unofficial role as adviser to him?

A. Martha Washington

B. Abigail Adams

C. Dolley Madison

D. Hillary Clinton

12. Both the press and the public loved this First Lady. She said it was because of her image as everyone's grandmother.

A. Bess Truman

B. Nancy Reagan

C. Mamie Eisenhower

D. Barbara Bush

13. Which First Lady could trace her lineage back to Pocahontas?

    A. Edith Wilson   *C. Dolley Madison*

    B. Lou Hoover   *D. Letitia Tyler*

14. Which First Lady was the only incumbent First Lady to never set foot in the White House?

    A. Anna Harrison   *C. Peggy Taylor*

    B. Melania Trump   *D. Lucretia Garfield*

15. Who was the youngest First Lady in American history?

    A. Jackie Kennedy   *C. Frances Cleveland*

    B. Grace Coolidge   *D. Melania Trump*

16. Which First Lady had a benevolent side to her that few ever saw or knew about? She worked towards aiding freed slaves and visiting hospitals to visit soldiers. She did this on her own without the knowledge of journalists or of those who would publicize her good works.

    A. Jane Pierce   *C. Hannah Van Buren*

    B. Eliza Johnson   *D. Mary Todd Lincoln*

17. Which First Lady encouraged people to follow her on her social media with Twitter, Facebook, and Instagram?

    A. Michelle Obama   *C. Barbara Bush*

    B. Melania Trump   *D. Betty Ford*

18. Which First Lady was a pack rat and with no rhyme or reason stuck her husband's letters, 1,200 in all, in the cushions of the sofa, behind chairs, under beds, in closets, and the attic – wherever was convenient at the time. They were a collection of letters her husband had written to her over a period of almost fifty years.

A. Mamie Eisenhower   C. Eleanor Roosevelt

B. Bess Truman   D. Nancy Reagan

19. Which First Lady had a dancing lesson from Chinese ballet students when she visited China?

A. Michelle Obama   C. Betty Ford

B. Pat Nixon   D. Laura Bush

20. How many First Ladies have there been that weren't married to the President?

A. 5   C. 6

B. 14   D. 9

21. Which First Lady was the youngest of the First Ladies to marry at the age of sixteen?

A. Eliza Johnson   C. Frances Cleveland

B. Martha Washington   D. Sarah Polk

22. Which First Lady was known to snuff tobacco?

A. *Eliza Johnson*   C. *Nancy Reagan*

B. *Dolley Madison*   D. *Rachel Jackson*

23. Which First Lady was the first born in the 19th century?

A. *Grace Coolidge*   C. *Mamie Eisenhower*

B. *Jackie Kennedy*   D. *Bess Truman*

24. Which two First Ladies lived at one time in China?

A. *L. Adams & C. Arthur*   C. *P. Taylor & M. Eisenhower*

B. *S. Polk & N. Taft*   D. *L. Hoover & B. Bush*

25. Which First Lady was accused of being a Confederate spy?

A. *Peggy Taylor*   C. *Julia Tyler*

B. *Mary Todd Lincoln*   D. *Julia Grant*

26. Which First Lady was originally a member of the Republican Party and even campaigned for the Republican presidential candidate Barry Goldwater?

A. *Lady Bird Johnson*   C. *Laura Bush*

B. *Bess Truman*   D. *Hillary Clinton*

27. Which First Lady's tiara was sold to a pawn shop in Las Vegas, of 'Pawn Stars' from the History Channel? They in turn sold it to the McKinley Presidential Library and Museum for the same amount they purchased it for.

A. Jackie Kennedy   C. Ida McKinley

B. Nancy Reagan   D. Melania Trump

28. Widely disliked in the White House, which First Lady was emotional, outspoken, and spent large sums of money at a time when budgets were tightened to fight the Civil War?

A. Mary Todd Lincoln   C. Hillary Clinton

B. Julia Grant   D. Harriet Lane

29. Which First Lady loved baseball? The American League sent her a yearly pass in a gold trimmed purse.

A. Bess Truman   C. Grace Coolidge

B. Laura Bush   D. Pat Nixon

30. Which First Lady, an immigrant herself though she very proudly announces she was a *legal immigrant* who became an American citizen, supported her husband on his stance on immigation?

A. Louisa Adams   C. Elizabeth Monroe

B. Melania Trump   D. Jackie Kennedy

31. Which First Lady when a teenager ran a stop sign causing an accident that killed the driver in the other car? The driver that was killed was a class mate and friend of hers.

A. Betty Ford   C. Hillary Clinton

B. Jackie Kennedy   D. Laura Bush

32. This woman acted as First Lady or hostess for her uncle, the only President who never married. Name the woman who served as the only bachelor president's First Lady.

A. Louisa Adams

C. Harriet Lane

B. Eliza Johnson

D. Caroline Harrison

33. When she was First Lady the only White House function she attended was the wedding of her daughter.

A. Letitia Tyler

C. Ellen Wilson

B. Elizabeth Monroe

D. Jane Pierce

34. Which First Lady was fluent in the Chinese language?

A. Barbara Bush

C. Pat Nixon

B. Lou Hoover

D. Melania Trump

35. Which First Lady was told her son died of a heart attack, when he had actually committed suicide?

A. Julia Grant

C. Edith Roosevelt

B. Anna Harrison

D. Rosalynn Carter

36. Which First Lady was in a musical that starred Yul Brenner and Mary Martin?

A. Betty Ford

C. Nellie Taft

B. Grace Coolidge

D. Nancy Reagan

37. Which First Lady worked as a model?

    A. Betty Ford   *C. Frances Cleveland*

    B. Jackie Kennedy   *D. Melania Trump*

38. Which First Lady while on the way to the Capitol building to give a speech learned of the 9/11 attacks? She spent some time in an office with Senator Kennedy waiting to be moved to a safe building. She realized that was the worst tragedy the nation had suffered since Senator Kennedy's brother, President John F. Kennedy, was assassinated.

    A. Barbara Bush   *C. Pat Nixon*

    B. Laura Bush   *D. Hillary Clinton*

39. The President stated that "the nation got two for the price of one," implying the First Lady would have a large role in his administration which American citizens were not too happy about.

    A. Hillary Clinton   *C. Edith Wilson*

    B. Michelle Obama   *D. Eleanor Roosevelt*

40. Which First Lady sat with a historian months after the President's death recording the story of their family? The tapes were supposed to be kept under lock and key in a vault until fifty years after his death, but her daughter had the vault opened early. In the tapes the First Lady reveals who she believes was the *'real'* killer of her husband.

    A. Pat Nixon   *C. Jackie Kennedy*

    B. Lucretia Garfield   *D. Nancy Reagan*

41. When her husband became President she was the oldest First Lady up to that time, at the age of sixty-five.

    A. Anna Harrison   *C. Nancy Reagan*

    B. Mamie Eisenhower   *D. Barbara Bush*

42. Which First Lady was slightly cross-eyed and when being photographed insisted it was in profile?

    A. Michelle Obama   *C. Edith Roosevelt*

    B. Bess Truman   *D. Julia Grant*

43. Which First Lady had a screwdriver to drink before going to church on Sundays, and yet they had alcohol removed from the White House? (There must have been a stash in the Family Quarters.)

    A. Betty Ford   *C. Rosalynn Carter*

    B. Lucy Hayes   *D. Barbara Bush*

44. Which First Lady was viewed by the American citizens as too European and elitist? She didn't help dissuade their opinion of her as she preferred to distance herself from those she considered unsophisticated.

    A. Melania Trump   *C. Jackie Kennedy*

    B. Elizabeth Monroe   *D. Louisa Adams*

45. Which two First Ladies consulted astrologers?

    A. M. Lincoln & L. Harding   *C. M. Lincoln & N. Reagan*

    B. E. Wilson & N. Reagan   *D. L. Harding & N. Reagan*

46. J. Edgar Hoover, the director of the FBI, considered this First Lady's views dangerous. He had his agents keep an extensive file on her. Who was she?

A. Eleanor Roosevelt

C. Hillary Clinton

B. Betty Ford

D. Mary Todd Lincoln

47. Which First Lady drove a coach of matching white Arabian horses?

A. Julia Tyler

C. Julia Grant

B. Sarah Polk

D. Martha Washington

48. She became First Lady when one President resigned and her husband became acting President.

A. Eliza Johnson

C. Ida McKinley

B. Lucretia Garfield

D. Betty Ford

49. Even though her husband was a graduate from Harvard, this First Lady had no formal education.

A. Pat Nixon

C. Mary Todd Lincoln

B. Ellen Wilson

D. Abigail Adams

50. Which First Lady's loyalties lay to the South, as she had grown up by slave laborers? This became a problem when the Civil War broke out. Later when she wished to return to Washington, D.C., she was denied unless she swore allegiance to the North. She did not do so and stayed loyal to the South.

A. Eliza Johnson

B. Julia Grant

C. Julia Tyler

D. Peggy Taylor

Answers

Chapter 23 — Do You Know...

1. C - Melania Trump, wife of Donald Trump

2. A - Mary Todd Lincoln, wife of Abraham Lincoln

3. B - Barbara Bush, wife of George H.W. Bush

4. A - Bess Truman, wife of Harry Truman

5. D - *6*

As of the printing of this book there are six, which include:

The current First Lady Melania Trump, Rosalynn Carter, Barbara Bush, Hillary Clinton, Laura Bush, and Michelle Obama.

6. A - Lucy Hayes, wife of Rutherford B. Hayes

7. C - Lou Hoover, wife of Herbert Hoover

She hired staff to help with the overflow of letters. Requests for help were sent to the correct organizations. Her office coordinated with more than forty federal, state, local, and private groups that could help those in need. In instances where no help could be found she forwarded the letter to a friend asking for their help. She also sent money herself in addition to asking others to help.

8. B - Bess Truman, wife of Harry Truman

9. D - Martha Washington, wife of George Washington and Abigail Adams, wife of John Adams

10. A - Eleanor Roosevelt, wife of Franklin D. Roosevelt

11. B - Abigail Adams, wife of John Adams

12. D - Barbara Bush, wife of George H.W. Bush

13. A - Edith Wilson, second wife of Woodrow Wilson

Unlike Senator Elizabeth Warren who claimed to be Native American related to Pocahontas when she was applying to get into Harvard. Warren has failed to have been able to back up these claims of being Native American with verifiable documentation stating only that she heard it from family members, but First Lady Edith Wilson was indeed a descendant of Pocahontas.

14. A - Anna Harrison, wife of William H. Harrison

15. C – Frances Cleveland, wife of Grover Cleveland

She was only twenty-one years of age when she married the sitting president and became the youngest First Lady in American history.

16. D - Mary Todd Lincoln, wife of Abraham Lincoln

17. A - Michelle Obama, wife of Barack Obama

18. B - Bess Truman, wife of Harry Truman

19. C - Betty Ford, wife of Gerald Ford

20. D – 9

There were 9 officially, but sometimes these stand-in First Ladies also had help for a short period of time. First Ladies that weren't married to the president were used when the presidents were widowers, a bachelor, or when the First Lady was too ill to take on the role.

First Ladies who assumed the role that weren't wives to the presidents were: *Dolley Madison to Thomas Jefferson, Emily Donelson (niece) to Andrew Jackson, Angelica Van Buren (daughter-in-law) to Martin Van Buren, Priscilla Tyler (daughter-in-law) to John Tyler, Harriet Lane (niece) to bachelor president James Buchanan, Martha Johnson Patterson (daughter) to Andrew Johnson, Mary Arthur McElroy (sister) to Chester Arthur, Rose Cleveland (sister) to Grover Cleveland before his marriage to Frances Cleveland, and Margaret Wilson (daughter) in the days before her father's marriage to his second wife Edith. There were a few others who assumed the role on occasion or for a short period of time to aid those mentioned above.*

21. A - Eliza Johnson, wife of Andrew Johnson

22. B - Dolley Madison, wife of James Madison

23. C - Mamie Eisenhower, wife of Dwight D. Eisenhower

24. D - Lou Hoover, wife of Herbert Hoover **&** Barbara Bush, wife of George H.W. Bush

25. B - Mary Todd Lincoln, wife of Abraham Lincoln

26. D - Hillary Clinton, wife of Bill Clinton

27. C - Ida McKinley, wife of William McKinley

28. A - Mary Todd Lincoln, wife of Abraham Lincoln

29. C - Grace Coolidge, wife of Calvin Coolidge

30. B - Melania Trump, wife of Donald Trump

She initially came to the U.S. with a visa to work, applied for a green card, and eventually studied and applied for American citizenship which she is very proud of. She stated that it is important to come to this country in a legal manner.

31. D - Laura Bush, wife of George W. Bush

32. C - Harriet Lane, First Lady to James Buchanan

James Buchanan became her guardian when she was orphaned at the age of eleven.

Grover Cleveland was also a bachelor when first elected as president, but married during his first administration.

33. A - Letitia Tyler, first wife of John Tyler

34. B - Lou Hoover, wife of Herbert Hoover

35. C - Edith Roosevelt, wife of Theodore Roosevelt

36. D - Nancy Reagan, wife of Ronald Reagan

37. Either one of these would be correct: A - Betty Ford, wife of Gerald Ford or D - Melania Trump, wife of Donald Trump

Melania Trump began her professional modeling career at the age of sixteen and is the only First Lady to have a major layout in Sports Illustrated Swimsuit Edition.

38. B - Laura Bush, wife of George W. Bush

39. A - Hillary Clinton, wife of Bill Clinton

40. C - Jackie Kennedy, wife of John F. Kennedy

In the tapes she reveals that after an independent investigation of the assassination she believes Lyndon B. Johnson and his cabal of Texas cronies were to blame for her husband's assassination.

41. A - Anna Harrison, wife of William H. Harrison

42. D - Julia Grant, wife of Ulysses S. Grant

43. C - Rosalynn Carter, wife of Jimmy Carter

44. B - Elizabeth Monroe, wife of James Monroe

45. D - Florence Harding, wife of Warren Harding **&** Nancy Reagan, wife of Ronald Reagan

46. A - Eleanor Roosevelt, wife of Franklin D. Roosevelt

47. A - Julia Tyler, second wife of John Tyler

48. D - Betty Ford, wife of Gerald Ford

49. D - Abigail Adams, wife of John Adams

50. C - Julia Tyler, second wife of John Tyler

24

Works & Achievements Of First Ladies

Answers are given on pages 265 - 266.

1. Her work toward the highway beautification became the first major legislative campaign by a First Lady.

A. Nellie Taft

C. Florence Harding

B. Lady Bird Johnson

D. Rosalynn Carter

2. Which First Lady wrote a monthly column for a women's magazine? The article was titled, *'I Want You To Write To Me'*? She received over 300,000 letters letting the First Lady know about the women, their lives, and the conditions in the world. This gave the President valuable insight for his New Deal agenda.

A. Lou Hoover

C. Bess Truman

B. Grace Coolidge

D. Eleanor Roosevelt

3. Which First Lady's main cause has been that of literacy?

A. Lucy Hayes

C. Eliza Johnson

B. Barbara Bush

D. Lady Bird Johnson

4. Which First Lady supported the causes of the care of wounded WWI veterans, humane treatment of animals, and was involved in the creation of the first federal prison for women?

    A. Lucretia Garfield   *C. Florence Harding*

    B. Caroline Harrison   *D. Edith Roosevelt*

5. During WWII which First Lady traveled abroad to visit the U.S. troops?

    A. Edith Wilson   *C. Bess Truman*

    B. Mamie Eisenhower   *D. Eleanor Roosevelt*

6. Which First Lady helped found (DAR) National Society of the Daughters of the American Revolution?

    A. Caroline Harrison   *C. Ida McKinley*

    B. Frances Cleveland   *D. Edith Roosevelt*

7. Which First Lady's greatest legacy is the Japanese Cherry Blossoms she arranged to have planted along the Tidal Basin in Washington, D.C.?

    A. Edith Roosevelt   *C. Grace Coolidge*

    B. Nellie Taft   *D. Ellen Wilson*

8. Which First Lady's most significant contribution as First Lady was overseeing an extensive renovation of the White House saving it from demolition?

A. Bess Truman   C. Jackie Kennedy

B. Melania Trump   D. Nancy Reagan

9. Which First Lady arranged for two important displays in the White House? One was the hanging of portraits of each First Lady and the other was an exhibit of the collection of presidential china?

A. Lucy Hayes   C. Edith Roosevelt

B. Jane Pierce   D. Nellie Taft

10. Which First Lady supported the emancipation of slaves, which she considered a threat to democracy?

A. Martha Washington   C. Lucy Hayes

B. Lou Hoover   D. Abigail Adams

11. Which First Lady pressured John Hopkins University to admit women to their medical school?

A. Frances Cleveland   C. Caroline Harrison

B. Ellen Wilson   D. Ida McKinley

12. Which First Lady's platform is to work on helping children, women, and to address fighting cyber bullying among the youth?

A. Laura Bush   C. Michelle Obama

B. Betty Ford   D. Melania Trump

13. In Lafayette Square across from the White House, which First Lady

helped stop the destruction of historic buildings along the square?

A. Jackie Kennedy   C. Eleanor Roosevelt

B. Bess Truman   D. Edith Wilson

14. Which First Lady launched a program to address the challenge of childhood obesity?

A. Laura Bush   C. Barbara Bush

B. Michelle Obama   D. Nancy Reagan

15. Which First Lady was strong on her stance opposing prohibition and promoting women's suffrage?

A. Lucy Hayes   C. Eliza Johnson

B. Lou Hoover   D. Nellie Taft

16. Which First Lady had electricity installed in the White House and made up detailed plans to enlarge the existing building by adding an east and west wing?

A. Caroline Harrison   C. Sarah Polk

B. Lady Bird Johnson   D. Nellie Taft

17. One of this First Lady's most important contributions to her husband's administrations came about from her correspondence with a junior British ambassador who had been best man at their wedding. He kept her up to date on the Russo-Japanese War. Through the First Lady, the President negotiated an end to the conflict for which he was awarded the Nobel Peace Prize. Which First Lady was this?

A. *Frances Cleveland*   C. *Edith Roosevelt*

B. *Edith Wilson*   D. *Bess Truman*

18. Which First Lady was involved in the women's movement to abolish slavery, and was also one of the 1st First Ladies to fight for the cause of women's rights?

A. *Louisa Adams*   C. *Abigail Adams*

B. *Eliza Johnson*   D. *Caroline Harrison*

19. Which First Lady added 600 paintings and antiques to the White House?

A. *Jackie Kennedy*   C. *Bess Truman*

B. *Pat Nixon*   D. *Nancy Reagan*

20. Which First Lady worked on *'Head Start'*, a program aimed at helping preschool children from disadvantaged homes?

A. *Rosalynn Carter*   C. *Pat Nixon*

B. *Michelle Obama*   D. *Lady Bird Johnson*

21. When the U.S. first entered WWI, this First Lady encouraged women to cut back on food so soldiers could eat better. She had a flock of sheep on the White House lawn, and when it came time to shear them the money brought in from the wool ($50,000) went to the war effort. Who was she?

A. *Edith Wilson*   C. *Eleanor Roosevelt*

B. *Lou Hoover*   D. *Caroline Harrison*

22. Which First Lady worked towards encouraging American youth to stay off drugs in her *'Just Say No'* program?

A. Melania Trump

B. Betty Ford

C. Nancy Reagan

D. Laura Bush

23. Which First Lady when keeping in mind what the White House represented to its many visitors, her first major project as First Lady was to restore and preserve the White House? She restored all the public rooms of the White House, and with the aid of many experts she included many items that had belonged to past Presidents.

A. Nancy Reagan

B. Jackie Kennedy

C. Melania Trump

D. Bess Truman

24. It is said and thought by many, that this First Lady was not only acting President for six and a half months while her husband was laid up, but also took on the role of Secretary to the President, and Secretary of State. Who was she?

A. Edith Wilson

B. Nancy Reagan

C. Jackie Kennedy

D. Lou Hoover

25. Which First Lady took a trip to Peru to bring relief supplies to earthquake victims?

A. Caroline Harrison

B. Edith Roosevelt

C. Lou Hoover

D. Pat Nixon

26. Wanting to make the White House more accessible, which First Lady opened it to public tours? She would often join in the tours herself and

invited thousands of guests to garden parties.

A. Lady Bird Johnson   *C. Florence Harding*

B. Betty Ford   *D. Pat Nixon*

27. Which First Lady was a strong advocate for the program No Child Left Behind Act and NCLB's Reading First Program – the largest early reading initiative in American history?

A. Nancy Reagan   *C. Bess Truman*

B. Laura Bush   *D. Barbara Bush*

28. With the approach of WWII, which First Lady did what she could to help European refugees, which included helping Jews who were trying to escape Nazi-occupied Europe?

A. Grace Coolidge   *C. Eleanor Roosevelt*

B. Mamie Eisenhower   *D. Lou Hoover*

29. Instead of worrying about setting fashion trends, as First Lady she worked on different causes, such as: advocate for the right for women to participate in sporting events such as the Olympics and teaching women to respond to crises and disasters?

A. Lucretia Garfield   *C. Eleanor Roosevelt*

B. Edith Roosevelt   *D. Lou Hoover*

30. Which First Lady led a fundraising effort to create a memorial for the victims of the Titanic?

A. Nellie Taft

B. Edith Wilson

C. Ida McKinley

D. Grace Coolidge

Answers

Chapter 24 — Works & Achievements Of First Ladies

1. B - Lady Bird Johnson, wife of Lyndon B. Johnson

2. D - Eleanor Roosevelt, wife of Franklin D. Roosevelt

3. B - Barbara Bush, wife of George H.W. Bush

4. C - Florence Harding, wife of Warren Harding

5. D - Eleanor Roosevelt, wife of Franklin D. Roosevelt

6. A - Caroline Harrison, wife of Benjamin Harrison

7. B - Nellie Taft, wife of William H. Taft

8. A - Bess Truman, wife of Harry Truman

9. C - Edith Roosevelt, wife of Theodore Roosevelt

10. D - Abigail Adams, wife of John Adams

11. C - Caroline Harrison, wife of Benjamin Harrison

12. D - Melania Trump, wife of Donald Trump

13. A - Jackie Kennedy, wife of John F. Kennedy

14. B - Michelle Obama, wife of Barack Obama

15. D -Nellie Taft, wife of William H. Taft

16. A - Caroline Harrison, wife of Benjamin Harrison

17. C - Edith Roosevelt, wife of Theodore Roosevelt

18. A - Louisa Adams, wife of John Quincy Adams

Another First Lady who fought for women's rights was her mother-in-law, Abigail Adams.

19. B - Pat Nixon, wife of Richard Nixon

20. D - Lady Bird Johnson, wife of Lyndon B. Johnson

21. A - Edith Wilson, second wife of Woodrow Wilson

22. C - Nancy Reagan, wife of Ronald Reagan

23. B - Jacqueline Kennedy, wife of John F. Kennedy

A tour of the restored White House aired on national television with 80,000,000 viewers watching; earning Jackie Kennedy an honorary Emmy Award.

24. A - Edith Wilson, second wife of Woodrow Wilson

25. D - Pat Nixon, wife of Richard Nixon

26. C - Florence Harding, wife of Warren Harding

27. B - Laura Bush, wife of George W. Bush

28. C - Eleanor Roosevelt, wife of Franklin D. Roosevelt

29. D - Lou Hoover, wife of Herbert Hoover

30. A - Nellie Taft, wife of William H. Taft

25

United States At War

Answers are given on page 270.

1. Which First Lady visited a war zone in South Vietnam riding in on a helicopter? She was the 1st First Lady to ever visit a combat zone.

    A. Hillary Clinton   *C. Pat Nixon*

    B. Mamie Eisenhower   *D. Eleanor Roosevelt*

2. She was the First Lady when the President decided to drop the atomic bomb on Japan which led to the end of WWII.

    A. Mamie Eisenhower   *C. Eleanor Roosevelt*

    B. Bess Truman   *D. Lou Hoover*

3. During the Civil War which First Lady, who was now a widow, received visits from leaders of both Confederate and Union armies?

    A. Sarah Polk   *C. Anna Harrison*

    B. Mary Todd Lincoln   *D. Peggy Taylor*

4. Who was First Lady when WWII broke out?

A. *Lou Hoover*   C. *Mamie Eisenhower*

B. *Edith Wilson*   D. *Eleanor Roosevelt*

5. During the Revolutionary War she provided meals and lodging to soldiers who stopped at their home.

A. *Martha Washington*   C. *Abigail Adams*

B. *Dolley Madison*   D. *Hannah Van Buren*

6. During the Civil War, her husband away at Congress, she was given thirty-six hours notice to vacate her home. In frail health on the journey she had to ask strangers for food and shelter.

A. *Eliza Johnson*   C. *Rachel Jackson*

B. *Hannah Van Buren*   D. *Anna Harrison*

7. Her husband's presidency saw the beginning of the Cold War and at the end of his presidency the Korean War.

A. *Mamie Eisenhower*   C. *Bess Truman*

B. *Eleanor Roosevelt*   D. *Lou Hoover*

8. Her husband was Commander of the Union Army during the Civil War.

A. *Julia Grant*   C. *Peggy Taylor*

B. *Martha Washington*   D. *Martha Jefferson*

9. The President left the White House during the War of 1812 to meet

with his generals on the battlefield. The First Lady stayed behind to gather important state papers so they wouldn't fall into the hands of the British.

A. Elizabeth Monroe   *C. Martha Washington*

B. Dolley Madison   *D. Abigail Adams*

10. Her husband was the Supreme Commander of the Allied forces during WWII.

A. Dolley Madison   *C. Mary Todd Lincoln*

B. Julia Grant   *D. Mamie Eisenhower*

Answers

Chapter 25 — United States At War

1. C - Pat Nixon, wife of Richard Nixon

2. B - Bess Truman, wife of Harry Truman

3. A - Sarah Polk, wife of James Polk

4. D - Eleanor Roosevelt, wife of Franklin D. Roosevelt

5. C - Abigail Adams, wife of John Adams

6. A - Eliza Johnson, wife of Andrew Johnson

7. C - Bess Truman, wife of Harry Truman

8. A - Julia Grant, wife of Ulysses S. Grant

9. B - Dolley Madison, wife of James Madison

Dolley Madison is best remembered for her role in saving a portrait of George Washington and other treasures from the White House as the British troops descended upon Washington, D.C. during the War of 1812. She was literally watching the British soldiers descend on Washington through binoculars before she could be convinced to leave the White House.

10. D - Mamie Eisenhower, wife of Dwight D. Eisenhower

26

Rumors & Gossip

Answers are given on pages 278 - 279.

1. She was pregnant at the age of nineteen and later claimed she had eloped with the baby's father. She said he left her shortly afterward, so she divorced him. Some historians accept this, while others question whether the marriage and divorce of this First Lady ever took place.

   A. Lucretia Garfield   *C. Florence Harding*

   B. Edith Roosevelt   *D. Pat Nixon*

2. Which First Lady was accused of being a Confederate spy?

   A. Peggy Taylor   *C. Julia Tyler*

   B. Mary Todd Lincoln   *D. Anna Harrison*

3. J. Edgar Hoover, director of the FBI, thought this First Lady's views dangerous. He ordered his FBI agents to keep a file on her. Who was she?

   A. Lou Hoover   *C. Jackie Kennedy*

   B. Nellie Taft   *D. Eleanor Roosevelt*

4. Which First Lady was said to have ruled the White House with a Gucci-clad fist?

A. Jackie Kennedy   *C. Nancy Reagan*

B. Melania Trump   *D. Michelle Obama*

5. When her husband the sitting president suffered from a major stroke and was incapacitated for five months she kept it a secret from the public.

A. Lou Hoover   *C. Lady Bird Johnson*

B. Edith Wilson   *D. Abigail Fillmore*

6. At the age of seventeen she married a man who was abusive. They separated, and she learned he had filed for divorce. Two years after she married again she discovered he never followed through with the divorce. After the divorce was finally finalized, she and the future President remarried. During her husband's election campaign accusations of adultery and bigamy were used against her with his political opponents. Those that knew her, respected her for her kindness and honesty.

A. Rachel Jackson   *C. Florence Harding*

B. Jane Pierce   *D. Hannah Van Buren*

7. Which First Lady and President enjoyed poker games in the White House where liquor was served; even though the Eighteenth Amendment made it illegal to do so?

A. Ellen Arthur   *C. Caroline Harrison*

B. Florence Harding   *D. Edith Wilson*

8. Which First Lady, the President's second wife, was entrusted by the President with a secret code which gave her access to confidential war documents?

A. Eleanor Roosevelt   C. Julia Grant

B. Julia Tyler   D. Edith Wilson

9. This prim and proper First Lady *'had'* to get married as she was already pregnant when they said their 'I do's'?

A. Melania Trump   C. Nancy Reagan

B. Laura Bush   D. Jackie Kennedy

10. Which First Lady found another woman's underwear in her bed in the White House, and told the President he should find out who they belonged to because they weren't her size?

A. Lou Hoover   C. Lady Bird Johnson

B. Jackie Kennedy   D. Hillary Clinton

11. Which First Lady was whispered about behind closed doors accused of being a lesbian? Later in life, against the will of his siblings, her own son wrote a book exposing her secret life. Letters discovered that the First Lady had written to her confidante and companion were made into a book by another author.

A. Eleanor Roosevelt   C. Hillary Clinton

B. Florence Harding   D. Eliza Johnson

12. The rumor was that the First Lady poisoned the President; whether

because she was angry over his numerous affairs or to save him on charges of corruption as scandals were being revealed is speculation. When she insisted on no autopsy, even though his doctors tried to convince her otherwise, she remained firm and insisted on him being embalmed right away which only fueled the flames of doubt.

A. Eleanor Roosevelt   C. Nellie Taft

B. Florence Harding   D. Jane Pierce

13. Which First Lady is the most notorious for being involved in scandals? A very small list of her *long* list of scandals, but by far not all of her scandals are: Abuse of power of the IRS, Filegate, Travelgate, covering up the information on the women that the President allegedly raped, seduced, or had sexual improprieties with; and then going so far as to stalk them, threaten, and attempting to discredit them, Benghazi, pay-to-play allegations, and looting the White House when she and the president moved out. This is the short list of scandals which the First Lady was connected with?

A. Lou Hoover   C. Mary Todd Lincoln

C. Pat Nixon   D. Hillary Clinton

14. Her name was on Hollywood's Blacklist which was put out to warn producers of actors and actresses suspected of being communist sympathizers.

A. Nancy Reagan   C. Betty Ford

B. Melania Trump   D. Eleanor Roosevelt

15. During her time as First Lady she received a lot of criticism. During the Civil War, Southerns labeled her a traitor to her birth while citizens loyal to the Union suspected her of treason. When she entertained, she

was accused of unpatriotic extravagance. When she stopped entertaining after her son's death, she was accused of shirking her duties as First Lady. It seemed everything she did was up for criticism. Who was this First Lady?

A. Eliza Johnson

C. Mary Todd Lincoln

B. Harriet Lane

D. Peggy Taylor

16. Which First Lady said she knew nothing about the scandal her husband was involved in until hearing about it in the press?

A. Melania Trump

C. Hillary Clinton

B. Pat Nixon

D. Eleanor Roosevelt

17. Which First Lady after putting up with her husband's numerous affairs retaliated and had affairs of her own, one of them being with the actor William Holden? Months after her husband's assassination she admitted to this on tapes that were to be kept locked in a vault and kept secret until 50 years after her husband's death, but which her daughter had opened early.

A. Jackie Kennedy

C. Nancy Reagan

B. Hillary Clinton

D. Edith Wilson

18. Which First Lady had to deal with her husband's numerous affairs including one with her best friend? Another woman later came forward claiming she had taken several trips with him when he was senator, and he was the father of her child which was later confirmed by DNA.

A. Eleanor Roosevelt

C. Florence Harding

B. Hillary Clinton

D. Lady Bird Johnson

19. Few people in Washington, D.C. would ever see this First Lady, who chose to remain out of the public's eye, causing rumors to start. Her husband died sixteen months into his presidency, and overwhelmed with grief she was too distraught to attend his funeral.

    A. Peggy Taylor   *C. Lucretia Garfield*

    B. Mary Todd Lincoln   *D. Ida McKinley*

20. Which First Lady, paranoid that her words and actions would be spread by the White House staff, made them all sign a confidentiality document? It was not legally enforceable, and the first one to break the agreement was her own personal secretary.

    A. Hillary Clinton   *C. Rosalynn Carter*

    B. Jackie Kennedy   *D. Pat Nixon*

21. There was concern on how much influence this First Lady had on her husband. The New York Times concluded a triumvirate was in charge at the White House: the President, his Chief of Staff, and the First Lady.

    A. Edith Wilson   *C. Florence Harding*

    B. Laura Bush   *D. Nancy Reagan*

22. Which First Lady after learning of her husband's infidelity moved into her own bedroom and became increasingly independent? She devoted herself to political and social causes that were important to her.

    A. Lady Bird Johnson   *C. Eleanor Roosevelt*

    B. Hillary Clinton   *D. Jackie Kennedy*

23. Which First Lady is ranked as the most stylish and glamorous of all, and on her first official visit to the White House before her husband took office she was "dissed" by the current First Lady who refused to parktake in the customary photo op with her?

A. Grace Coolidge

C. Jackie Kennedy

B. Melania Trump

D. Laura Bush

24. Which First Lady was witnessed by the White House staff leaning over the stairs yelling at the President that she knew about a girlfriend of his and demanded he not leave the White House that night?

A. Florence Harding

C. Hillary Clinton

B. Michelle Obama

D. Jackie Kennedy

25. Which First Lady suffered an inner-ear problem which affected her balance which sometimes caused her to stumble? This gave some the unfounded reason to believe she had a drinking problem.

A. Bess Truman

C. Mamie Eisenhower

B. Barbara Bush

D. Betty Ford

Answers

Chapter 26 — Rumors & Gossip

1. C - Florence Harding, wife of Warren Harding

2. B - Mary Todd Lincoln, wife of Abraham Lincoln

3. D - Eleanor Roosevelt, wife of Franklin D. Roosevelt

4. C - Nancy Reagan, wife of Ronald Reagan

5. B - Edith Wilson, second wife of Woodrow Wilson

6. A - Rachel Jackson, wife of Andrew Jackson

7. B - Florence Harding, wife of Warren Harding

8. D - Edith Wilson, second wife of Woodrow Wilson

9. C - Nancy Reagan, wife of Ronald Reagan

10. B - Jackie Kennedy, wife of John F. Kennedy

11. A - Eleanor Roosevelt, wife of Franklin D. Roosevelt

She wasn't the first lesbian in the White House. Rose Cleveland, sister to Grover Cleveland, who served as First Lady until he married Frances was also a lesbian.

12. B - Florence Harding, wife of Warren Harding

13. D - Hillary Clinton, wife of Bill Clinton

14. A - Nancy Reagan, wife of Ronald Reagan

Later it was found out that it was another actress with the same name who was supposed to be on the Blacklist, not the future First Lady.

15. C - Mary Todd Lincoln, wife of Abraham Lincoln

16. B - Pat Nixon, wife of Richard Nixon

17. A – Jackie Kennedy, wife of John F. Kennedy

18. C - Florence Harding, wife of Warren Harding

19. A - Peggy Taylor, wife of Zachary Taylor

20. B - Jackie Kennedy, wife of John F. Kennedy

21. D - Nancy Reagan, wife of Ronald Reagan

22. C - Eleanor Roosevelt, wife of Franklin D. Roosevelt

23. B - Melania Trump, wife of Donald Trump

Michelle Obama refused to appear on camera or to be a part of the customary photo op between the current and in-coming First Lady.

24. A - Florence Harding, wife of Warren Harding

25. C - Mamie Eisenhower, wife of Dwight D. Eisenhower

27

Life After The White House

Answers are given on pages 286 - 287.

1. After she moved out of the White House, which First Lady visited the White House only once in her lifetime in a secret trip with her children to view portraits of her and her husband? When in the Washington, D.C. area at another time; rather than drive by the White House she asked her driver to avoid routes where she would see the White House.

   A. Frances Cleveland   *C. Grace Coolidge*

   B. Jackie Kennedy   *D. Betty Ford*

2. Which First Lady had seventeen people testify against her, including her own son? They said she was insane and after only ten minutes of deliberation she was committed to a state hospital for the insane.

   A. Barbara Bush   *C. Mary Todd Lincoln*

   B. Jane Pierce   *D. Ida McKinley*

3. This First Lady's husband published his memoirs when he knew he was dying so his wife would have financial stability. She was also the *first* First Lady to write her memoirs, but they wouldn't be published until 1975.

A. *Julia Grant*   C. *Lady Bird Johnson*

B. *Mamie Eisenhower*   D. *Julia Tyler*

4. Which President's wife freed the slaves they owned a year after her husband's death fearing for her life after his will revealed the slaves were to be set free after her death? Fearing her life could be in danger she decided to free them immediately.

A. *Julia Tyler*   C. *Dolley Madison*

B. *Anna Harrison*   D. *Martha Washington*

5. In her early days as First Lady she had recorded her thoughts in daily tape recordings, and after she left the White House she wrote an 800 page White House Diary which was a revealing account of life in the White House by a President's wife.

A. *Laura Bush*   C. *Lady Bird Johnson*

B. *Julia Grant*   D. *Frances Cleveland*

6. When she was a widow she remarried a man twenty-eight years older than her. He was not only one of the wealthiest men in the world, but he was a foreigner.

A. *Frances Cleveland*   C. *Betty Ford*

B. *Jackie Kennedy*   D. *Melania Trump*

7. Which First Lady when an impoverished widow planned to sell a slave that had been with her husband since he was a child, and was only saved when Daniel Webster stepped in and gave her the cash she needed and permitted the slave to buy his own freedom?

A. *Martha Washington*   C. *Julia Tyler*

B. *Peggy Taylor*   D. *Dolley Madison*

8. After her days as First Lady she was elected to the U.S. Senate and held the position of Secretary of State; and even ran for President herself.

A. *Nellie Taft*   C. *Hillary Clinton*

B. *Eleanor Roosevelt*   D. *Michelle Obama*

9. One of her closest friends was a black woman who had been a slave for thirty years and a seamstress in the White House for the First Lady.

A. *Mary Todd Lincoln*   C. *Dolley Madison*

B. *Louisa Adams*   D. *Anna Harrison*

10. After the death of the President, she accepted an appointment to the United States delegation to the United Nations.

A. *Hillary Clinton*   C. *Nellie Taft*

B. *Eleanor Roosevelt*   D. *Grace Coolidge*

11. As a widow she rode in an airplane, an activity the President had declared improper for a First Lady.

A. *Bess Truman*   C. *Edith Wilson*

B. *Grace Coolidge*   D. *Eleanor Roosevelt*

12. Years after the death of her husband, this First Lady walked around town with over $50,000 worth of government bonds sewn into the

pockets of her petticoats.

A. Anna Harrison   *C. Anna Harrison*

B. Jane Pierce   *D. Mary Todd Lincoln*

13. When she was First Lady she was the most famous woman on earth, yet after her husband's death she never publicly spoke about her marriage to the President or of her times as First Lady.

A. Jackie Kennedy   *C. Pat Nixon*

B. Eleanor Roosevelt   *D. Frances Cleveland*

14. When this First Lady was to attend a luncheon in China she was taken to a palace through the streets of Shanghai in a carved chair on a raised platform with yellow silk curtains hiding her from the eyes of the curious while four strong men carried her sedan, much as they used to do with the Empress of China.

A. Lou Hoover   *C. Florence Harding*

B. Julia Grant   *D. Barbara Bush*

15. Which First Lady helped draft the Universal Declaration of Human Rights?

A. Hillary Clinton   *C. Eleanor Roosevelt*

B. Michelle Obama   *D. Nellie Taft*

16. Between her husband's first and second terms of presidency, their primary residence was farmland where the First Lady and President gardened and ate the produce they grew.

A. *Frances Cleveland*   C. *Bess Truman*

B. *Grace Coolidge*   D. *Mamie Eisenhower*

17. As a widow, this First Lady did charity work for the Red Cross and her church, raised funds to bring refugee children to the United States from Germany in 1939, and raised money for the Queen Welhelmina Fund for the Dutch victims of Nazi invaders. She loaned her home to the WAVES during WWII.

A. *Lou Hoover*   C. *Edith Wilson*

B. *Bess Truman*   D. *Grace Coolidge*

18. After her husband's death, she was a living connection to the country's Founding Fathers and was awarded an honorary seat in Congress.

A. *Nellie Taft*   C. *Frances Harding*

B. *Dolley Madison*   D. *Grace Coolidge*

19. After her husband's death, she spent her remaining years with her only surviving son helping him raise her grandson who would one day become President himself.

A. *Anna Harrison*   C. *Julia Tyler*

B. *Barbara Bush*   D. *Eliza Johnson*

20. After leaving the White House, she and her husband traveled the world for over two years.

A. *Rosalynn Carter*

C. *Julia Grant*

B. *Mary Todd Lincoln*

D. *Elizabeth Monroe*

Answers

Chapter 27 — Life After the White House

1. B - Jackie Kennedy, wife of John F. Kennedy

2. C - Mary Todd Lincoln, wife of Abraham Lincoln

Mary Lincoln spent four months in the asylum. There are many circumstances she dealt with which could have attributed to her mental state.

Her son Willie died while living in the White House, she lost a son previous to their White House days, she was a loving mother and lost three of her sons at early ages.

She was sitting next to her husband at Ford's Theater holding his hand when he was shot.

She also was in a horse and carriage accident where she was thrown from the carriage and hit her head on a rock.

Her only son that lived to adulthood, Robert Lincoln, is the one who had her committed to the state hospital.

3. A - Julia Grant, wife of Ulysses S. Grant

4. D - Martha Washington, wife of George Washington

5. C - Lady Bird Johnson, wife of Lyndon B. Johnson

6. B - Jackie Kennedy, wife of John F. Kennedy

7. D - Dolley Madison, wife of James Madison

8. C - Hillary Clinton, wife of Bill Clinton

9. A - Mary Todd Lincoln, wife of Abraham Lincoln

10. B - Eleanor Roosevelt, wife of Franklin D. Roosevelt

11. B - Grace Coolidge, wife of Calvin Coolidge

12. D - Mary Todd Lincoln, wife of Abraham Lincoln

13. A - Jackie Kennedy, wife of John F. Kennedy

14. B - Julia Grant, wife of Ulysses S. Grant

15. C - Eleanor Roosevelt, wife of Franklin D. Roosevelt

16. A - Frances Cleveland, wife of Grover Cleveland

17. D - Grace Coolidge, wife of Calvin Coolidge

18. B - Dolley Madison, wife of James Madison

19. A - Anna Harrison, wife of William H. Harrison

20. C - Julia Grant, wife of Ulysses S. Grant

28

Let Me Introduce You To The President

The First Ladies will tell you about their husbands and what they are most remembered for from their presidential years. The years their husbands were President are given as additional clues. See if you can name the President.

Answers are given on pages 304 - 306.

1. **1825 – 1829** My husband was the 6th President. I'm afraid one of the things my husband is most remembered for is him swimming nude in the Potomac and that his father was also President. After his days in the White House he became a Congressman. Even though not a very popular man, he spent his life serving his country. He watched it's inception as a child witnessing the Battle of Bunker Hill with his mother from a hilltop near their family farm. He served as a diplomat, President, then Congressman until he collapsed and died still serving his country.

   A. George Washington   *C. John Quincy Adams*

   B. Thomas Jefferson   *D. James Madison*

2. **1981 – 1989** My husband was the 40th President, the first President who had been an actor and the oldest President. I'm proud to say my husband was a President most liked by the public by both Republicans and Democrats. He may have been the oldest President, but he was an effective President. He saw the American hostages in Iran brought home, saw the end of the Cold War, and to get employment up and inflation down he had an economic policy called "Reganomics."

A. George H.W. Bush

C. Jimmy Carter

B. Ronald Reagan

D. Gerald Ford

3. **2009 - 2017** My husband was the 44th President. My husband is most well-known for being the first African-American President in American history. He pushed through the Health Care Reform. Unemployment was at a record high and the economy has suffered. He pushed for higher taxes and stimulus plans to help the economy.

A. Warren Harding

C. Zachary Taylor

B. Andrew Johnson

D. Barack Obama

4. **1789 – 1797** My husband was the 1st President of the United States. He had a big responsibility for setting the precedent for all future Presidents. He is most remembered for leading the Continental Army in the American Revolution during his pre-presidential days and for being the first President. He was the only President unanimously elected.

A. George Washington

C. James Madison

B. Thomas Jefferson

D. James Monroe

5. **1974 – 1977** My husband was the 38th President. He is the only man to become President without having been elected to the office of the President or the Vice President. My husband being a good, honest man

wanted more than anything to restore the people's faith in their leaders in Washington, D.C.

A. Richard Nixon

C. Ronald Reagan

B. Gerald Ford

D. Lyndon B. Johnson

6. **1901 – 1909** My husband was the 26th President. He became President after the previous President was assassinated. One of my husband's main concerns was making life better for the average American. He saw to it that a large amount of land out west was set aside for natural forests. He set safety standards for food and medicine. He negotiated peace between Russia and Japan. He saw to it that the Panama Canal was built.

A. William McKinley

C. Theodore Roosevelt

B. Franklin D. Roosevelt

D. Lyndon B. Johnson

7. **1993 – 2001** My husband was the 42nd President. My husband balanced the budget, the first time to have been done so in years. He was President during one of the longest periods of peace. He was the first two term President from the Democratic party since President Franklin D. Roosevelt. He was impeached, but the Senate allowed him to remain in office. He was the first President born after the end of WWII.

A. George W. Bush

C. Donald Trump

B. Bill Clinton

D. Gerald Ford

8. **1893 – 1897** My husband was the 24th president. My husband's second term began with the worst financial crises in the nation's history to date. The Panic of 1893 started with a railroad bankruptcy, then several banks failed, the stock market crashed, and three more railroads failed. Unemployment rose and the economy didn't recover until near the

end of his second term. He is the only president to have served two non-consecutive terms.

A. *Grover Cleveland*   C. *Herbert Hoover*

B. *James Buchanan*   D. *Franklin D. Roosevelt*

9. **2017-** . My husband is the 45th President. He is the first President to have been elected who was not previously a politician. Many Americans not happy to see their country going in the direction it was, voted for my husband so he could fulfill his promise to 'Make America Great Again.' Two of his campaign promises was to vet all incoming immigrants in order to keep the country safe and to replace the Affordable Care Act otherwise known as Obamacare. He has only been in office a short time, but to date has met some of his campaign promises and fighting his political opponents to accomplish the others.

A. *Gerald Ford*   C. *Ronald Reagan*

B. *Dwight D. Eisenhower*   D. *Donald Trump*

10. **1861 – 1865**   My husband was the 16th President until he was assassinated. You may remember him for his famous Emancipation Proclamation or his presentation of the Gettysburg Address. Or perhaps you remember him as being the tallest President at 6'4", which was 2" taller than our first President George Washington. He wore a full beard and wore a stovepipe hat which easily identified him. But his accomplishments are what kept the United States intact. You see, the Southern states seceded from the Union to form their own country, the Confederate States of America. More than anything he wanted to preserve the Union. He led our country during the Civil War, and did reunite the Union and the Confederacy back into the United States. Slavery was another issue of the times, but was not the cause of the Civil War. Though as a result of the Civil War and the Emancipation Proclamation, the slaves were freed. My husband's death was as well-

known as his life. He was the first President to be assassinated.

A. *Thomas Jefferson*

C. *Barack Obama*

B. *Abraham Lincoln*

D. *Ulysses S. Grant*

11. **1797 – 1801**   My husband was the first Vice President and the 2nd President. He is only one of two Presidents in our history who had a son who also became President. Even before becoming President he was a patriot who fought for our nation's independence and one of our nation's Founding Fathers.

A. *John Adams*

C. *Thomas Jefferson*

B. *George H.W. Bush*

D. *James Madison*

12. **1897 – 1901**   My husband was the 25th President. My husband was President during the Spanish-American War which gained the U.S. quite a bit of territory. This additional territory made the U.S. a world power. Before he was assassinated, the U.S. annexed the Hawaiian islands and began the work towards building the Panama Canal.

A. *William McKinley*

C. *Theodore Roosevelt*

B. *James Garfield*

D. *John F. Kennedy*

13. **2001 – 2009**   My husband was the 43rd President and his father was the 41st President. My husband was President during the terrorist attacks of 9/11. He ordered the invasion of Afghanistan as retaliation. The U.S. invaded Iraq and overthrew the dictator Saddam Hussein in the Second Gulf War. His father was President and he is only the second son in American history to also become President after his father. He had an attempted assassination attempt on his life when a man threw a grenade at him. It didn't explode, which I am very grateful for.

A. Bill Clinton

B. Lyndon B. Johnson

C. George W. Bush

D. Benjamin Harrison

14. **1801 – 1809** My husband was the 3rd President, though I did not live to see him become President. He is most well-known for writing the Declaration of Independence. During the years of his presidency, he purchased the land that became known as the Louisiana Purchase and sent Lewis and Clark out to explore and map the areas acquired.

A. James Madison

B. Thomas Jefferson

C. John Quincy Adams

D. John Adams

15. **1881 – 1881** My husband was the 20th President until he was assassinated. He was assassinated after only two hundred days in office. He was determined to put an end to political corruption. He was the last President to be born in a log cabin. He knew Latin and Greek and could write with both hands simultaneously and in different languages. After being shot by his assassin, Alexander Graham Bell tried to locate the bullet with a type of metal detector, but was unsuccessful. My husband died a few days later.

A. Abraham Lincoln

B. William McKinley

C. James Garfield

D. John F. Kennedy

16. **1969 – 1974** My husband was the 37th President, and the only President to resign. He will always be most remembered for being the first President to resign due to the Watergate scandal. Most people remember the scandal and forget that he ended the Vietnam War. He also improved relations between the U.S. and the Soviet Union and China.

A. Donald Trump

C. John F. Kennedy

B. Andrew Johnson

D. Richard Nixon

17. **1817 – 1825**   My husband was the 5ᵗʰ President. He was the only person in history to have held two cabinet positions at once – Secretary of State and Secretary of War. His first presidential term was called, 'The Era of Good Feelings'. When he ran for a second term he had no opposing candidates, the only President besides George Washington to be able to make that claim. My husband was the last of the Founding Fathers.

A. James Monroe

C. John Quincy Adams

B. James Madison

D. Andrew Jackson

18. **1933 – 1945**   My husband was the 32ⁿᵈ President, the only President elected to a third term. He became President during the Great Depression. He instituted the New Deal which introduced the program Social Security. He led the U.S. and the Allied Powers against the Axis Powers of Germany and Japan during WWII. He spoke to the American people over the radio in talks called "fireside chats."

A. Harry Truman

C. Herbert Hoover

B. Dwight D. Eisenhower

D. Franklin D. Roosevelt

19. **1963 – 1969**   My husband was the 36ᵗʰ President, the only President who was sworn into office aboard Air Force One. He will always be most remembered for his role in the Vietnam War. He worked towards civil rights so everyone would have equal opportunities. He appointed the first African-American to the Supreme Court and the first African-American cabinet member.

A. *John F. Kennedy*   C. *Harry Truman*

B. *Lyndon B. Johnson*   D. *Gerald Ford*

20. **1837 – 1841** My husband was the 8ᵗʰ President, though I did not live to see him become President. My husband continued with President Jackson's policy of forcing American Indians to move to new lands out west. The Trail of Tears in which many thousands of Indians died along the way happened during his administration. He was actually the first President to be born a citizen of the United States. A short time after he became President, the nation was in a financial depression due partially to the transfer of federal funds to state banks.

A. *Andrew Jackson*   C. *Martin Van Buren*

B. *William H. Harrison*   D. *John Tyler*

21. **1977 – 1981**   My husband was the 39ᵗʰ President and a peanut farmer. He was the first President from the deep South in over one hundred years. When he was President economic problems were escalating. The price of gas was high with long lines at the gas pumps. Unemployment was also an issue. Did you know he was the first President born in a hospital?

A. *Andrew Jackson*   C. *John Tyler*

B. *Grover Cleveland*   D. *Jimmy Carter*

22. **1909 – 1913** My husband was the 27ᵗʰ President. He is the only President who went on to serve on the Supreme Court after his term as President was over. He was the first President to serve over forty-eight states once New Mexico and Arizona were added to the United States.

A. *Woodrow Wilson*   C. *William McKinley*

B. *Willaim H. Taft*   D. *Benjamin Harrison*

23. **1850 – 1853**   My husband was the 13th President. My husband was an "accidental" President. The previous President dead after eating contaminated cherries, my husband found himself to be President. He opposed slavery, but refused to touch it in states where it already existed. He thought this would preserve the Union. He went down in history as an ineffective President.

A. *Millard Fillmore*   C. *John Tyler*

B. *Franklin Pierce*   D. *Martin Van Buren*

24. **1829 – 1837**   My husband was the 7th President. I am proud to say my husband was considered to be the most "common man" to become President. Unfortunately, I didn't live to see him become President. I passed away just weeks before his inauguration. He was a war hero in the War of 1812. He was given the nickname 'Old Hickory' for being so tough. He is the only President who had been a prisoner of war. An assassin tried to shoot him with two different pistols in his presidential days. Luckily for him, both pistols misfired.

A. *John Quincy Adams*   C. *Andrew Jackson*

B. *Millard Fillmore*   D. *Zachary Taylor*

25. **1841 – 1845**   My husband was the 10th President. He had two First Ladies. My husband was the first President to serve without being elected. When President Harrison died just days into his presidency my husband had to pick up the reins and take over the office of the President. While he was President, he signed a bill which enabled settlers the right to claim land which helped settle the west. He also worked for the annexation of Texas to make it a part of the United States.

A. James Polk   C. Andrew Jackson

B. Franklin Pierce   D. John Tyler

26. **1989 – 1993**   My husband was the 41st President and my son would become the 43rd President. My husband was President during the Persian Gulf War. The Soviet Union and communism were collapsing while new nations were forming. The U.S. began building relationships with them. My husband and I have been married for over seventy years, the longest of any President and First Lady. Now that's something to be proud of.

A. George W. Bush   C. Benjamin Harrison

B. George H.W. Bush   D. Franklin D. Roosevelt

27. **1841 – 1841**   My husband was the 9th President, and my grandson would become the 23rd President. My husband, some called him 'Old Tippecanoe', was the first President to die in office. He spoke for over an hour at his inauguration with no coat or hat and caught a cold which turned into pneumonia. He died just thirty-two days after becoming President, the shortest presidency in American history.

A. William H. Harrison   C. Benjamin Harrison

B. John Quincy Adams   D. John Adams

28. **1929 - 1933**   My husband was the 31st President. He was President during the Stock Market Crash of 1929 which was the start of the Great Depression. This was the country's worst economic crisis in history. He donated his salary to charity. The Star Spangled Banner became the national anthem. Many of you may not know this, but Charles Curtis, his Vice President, his ancestry was largely from Native American blood from the Kaw tribe.

A. Theodore Roosevelt

C. Andrew Jackson

B. Warren Harding

D. Herbert Hoover

29. **1849 – 1850** My husband was the 12th President. 'Old Rough & Ready,' that's what they called him. He fought in the War of 1812, the Black Hawk War, the Second Seminole War in Florida and commanded several battles in the Mexican-American War. You would think the old guy would be ready to retire and enjoy the rest of his life after that. I actually prayed for his defeat, but he went on to become President. While President, he tried to resolve the slavery issue. After only sixteen months in office he died from cholera after eating contaminated cherries and drinking buttermilk. Some suspected he had been poisoned.

A. Andrew Jackson

C. Zachary Taylor

B. Andrew Johnson

D. Ulysses S. Grant

30. **1961 – 1963** My husband was the 35th President until he was assassinated. When my husband was President the Cold War was a major concern to Americans. It was uneasy times during these days. Some of the events that occurred during his presidency were: the Berlin Wall went up in Germany, the Bay of Pigs, and the Cuban Missile Crisis. These are events that people who lived during these times won't soon forget, but I think what they will remember most was where they were when they heard of the news of his assassination.

A. William McKinley

C. James Garfield

B. John F. Kennedy

D. Dwight D. Eisenhower

31. **1857 – 1861** My uncle was the 15th President, the only President who never married. He was the last President before the start of the Civil War. While he was President, the Supreme Court issued the Dred Scott ruling. This ruling stated African-Americans could not be American

citizens, and the federal government had no power to regulate slavery in the federal territories acquired after the creation of the United States. My uncle thought this would solve the problem, but it did not.

A. *James Buchanan*   C. *John Quincy Adams*

B. *James Polk*   D. *Martin Van Buren*

32. **1921 – 1923** My husband was the 29th President. Some people seem to think I poisoned him. I'm sorry to say my husband has the reputation of being one of the worst Presidents in history. Some go as far as to say I murdered him just as the scandals of the presidency were being discovered, or maybe because of his many mistresses. They say I tried to cover up how he died by not allowing the doctors to perform an autopsy and insisting that he be embalmed and buried immediately. I have nothing to say on the matter.

A. *Franklin D. Roosevelt*   C. *Zachary Taylor*

B. *Woodrow Wilson*   D. *Warren Harding*

33. **1953 – 1961** My husband was the 34th President. He is best known for being the Supreme Commander of the Allied forces during WWII. During his presidency, he helped negotiate an end to the Korean War. During his presidency times were peaceful and it was a time of economic prosperity.

A. *Ulysses S. Grant*   C. *Zachary Taylor*

B. *Dwight D. Eisenhower*   D. *Andrew Jackson*

34. **1809 – 1817** My husband was our nation's 4th President. He is well-known for his work on the Constitution and the Bill of Rights and became known as 'Father of the Constitution.' During his presidency was the War of 1812. He didn't want to go to war, but Britain was seizing

U.S. ships and he felt he had no alternative. During the war the British marched into Washington, D.C. and burned the White House. Thankfully, before they did so I was able to get some important treasures out and save them.

A. *John Adams*   C. *James Madison*

B. *James Monroe*   D. *Abraham Lincoln*

35. **1869 – 1877**   My husband was the 18th President. My husband was U.S. General and Commander of the Union armies during the Civil War and as a war hero would go on to become President. He helped establish national parks, such as Yellowstone. He fought for civil rights for African-Americans and Native Americans.

A. *Ulysses S. Grant*   C. *Zachary Taylor*

B. *Andrew Jackson*   D. *Theodore Roosevelt*

36. **1885 – 1889**   My husband was the 22nd President. He was the second President to earn the nickname 'The Veto President.' He vetoed more than twice as many laws as all the previous Presidents. He must have done all right though, as he was the only President to serve non-consecutive terms. He was also the only President to marry in the White House when he married me when I was just 21 years of age making me the youngest First Lady in history. When we left the White House after his first term I told the White House staff to leave everything just as it was because we would be back, and sure enough my husband was voted in again as President four years later.

A. *John Tyler*   C. *Martin Van Buren*

B. *Franklin Pierce*   D. *Grover Cleveland*

37. **1881 – 1885**   My husband was the 21st President. He was a bit of a

dandy and changed clothes several times throughout the day. He had as many as eighty pairs of pants hanging in his closet. Unfortunately, I didn't live to see him become President or I would most assuredly have put a stop to him auctioning off many priceless items of past Presidents from the White House when he decided to redecorate. Why, some of those items dated back as far as our second president when John Adams was President.

A. Donald Trump

C. William H. Taft

B. Chester Arthur

D. Martin Van Buren

38. **1865 – 1869**   My husband was the 17th President. It was a hard act to follow to try to take over after the President was assassinated. The Civil War was over, but now the nation needed to heal. The country was going through many changes, still a lot of bitterness over the Civil War, preserving the Union, the slaves way of life had completely changed and they would need help in finding their way. In his time as President, my husband vetoed so many bills passed by Congress he began to be known as 'The Veto President.' Congress impeached him; however the Senate voted to keep him on as President.

A. Andrew Johnson

C. Chester Arthur

B. James Garfield

D. Theodore Roosevelt

39. **1877 – 1881**   My husband was the 19th President. The election was one of the closest in history. Congress ended up having to make the final decision on who would become the next President. This made some people none too happy with the decision. Some people would go so far as to say my husband was a 'fraudulent President.' No alcohol was served in the White House. People seemed to love labeling others with nicknames, such as 'His Fraudulency' for my husband and 'Lemonade Lucy' for me.

A. George W. Bush   C. Rutherford B. Hayes

B. John Tyler   D. Donald Trump

40. **1923 – 1929**   My husband was the 30th President. He was a man of few words. He had his hands full cleaning up after the previous President's mess he left behind. My husband was an honest man. He signed the Indian Citizenship Act, which gave citizens rights to all Native Americans. The time he was President was the era known as 'The Roaring Twenties.' A funny thing, my husband such a silent man, was the first President to be in a movie with sound.

A. Calvin Coolidge   C. Woodrow Wilson

B. Franklin D. Roosevelt   D. William McKinley

41. **1889 – 1893**   My husband was the 23rd President. My husband was the grandson of the 9th President. Six states from out west were added to the country while he was President. He signed the Sherman Antitrust Act which was to prevent large monopolies where big companies come in and bought up their competition and then raised prices.

A. William H. Harrison   C. Andrew Johnson

B. Lyndon B. Johnson   D. Benjamin Harrison

42. **1913 – 1921**   My husband was the 28th President. My husband was President during WWI. He helped form the League of Nations. Some say that I ran the executive branch of our government after my husband suffered a stroke.

A. Harry Truman   C. Woodrow Wilson

B. Franklin D. Roosevelt   D. Theodore Roosevelt

43. **1853 – 1857**   My husband was the 14ᵗʰ President. During his presidency, Commander Perry led the negotiation of a treaty that opened trade with Japan. The greatest tensions, and ultimately his downfall, can be attributed to the Kansas-Nebraska Act.

A. *Franklin Pierce*   C. *Millard Fillmore*

B. *James Polk*   D. *William H. Harrison*

44.   **1945 – 1953**   My husband was the 33ʳᵈ President. He became President when the previous President died. He is most known for putting an end to WWII in the Pacific by dropping the atomic bomb on Japan. He was the only President in the 1900's who never went to college.

A. *Lyndon B. Johnson*   C. *Dwight D. Eisenhower*

B. *Harry Truman*   D. *Warren Harding*

45. **1845 – 1849**   My husband was the 11ᵗʰ President. I'm proud to say my husband added over a million square miles to the United States. His goal had been to expand the borders of the United States all the way to the Pacific Ocean. He granted Texas it's statehood which made the Mexicans angry, so it wasn't long before the Mexican-American War broke out. Although many people don't know a lot about him, he's considered by many historians to be one of the most important Presidents.

A. *James Polk*   C. *John Tyler*

B. *Millard Fillmore*   D. *Franklin Pierce*

Answers

Chapter 28 — Let Me Introduce You To The President

These questions are given as descriptions the First Ladies may have used in describing their husbands during their time as the president. Clues are given in each description.

1. C - John Quincy Adams

2. B - Ronald Reagan

3. D - Barack Obama

4. A - George Washington

5. B - Gerald Ford

6. C - Theodore Roosevelt

7. B - Bill Clinton

8. A - Grover Cleveland

9. D - Donald Trump

10. B - Abraham Lincoln

11. A - John Adams

12. A - William McKinley

13. C - George W. Bush

14. B - Thomas Jefferson

15. C - James Garfield

16. D - Richard Nixon

17. A - James Monroe

18. D - Franklin D. Roosevelt

19. B - Lyndon B. Johnson

20. C - Martin Van Buren

21. D - Jimmy Carter

22. B - William H. Taft

23. A - Millard Fillmore

24. C - Andrew Jackson

25. D - John Tyler

26. B - George H.W. Bush

27. A - William H. Harrison

28. D - Herbert Hoover

29. C - Zachary Taylor

30. B - John F. Kennedy

31. A - James Buchanan

32. D - Warren Harding

33. B - Dwight D. Eisenhower

34. C - James Madison

35. A - Ulysses S. Grant

36. D - Grover Cleveland

37. B - Arthur Chester

38. A - Andrew Johnson

39. C - Rutherford B. Hayes

40. A - Calvin Coolidge

41. D - Benjamin Harrison

42. C - Woodrow Wilson

43. A - Franklin Pierce

44. B - Harry Truman

45. A - James Polk

29

Illness, Accidents, & Death

Some of these events happened while they were living in the White House; while other events may have been before or after their days in the White House.

Answers are given on pages 317 - 319.

1. At the funeral of her husband, which First Lady walked behind the horse-drawn caisson down Constitution Avenue?

    A. Mary Todd Lincoln   *C. Jackie Kennedy*

    B. Mamie Eisenhower   *D. Edith Wilson*

2. After her death, the President was astonished to find hundreds of checks from people she had helped over the years wanting to repay her. She never cashed any of the checks, and even her family had not been aware of all the people she had helped over the years.

    A. Lou Hoover   *C. Bess Truman*

    B. Betty Ford   *D. Martha Washington*

3. As the First Lady read a newspaper article about him to the President, he suddenly dropped dead.

A. Eleanor Roosevelt

B. Mamie Eisenhower

C. Lady Bird Johnson

D. Florence Harding

4. After the First Lady's death, the President presented a stained glass window to St. John's Church where she had sung in their choir. As a special request, he asked that the window be hung in the south transept so he could see it at night. He never remarried.

A. Ellen Arthur

B. Grace Coolidge

C. Sarah Polk

D. Ellen Wilson

5. Which First Lady had an inner-ear disease that affected her balance? Critics noticed her balance problem and spread rumors that she had a drinking problem.

A. Bess Truman

B. Mamie Eisenhower

C. Barbara Bush

D. Pat Nixon

6. She was First Lady for only nine months. During that time, she was ill with malaria and spent the last weeks of her husband's life by his side nursing him.

A. Anna Harrison

B. Ida McKinley

C. Lucretia Garfield

D. Eliza Johnson

7. Twenty-six days after leaving the White House, which First Lady died after attending the ceremonies of the incoming President's inauguration

where there had been a strong wind and snow? She caught a chill which turned into pneumonia.

A. Abigail Fillmore   C. Jane Pierce

B. Pat Nixon   D. Ellen Wilson

8. Her first husband and son died of yellow fever on the same day. She was a widow with a young son when she married her second husband, the future President.

A. Martha Washington   C. Jane Pierce

B. Martha Jefferson   D. Dolley Madison

9. Ninety-nine minutes after her husband had been assassinated, she stood by the side of the Vice President as he took the oath of office. Who was the widowed First Lady?

A. Lucretia Garfield   C. Mary Todd Lincoln

B. Jackie Kennedy   D. Ida McKinley

10. When the First Lady was a teenager, her father was asphyxiated by carbon monoxide while working on a car in a closed garage. It was never determined whether it was accidental or a suicide. Who was this First Lady?

A. Bess Truman   C. Jackie Kennedy

B. Eleanor Roosevelt   D. Betty Ford

11. Which First Lady was buried in the dress she had bought to wear to her husband's inaugural ceremony, but wouldn't live to see him become

President?

A. Rachel Jackson   *C. Hannah Van Buren*

B. Martha Jefferson   *D. Ellen Arthur*

12. With the First Lady's deteriorating health a doctor moved into the White House. The President wasn't notified of the truth of how serious her condition was until days before her death. She was the third First Lady to die while a resident in the White House.

A. Letitia Tyler   *C. Ellen Wilson*

B. Eliza Johnson   *D. Ellen Arthur*

13. Which First Lady hid the fact that she was a smoker and eventually died of lung cancer?

A. Jackie Kennedy   *C. Betty Ford*

B. Pat Nixon   *D. Lady Bird Johnson*

14. Which three First Ladies passed away while their husbands were in office?

A. Letitia Tyler, Caroline Harrison, & Ellen Wilson

B. Rachel Jackson, Anna Harrison, & Ida McKinley

C. Ellen Wilson, Ida McKinley, Ellen Arthur

D. Letitia Tyler, Ellen Wilson, & Ellen Arthur

15. Which First Lady came down with a cold which turned into pneumonia after waiting outside in the cold for a carriage one evening?

She died at the age of forty-two. Her husband, devastated by her death, hung a portrait of her in the White House and left flowers by the painting in honor of her.

A. Eliza Johnson

C. Ellen Wilson

B. Ellen Arthur

D. Lucretia Garfield

16. Which First Lady's parents were killed in a car accident? She was seven months pregnant and advised not to travel so was unable to attend her parents' funeral.

A. Rosalynn Carter

C. Barbara Bush

B. Jackie Kennedy

D. Grace Coolidge

17. Which First Lady was addicted to alcohol and pain killers? After battling her dependency of drugs and alcohol, she then established a center for people suffering from the same problem?

A. Pat Nixon

C. Mary Todd Lincoln

B. Jane Pierce

D. Betty Ford

18. Which First Lady died at the age of thirty-five from tuberculosis and didn't live to see her husband become President?

A. Martha Jefferson

C. Ellen Arthur

B. Hannah Van Buren

D. Rachel Jackson

19. Which First Lady was pregnant fourteen times; with nine miscarriages, one stillborn, and another child that died around one year of age?

A. Martha Washington   C. Louisa Adams

B. Jackie Kennedy   D. Eleanor Roosevelt

20. Which First Lady's epitaph read: *'A being so gentle and so virtuous slander might wound but could not dishonor,'* showing the bitterness the President felt at the slander she had endured during his campaign?

A. Ellen Arthur   C. Pat Nixon

B. Rachel Jackson   D. Martha Jefferson

21. Which First Lady greeted guests at the White House while seated in a blue velvet chair holding a bouquet of flowers, so she wouldn't have to shake hands? She sat beside the President where he kept a watchful eye out for signs of a seizure and covered her face with a handkerchief at those times.

A. Mary Todd Lincoln   C. Elizabeth Monroe

B. Harriet Lane   D. Ida McKinley

22. Which First Lady was diagnosed with breast cancer and was very open with the public about her mastectomy and treatment bringing insight and visibility to a disease that people had been previously reluctant to talk about?

A. Betty Ford   C. Nancy Reagan

B. Laura Bush   D. Eleanor Roosevelt

23. Anyone who was alive in 1961 remembers well the scene of the First Lady veiled in black holding the hands of her two young children as her husband's coffin was paraded past; her toddler son saluting his dad's

coffin.

A. Lucretia Garfield   C. Jackie Kennedy

B. Mary Todd Lincoln   D. Ida McKinley

24. Which First Lady suffered a seizure and fell near an open fireplace leading to severe burns?

A. Ida McKinley   C. Hillary Clinton

B. Elizabeth Monroe   D. Nellie Taft

25. She was sick when her husband left on his journey to his inauguration. She never made the journey to join him, as one month after his inauguration he was dead.

A. Anna Harrison   C. Jane Pierce

B. Hannah Van Buren   D. Lucy Hayes

26. She died less than three months before her husband's inauguration.

A. Rachel Jackson   C. Caroline Harrison

B. Ellen Arthur   D. Abigail Fillmore

27. As the First Lady sat in the theater holding the hand of the President, he was shot by an assassin.

A. Jackie Kennedy   C. Mary Todd Lincoln

B. Ida McKinley   D. Lucretia Garfield

28. When this President was shot by an assassin, his last words and thoughts were spoken of taking care how his wife would be informed. Who was his wife?

    A. Lucretia Garfield   *C. Edith Roosevelt*

    B. Caroline. Harrison   *D. Ida McKinley*

29. She was the 1st First Lady to die in the White House.

    A. Martha Jefferson   *C. Abigail Fillmore*

    B. Letitia Tyler   *D. Ellen Wilson*

30. When she was only eighteen years old, her father shot himself in the family bathtub. She never spoke of it, even to her family.

    A. Eleanor Roosevelt   *C. Hillary Clinton*

    B. Betty Ford   *D. Bess Truman*

31. Unsure of the true cause of death of the President, she made the unusual decision to not have an autopsy. Some secretly, and some not so secretly, accused the First Lady of poisoning the President after learning of his numerous affairs. So; food poisoning, heart attack, or murder – the true cause of the President's death will remain a mystery.

    A. Peggy Taylor   *C. Eleanor Roosevelt*

    B. Florence Harding   *D. Anna Harrison*

32. Name the only two First Ladies to be buried by their husbands at Arlington Cemetery.

A. N. Taft & J. Kennedy	*C. E. Wilson & J. Kennedy*
B. M. Washington & J. Kennedy	*D. D. Madison & M. Jefferson*

33. It is believed that two First Ladies suffered from epilepsy. Can you name them?

A. I. McKinley & J. Pierce	*C. J. Grant & I. McKinley*
B. E. Monroe & I. McKinley	*D. M. Washington & N. Taft*

34. Which First Lady held the hand of the President after he had been shot until he passed away? After his death, she went into seclusion until her own death.

A. Mary Todd Lincoln	*C. Ida McKinley*
B. Lucretia Garfield	*D. Jackie Kennedy*

35. Which First Lady, after being declared insane, tried to commit suicide by overdose?

A. Anna Harrison	*C. Jane Pierce*
B. Hillary Clinton	*D. Mary Todd Lincoln*

36. After the death of her husband she became an advocate of stem cell research due to the scientific promise of treatment of Alzheimer patients.

A. Lady Bird Johnson	*C. Barbara Bush*
B. Nancy Reagan	*D. Mamie Eisenhower*

37. Which First Lady lost a newborn son just three months before her husband was assassinated?

 A. Lucretia Garfield   C. Jackie Kennedy

 B. Mary Todd Lincoln   D. Edith Roosevelt

38. Weeks before her husband's inauguration the family was involved in a train accident in which their eleven year old son was killed right in front of them. She went into a deep depression and did not attend her son's funeral or her husband's inauguration.

 A. Jane Pierce   C. Julia Grant

 B. Peggy Taylor   D. Anna Harrison

39. Holding the title of being the oldest former First Lady living to the ripe old age of ninety-seven, respects were paid at her funeral by her successors Betty Ford, Rosalynn Carter, and Nancy Reagan.

 A. Barbara Bush   C. Bess Truman

 B. Lady Bird Johnson   D. Mamie Eisenhower

40. When her young daughter died of leukemia, her hair started turning white at the age of twenty-eight. Who is she?

 A. Abigail Adams   C. Frances Cleveland

 B. Ida McKinley   D. Barbara Bush

Answers

Chapter 29 – Illness, Accidents, & Death

1. C - Jackie Kennedy, wife of John F. Kennedy

2. A - Lou Hoover, wife of Herbert Hoover

3. D - Florence Harding, wife of Warren Harding

4. A - Ellen Arthur, wife of Chester Arthur

5. B - Mamie Eisenhower, wife of Dwight D. Eisenhower

6. C - Lucretia Garfield, wife of James Garfield

7. A - Abigail Fillmore, wife of Millard Fillmore

8. D - Dolley Madison, wife of James Madison

9. B - Jackie Kennedy, wife of John F. Kennedy

10. D - Betty Ford, wife of Gerald Ford

11. A - Rachel Jackson, wife of Andrew Jackson

12. C - Ellen Wilson, first wife of Woodrow Wilson

13. B - Pat Nixon, wife of Richard Nixon

14. A - Letitia Tyler first wife of John Tyler, Caroline Harrison wife of Benjamin Harrison, & Ellen Wilson first wife of Woodrow Wilson

15. B - Ellen Arthur, wife of Chester Arthur

16. C - Barbara Bush, wife of Geore H.W. Bush

17. D - Betty Ford, wife of Gerald Ford

18. B - Hannah Van Buren, wife of Martin Van Buren

19. C - Louisa Adams, wife of John Quincy Adams

Two of her sons were raised by John and Abigail Adams, her in-laws, while John Quincy Adams and Louisa were in foreign countries. Louisa blamed her long absence for the early death of the two oldest sons.

20. B - Rachel Jackson, wife of Andrew Jackson

21. D - Ida McKinley, wife of William McKinley

22. A - Betty Ford, wife of Gerald Ford

23. C - Jackie Kennedy, wife of John F. Kennedy

24. B - Elizabeth Monroe, wife of James Monroe

25. A - Anna Harrison, wife of William H. Harrison

26. A - Rachel Jackson, wife of Andrew Jackson

27. C - Mary Todd Lincoln, wife of Abraham Lincoln

28. D - Ida McKinley, wife of William McKinley

29. B - Letitia Tyler, first wife of John Tyler

30. D - Bess Truman, wife of Harry Truman

31. B - Florence Harding, wife of Warren Harding

32. A - Nellie Taft wife of William H. Taft & Jackie Kennedy wife of John F. Kennedy

33. B - Elizabeth Monroe wife of James Monroe & Ida McKinley wife of William McKinley

34. C - Ida McKinley, wife of William McKinley

35. D - Mary Todd Lincoln, wife of Abraham Lincoln

36. B - Nancy Reagan, wife of Ronald Reagan

37. C - Jackie Kennedy, wife of John F. Kennedy

38. A - Jane Pierce, wife of Franklin Pierce

39. C - Bess Truman, wife of Harry Truman

40. D - Barbara Bush, wife of George H.W. Bush

Children of the Presidents &
First Ladies

30

Before The Days In The White House

Answers are given on pages 327 - 328.

1. Which president's daughter was baptized in China?

A. Dora Bush

C. Sasha Obama

B. Chelsea Clinton

D. Amy Carter

2. Which presidential daughter was in a ballet recital where Michael Jackson came to see her perform?

A. Caroline Kennedy

C. Chelsea Clinton

B. Jenna Bush

D. Ivanka Trump

3. When his father was in Congress, this future presidential son remembered his father taking him to visit the U.S. Patent Office where they would spend hours in the Model Room looking at models of American inventions. His father would one day have a patented invention of his own. Who was the son of the only president to have a patent registered in his name?

A. Peter Jefferson

C. Jeb Bush

B. Andrew Jackson Jr

D. Robert Lincoln

4. Which president's young daughter was cared for by a prisoner working on a trustee program who had received a life sentence for killing a man?

A. Chelsea Clinton

C. Amy Carter

B. Patti Davis Reagan

D. Dora Bush

5. Which president's daughter, in the days before his presidency, was good friends with the stepdaughter of the Emperor Napoleon Bonaparte?

A. Lynda Johnson

C. Nellie Grant

B. Eliza Monroe

D. Ivanka Trump

6. Which president's son lost his father's inaugural address speech notes on their trip to Washington for the inauguration?

A. George W Bush

C. Robert Lincoln

B. Calvin Coolidge Jr

D. Jacky Washington

7. Which presidential daughters stuffed paper down the toilets of the vice president's plane, Air Force Two, clogging them?

A. Barbara & Jenna Bush

C. Ivanka & Tiffany Trump

B. Lynda & Luci Johnson

D. Julie & Tricia Nixon

8. By the age of two, which president's son had already traveled around the world twice?

A. George W Bush

C. Herbert Hoover Jr

B. John F Kennedy Jr

D. John Eisenhower

9. Which presidential sons had their mouths washed out with soap by their mother when using foul language as young boys?

A. Sons of Donald Trump

C. Sons of Jimmy Carter

B. Sons of George H W Bush

D. Sons of F. D. Roosevelt

10. Which president's child was almost expelled from school for poor grades, using marijuana, and hashish?

A. Jeb Bush

C. Ron Reagan

B. Malia Obama

D. Amy Carter

11. Which presidential son was water boy for Stanford University's football team?

A. George W Bush

C. Herbert Hoover Jr

B. Michael Reagan

D. Steve Ford

12. While her father was vice president, which future president's daughter was threatened to be kidnapped by the SLA, Symbionese Liberation Army, the same group that kidnapped Patty Hearst the granddaughter of William Randolph Hearst?

A. Chelsea Clinton

C. Patsy Washington

B. Susan Ford

D. Maureen Reagan

13. Which president's sons were taught sign language by their mother?

A. John & Cal Coolidge Jr

C. Herbert Jr & Allan Hoover

B. Willie & Tad Lincoln

D. Jack & Chip Carter

14. Which presidential child was head cheerleader while a senior in high school?

A. Jenna Bush   *C. Barbara Bush*

B. Steve Ford   *D. George W Bush*

15. Two of which president's sons sailed with their father to Europe so he could help negotiate an end to the Revolutionary War?

A. Sons of Thomas Jefferson   *C. Sons of James Monroe*

B. Sons of John Adams   *D. Sons of Franklin Pierce*

Answers

Chapter 30 – Before The Days In The White House

1. A - Doro Bush

While China banned freedom of worship to their own countrymen at this time (1975), Doro became the first person to ever be publicly baptized in the People's Republic of China since the days the Communist party took over the country in 1949.

2. D - Ivanka Trump

Michael Jackson was a neighbor living in Trump Towers at the time.

3. D – Robert Lincoln

4. C - Amy Carter

5. B - Eliza Monroe

6. C - Robert Lincoln

* *The notes were later found before the inauguration.*

7. A - Barbara & Jenna Bush

8. C - Herbert Hoover Jr.

9. B – Sons of George H W Bush

10. A - Jeb Bush

11. C - Herbert Hoover Jr.

12. B - Susan Ford

13. A - John & Cal Jr Coolidge

14. D - George W Bush

15. B – Sons of John Adams

31

Inauguration & Inaugural Events

Answers are given on page 332.

1. Which president's sons had to work the day their father was sworn into office for his first administration, and didn't hear the news their father was about to become the president until after he had been sworn in?

A. Lincoln's sons

B. Coolidge's sons

C. Hoover's sons

D. None of the above

2. Which president's daughters were surprised to find the Jonas Brothers, a singing group, at the end of the scavenger hunt set up for them at the White House while their parents attended inaugural balls?

A. L. B. Johnson's daughters

B. R. Nixon's daughters

C. G. W. Bush's daughters

D. B. Obama's daughters

3. Which president was the first to have his children attend his inauguration?

A. Martin Van Buren

B. John Tyler

C. John F. Kennedy

D. Lyndon B. Johnson

4. This president's son wasn't invited to his father's inauguration and in turn the son didn't attend his father's funeral?

A. Ron Reagan

C. Dick Taylor

B. John Kennedy Jr

D. John Eisenhower

5. Which president along with his family was the first to get out of the presidential limo and walk to the White House during the inaugural parade?

A. Jimmy Carter

C. John F Kennedy

B. James Monroe

D. Warren Harding

6. Which First Daughter gave her father a thumbs-up sign after he took the oath of office?

A. Ivanka Trump

C. Chelsea Clinton

B. Sasha Obama

D. Susan Ford

7. Which president's son while working at Yellowstone as a park ranger was riding horseback patrol and oblivious to what was going on in the outside world was 'confiscated' by Secret Service agents, whisked aboard a helicopter, and rushed to the White House to attend his father's inauguration?

A. Michael Reagan

C. Alan Arthur

B. Archie Roosevelt

D. Jack Ford

8. Which First Son had to hold up his father and help him to the rostrum to be sworn into office due to the fact that his father was handicapped?

A. *Jeff Carter*   C. *Jimmy Roosevelt*

B. *Russell Harrison*   D. *Fred Grant*

9. Which president's daughter was preparing for a date when her father telephoned changing her plans, where instead of going on a date she went to the Cabinet Room of the White House to witness her father sworn into office due to the death of the previous president?

A. *Lynda Johnson*   C. *Nell Arthur*

B. *Martha Johnson*   D. *Margaret Truman*

10. Name one of the president's sons (there were two) who was a college student at the time of his father's inauguration who had to turn around and return to college the morning after his father's inauguration, as his father didn't want him to miss school.

A. *Allan Hoover*   C. *John Coolidge*

B. *Jeb Bush*   D. *John Eisenhower*

Answers

Chapter 31 – Inauguration & Inaugural Events

1. B - Calvin Coolidge's sons

Vice President Calvin Coolidge was visiting at the home of his father when he was woken in the middle of the night to be informed the president was dead. Coolidge was sworn in immediately by his own father who was a notary public.

2. D – Barack Obama's daughters

3. A - Martin Van Buren

4. C - Dick Taylor

5. A - Jimmy Carter

6. B – Sasha Obama

7. D – Jack Ford

8. C – Jimmy Roosevelt

9. D – Margaret Truman

10. Either A - Allan Hoover *or* C – John Coolidge would be correct

32

College Days

Answers are given on page 336.

1. Which First Daughter has the highest educational credentials to date?

   A. Caroline Kennedy

   C. Ivanka Trump

   B. Chelsea Clinton

   D. Lynda Johnson

2. Which First Daughter attended Yale becoming the 4th generation of her family and the first female from her family to attend the Ivy League University?

   A. Tiffany Trump

   C. Barbara Bush

   B. Chelsea Clinton

   D. Malia Obama

3. Which president's son was a member of the Skull and Bones secret club at Yale?

   A. Dick Taylor

   C. George W Bush

   B. Robert Taft

   D. All of the above

4. As this presidential son was receiving his diploma from West Point, his father the Supreme Allied Commander of WWII was overseeing the invasion of the beaches of Normandy known as D-Day. Who was he?

A. *John Eisenhower*   C. *Robert Lincoln*

B. *Jeb Bush*   D. *Fred Grant*

5. Which president's son attended West Point military school?

A. *Martin Van Buren*   C. *John Eisenhower*

B. *Fred Grant*   D. *All of the above*

6. Which First Son having just moved into the White House changed his original plans to study oceanography at Duke University and instead moved out west to become a cowboy?

A. *Steve Ford*   C. *Fred Grant*

B. *Ron Reagan*   D. *John Kennedy, Jr*

7. A student at Yale, which First Son while attending the Yale/Princeton game was one of the spectators after the game who attempted to destroy the vintage wooden goalposts and was caught in the act by the police?

A. *Robert Lincoln*   C. *Franklin Roosevelt, Jr*

B. *George W Bush*   D. *Cal Coolidge, Jr*

8. Which First Son went to seminary school and became an ordained minister?

A. *Ron Reagan*   C. *Michael Ford*

B. *Neil Bush*   D. *John Eisenhower*

9. Which First Daughter arrived at Stanford University as a new college

student with an entourage including the President, First Lady, dozens of Secret Service agents, and over 200 reporters?

A. Chelsea Clinton   *C. Julie Nixon*

B. Amy Carter   *D. Caroline Kennedy*

10. Which First Son dropped out of Yale his first semester to become a ballet dancer?

A. Eric Trump   *C. Ron Reagan*

B. George W Bush   *D. Jack Ford*

Answers

Chapter 32 – College Days

1. B – Chelsea Clinton

2. C – Barbara Bush

3. D – All of the above

4. A – John Eisenhower

5. D – All of the above

6. A – Steve Ford

7. B – George W Bush

8. C – Michael Ford

9. A – Chelsea Clinton

10. C – Ron Reagan

33

Life In The White House

Answers are given on page 342 - 343.

1. Which presidential son brought hungry children, which the White House kitchen called "street urchins," in to be fed at the White House?

A. *Jacky Washington*   C. *Allan Hoover*

B. *Elliott Roosevelt*   D. *Tad Lincoln*

2. Which First Son on his first night in the White House went on the roof with his stereo playing Led Zeppelin?

A. *Chip Carter*   C. *Steve Ford*

B. *Donald Trump Jr*   D. *Michael Reagan*

3. Which First Daughter after staying overnight in the Lincoln Bedroom swore she had seen Lincoln's ghost?

A. *Martha Jefferson*   C. *Mollie Garfield*

B. *Maureen Reagan*   D. *Sasha Obama*

4. Which First Son had a butler replaced just because he didn't like the way he walked?

A. *Allan Hoover*   C. *Payne Madison*

B. *Smith Van Buren*   D. *Ron Reagan*

5. The First Lady gave her daughters the advice, "Don't do anything you wouldn't mind seeing on the front page of the newspaper?" Which president's daughters received this advice?

A. *Jessie & Margaret Wilson*   C. *Malia & Sasha Obama*

B. *Lynda & Luci Johnson*   D. *Julie & Tricia Nixon*

6. Which First Daughter was reclusive to the point that her sister referred to her as, "the Howard Hughes of the White House?"

A. *Caroline Kennedy*   C. *Tricia Nixon*

B. *Amy Carter*   D. *Luci Johnson*

7. Which First Daughter had a pony named Macaroni that she rode on the White House lawn?

A. *Ethel Roosevelt*   C. *Anna Roosevelt*

B. *Eleanor Wilson*   D. *Caroline Kennedy*

8. Which First Daughter milked the cows from the White House dairy every morning?

A. *Nell Arthur*   C. *Ruth Cleveland*

B. *Martha Johnson*   D. *Elizabeth Monroe*

9. Which First Daughter was taught to drive at Camp David in an

armored Secret Service car?

    A. Chelsea Clinton   *C. Tricia Nixon*

    B. Malia Obama   *D. Susan Ford*

10. Which First Son's most memorable experience while living in the White House was to see a Wright Brother's flying machine land on the South Lawn of the White House?

    A. Charlie Taft   *C. Manning Force Hayes*

    B. Smith Van Buren   *D. Archie Roosevelt*

11. Which First Daughter dated movie star George Hamilton?

    A. Tricia Nixon   *C. Alice Roosevelt*

    B. Margaret Truman   *D. Lynda Johnson*

12. Which First Son carved his initials in the presidential yacht?

    A. Chip Carter   *C. Charlie Taft*

    B. Tad Lincoln   *D. None of the above*

13. Which First Daughter was only the second in history to be an only child of a president?

    A. Margaret Truman   *C. Ivanka Trump*

    B. Luci Johnson   *D. Chelsea Clinton*

14. Which presidential daughter was scandalous, doing things such as

smoking in public that young women of the times didn't do; yet the public and the press loved her wondering what scandalous thing she would do next?

    A. Knoxie Taylor   *C. Nellie Grant*

    B. Alice Roosevelt   *D. Margaret Truman*

15. Which president's son tied goats to a chair and had them pull him through the East Room of the White House chariot style?

    A. John Kennedy Jr   *C. Barron Trump*

    B. Quentin Roosevelt   *D. Tad Lincoln*

16. Which president's sons and friends threw spitballs at President Andrew Jackson's portrait?

    A. Sons of T. Roosevelt   *C. Sons of F. D. Roosevelt*

    B. Sons of D. Trump   *D. Sons of J. Madison*

17. Name the only two presidents to have a child born during their administration.

    A. T. Jefferson & G. Cleveland   *C. W. Harding & B. Clinton*

    B. G. Cleveland & J.F Kennedy   *D. None of the above*

18. Which First Family member, along with the First Lady, was taught to dance the Charleston by the White House butler – even though the President refused to let his family dance in public?

A. *John Coolidge*   C. *Caroline Kennedy*

B. *Jessie Wilson*   D. *Herbert Hoover Jr*

19. During her father's administration, which president's daughter led marches for women's rights and organized protests and pushed her father into supporting the 19th Amendment giving women the right to vote?

A. *Anna Roosevelt*   C. *Jessie Wilson*

B. *Nell Arthur*   D. *Alice Roosevelt*

20. Name one of the president's sons who enjoyed going to the White House roof to watch the stars through a telescope.

A. *Allan Hoover*   C. *Jeff Carter*

B. *Marvin Bush*   D. *Jessie Grant*

Answers

Chapter 33 – Life In The White House

1. D – Tad Lincoln

2. C – Steve Ford

3. B – Maureen Reagan

4. A – Allan Hoover

5. B – Lynda & Luci Johnson

6. C – Tricia Nixon

7. D – Caroline Kennedy

8. B – Martha Johnson

9. A – Chelsea Clinton

10. A – Charlie Taft

11. D – Lynda Johnson

12. C – Charlie Taft

13. D – Chelsea Clinton

14. B – Alice Roosevelt

15. D – Tad Lincoln

16. A – Sons of Roosevelt

17. B – Grover Cleveland & John F Kennedy

18. A – John Coolidge

19. C – Jessie Wilson

20. Either one is correct: C – Jeff Carter *or*   D – Jessie Grant

34

Who Am I

Answers are given on page 347.

1. Which First Daughter was named after Tiffany's, the prestigious jewelry retailer?

    A. Daughter of D. Trump   *C. Daughter of J.F Kennedy*

    B. Daughter of G. Ford   *D. Daughter of R. Nixon*

2. Which First Son challenged the editor of a newspaper editor to a duel for insulting his father the president?

    A. George W Bush   *C. John Tyler, Jr*

    B. Jimmy Roosevelt   *D. Jacky Washington*

3. Which First Daughter was nicknamed 'Princess Alice'?

    A. Daughter of T. Roosevelt   *C. Daughter of L.B. Johnson*

    B. Daughter of G. Cleveland   *D. Daughter of B. Harrison*

4. Which president's son was adopted and was alive to see his father become president?

    A. Jacky Washington   *C. Andrew Jackson, Jr*

    B. Michael Reagan   *D. None of the above*

5. Which First Daughter holds the title, 'Most Influential First Daughter'?

    A. Martha Jefferson   *C. Chelsea Clinton*

    B. Margaret Truman   *D. Ivanka Trump*

6. Which First Son was part owner of the Texas Rangers baseball team?

    A. Don Trump, Jr   *C. Jeff Carter*

    B. George W Bush   *D. Alan Coolidge*

7. Which First Daughter ran for the Senate, but her own father refused to endorse her candidacy?

    A. Amy Carter   *C. Maureen Reagan*

    B. Margaret Truman   *D. Caroline Kennedy*

8. While in first grade, which First Son was teased by other children and one day punched one of the bullies. When asked where he learned to fight, he proudly answered, "The Secret Service."

A. *John F Kennedy, Jr*   C. *Tad Lincoln*

B. *Cal Coolidge, Jr*   D. *Barron Trump*

9. Which First Son was a member of the newly formed group 'Sons of the American Revolution'?

A. *Son of Dwight D. Eisenhower*   C. *Son of Abraham Lincoln*

B. *Son of Rutherford B Hayes*   D. *Son of Benjamin Harrison*

10. Which First Daughter is known for being one of "the Rich Kids of Instagram"?

A. *Malia Obama*   C. *Chelsea Clinton*

B. *Tiffany Trump*   D. *Tricia Nixon*

Answers

Chapter 34 – Who Am I

1. A – The daughter of Donald Trump (Tiffany Trump)

2. C – John Tyler, Jr

3. A – The daughter of Theodore Roosevelt (Alice Roosevelt)

4. Either B – Michael Reagan or C – Andrew Jackson, Jr would be correct.

5. D – Ivanka Trump

6. B – George W Bush

7. C – Maureen Reagan

8. A – John F Kennedy, Jr

9. D - The son of Benjamin Harrison

* *Members of the SAR, Sons of the American Revolution, are males whose ancestors served in the American Revolutionary War. His father's great-grandfather was a signer of the Declaration of Independence and Governor of Virginia and one of George Washington's chief adjutants.*

10. B – Tiffany Trump

35

Quotes Of The First Family

Answers are given on page 351.

1. Which First Daughter said: "I'll never throw away my blue jeans."

   A. Malia Obama   *C. Susan Ford*

   B. Patti Davis Reagan   *D. Caroline Kennedy*

2. Which First Son while hunting shot a protected species of songbird and afterward said, "Thank goodness it wasn't deer season. I might have shot a cow"?

   A. Eric Trump   *C. Ron Reagan*

   B. George W. Bush   *D. Kermit Roosevelt*

3. Which First Daughter said: "I hated the White House. It's like this tiny claustophic town. There are eyes and ears everywhere"?

   A. Sasha Obama   *C. Chelsea Clinton*

   B. Susan Ford   *D. Patti Davis Reagan*

4. Which First Daughter said: "We were well-behaved, but we didn't deserve any Academy Awards"?

A. *Julie Nixon*   C. *Malia Obama*

B. *Luci Johnson*   D. *Tiffany Trump*

5. Which First Son said: "I was never a great intellectual"?

A. *Eric Trump*   C. *John Eisenhower*

B. *George W Bush*   D. *Franklin Roosevelt, Jr*

6. Which First Daughter said: "Determination gets you a long way"?

A. *Mollie Garfield*   C. *Chelsea Clinton*

B.*Tiffany Trump*   D. *Lynda Johnson*

7. Which First Daughter while campaigning for her father said: "Like many of my fellow millennials, I do not consider myself categorically Republican or Democrat"?

A. *Ivanka Trump*   C. *Barbara Bush*

B. *Chelsea Clinton*   D. *Malia Obama*

8. When asked what it was like to live in the White House, which First Daughter said: "I feel like it's filled with millions of ghosts. I'm not kidding. I have heard ghosts, I really have"?

A. *Maureen Reagan*   C. *Amy Carter*

B. *Jenna Bush*   D. *Margaret Truman*

9. Which First Son when approached to run for the presidency himself is said to have responded with this quote: "It seems difficult for the average American to understand that it is possible for anyone not to desire the

Presidency, but I most certainly do not"?

<ul>
<li>A. John Kennedy, Jr</li>
<li>C. Robert Lincoln</li>
</ul>

<ul>
<li>B. John Eisenhower</li>
<li>D. John Quincy Adams</li>
</ul>

10. Which First Son said: "I am an unabashed atheist who is not afraid of burning in hell"?

<ul>
<li>A. Ron Reagan</li>
<li>C. Chip Carter</li>
</ul>

<ul>
<li>B. Payne Madison</li>
<li>D. George W Bush</li>
</ul>

11. Which alcoholic First Son when asked why he finally gave up drinking responded: "I'm afraid I might do something to embarrass my father"?

<ul>
<li>A. Benjamin Pierce</li>
<li>C. Chip Carter</li>
</ul>

<ul>
<li>B. Steve Ford</li>
<li>D. George W Bush</li>
</ul>

12. Which First Daughter said: "I refuse to let the opinions of others define how I see myself, how I carry myself, how I get through my days"?

<ul>
<li>A. Caroline Kennedy</li>
<li>C. Ivanka Trump</li>
</ul>

<ul>
<li>B. Lynda Johnson</li>
<li>D. Julie Nixon</li>
</ul>

Answers

Chapter 35 – Quotes Of The First Family

1. C – Susan Ford

2. B – George W Bush

3. D – Patti Davis Reagan

4. A – Julie Nixon

5. B – George W Bush

6. C – Chelsea Clinton

7. A – Ivanka Trump

8. B – Jenna Bush

9. C – Robert Lincoln

10. A – Ron Reagan

11. D – George W Bush

12. C – Ivanka Trump

36

The First Or The Only One To Do So

Answers are given on page 356.

1. Which First Daughter was the first Orthodox Jewish First Daughter?

    A. Patsy Washington   *C. Betsy Harrison*

    B. Ivanka Trump   *D. Pearl Tyler*

2. Which presidential sons were the first Boy Scouts to live in the White House?

    A. Willie & Tad Lincoln   *C. John & Cal Coolidge Jr*

    B. Harry & Abram Garfield   *D. Allan & Herbert Hoover Jr*

3. Who is the only president to have two of his children born during his administration?

    A. Grover Cleveland   *C. Franklin Pierce*

    B. John F Kennedy   *D. None of the above*

4. Which was the first presidential daughter to assume the role of hostess for the White House?

A. Martha Jefferson   C. Martha Johnson

B. Ivanka Trump   D. Eliza Monroe

5. Who was the first son of a president to have been in Little League?
Hint: He would one day be part owner of a baseball team.

A. Eric Trump   C. Ron Reagan

B. George W Bush   D. Michael Ford

6. Who is the only presidential daughter to have had her prom in the White House?

A. Malia Obama   C. Amy Carter

B. Chelsea Clinton   D. Susan Ford

7. The first child born in the White House was the son of which presidential daughter?

A. Patsy Washington   C. Martha Jefferson

B. Nabby Adams   D. Nellie Grant

8. Which First Daughter was the first and only child of a president born in the White House?

A. Esther Cleveland   C. Pearl Tyler

B. Fanny Hayes   D. Margaret Truman

9. Which president's daughters were the first African-Americans to live in the White House?

A. *Daughters of A. Johnson*   C. *Daughters of Z. Taylor*

B. *Daughters of W. H Harrison*   D. *Daughters of B. Obama*

10. Which president's adult children and grandchildren were the first to eat ice cream?

A. *George Washington*   C. *Abe Lincoln*

B. *Thomas Jefferson*   D. *Andrew Jackson*

11. Which president's daughter was the first to have her wedding take place at the White House?

A. *Maria Monroe*   C. *Nellie Grant*

B. *Alice Tyler*   D. *Alice Roosevelt*

12. Who was the first presidential son to also become president?

A. *George W Bush*   C. *John Quincy Adams*

B. *Abraham Van Buren*   D. *Benjamin Harrison*

13. Which two president's sons became the first brothers to be simultaneous governors?

A. *Herbert Jr & Allan Hoover*   C. *Quentin & Archie Roosevelt*

B. *George W & Jeb Bush*   D. *John & Smith Van Buren*

14. Which president's son was the first child ever born to a President-elect?

A. Son of Thomas Jefferson   C. Son of James Buchanan

B. Son of James Madison   D. Son of John F Kennedy

15. Which president's stepson was the first member of a presidential family to end up in debtor's prison due to gambling debts?

A. Jacky Washington   C. Charles Adams

B. Payne Madison   D. Benjamin Pierce

Answers

Chapter 36 – The First Or The Only One To Do So

1. B – Ivanka Trump

2. C – John & Cal Coolidge, Jr

3. A – Grover Cleveland

4. A – Martha Jefferson
Though not considered the "official" First Lady for her father as the majority of his administration she was giving birth or caring for her children and the role was mostly filled by Dolley Madison, though Martha did at times take over the role as First Lady.

5. B – George W Bush

6. D – Susan Ford

7. C – Martha Jefferson

8. A – Esther Cleveland

9. D – Daughters of Barack Obama

10. B - Thomas Jefferson

11. A – Maria Monroe

12. C – John Quincy Adams

13. B - George W & Jeb Bush

14. D – Son of John F Kennedy

15. B – Payne Madison

37

Holidays At The White House

Answers are given on page 360.

1. Which president's family spent each Christmas in Hawaii?

    A. Donald Trump family

    B. George H W Bush family

    C. Franklin Roosevelt family

    D. Barack Obama family

2. Which was the first president to decorate the White House with a Christmas tree for his grandchildren?

    A. Thomas Jefferson

    B. Andrew Jackson

    C. Benjamin Harrison

    D. Franklin Roosevelt

3. Who was the first president whose daughters enjoyed the first Christmas tree in the White House decorated with electric lights?

    A. Woodrow Wilson

    B. Grover Cleveland

    C. Andrew Johnson

    D. John Tyler

4. Which former president's son went to a Halloween party dressed as Michelangelo's *David* covered in talcum powder and dressed only in a fig leaf?

A. *Donald Trump Jr*   C. *John Kennedy Jr*

B. *George W Bush*   D. *Steve Ford*

5. On Memorial Day, which First Daughter would join the first lady to decorate the graves of Civil War soldiers at Arlington National Cemetery?

A. *Eliza Monroe*   C. *Anna Roosevelt*

B. *Fanny Hayes*   D. *Julie Nixon*

6. Which president threw a Christmas party for his children and grandchildren that included an indoor "snowball fight"?

A. *Andrew Jackson*   C. *Benjamin Harrison*

B. *Abraham Lincoln*   D. *George H W Bush*

7. Which First Daughter received a talking doll for Christmas that was one day left in the Oval Office and inadvertently recorded the president using foul language?

A. *Sasha Obama*   C. *Caroline Kennedy*

B. *Amy Carter*   D. *Nellie Grant*

8. Which president's son was responsible for saving the turkey given to the White House for the president's Thanksgiving dinner, initiating the practice of pardoning the turkey?

A. *John Kennedy, Jr*   C. *Cal Coolidge, Jr*

B. *Tad Lincoln*   D. *Quentin Roosevelt*

9. The first lady wanted her children to experience the same joys as other children, so when Halloween came around she dressed up along with her children so as to not be recognized and took her children to a nearby neighborhood of the White House to go trick-or-treating. Which presidential children were these?

A. Children of J. Garfield

C. Children of G. Cleveland

B. Children of T. Roosevelt

D. Children of J. F. Kennedy

10. A Christmas tradition of which presidential family, did their father read Charles Dickens 'A Christmas Carol' to his children and grandchildren?

A. Franklin D Roosevelt

C. Lyndon B Johnson

B. John F Kennedy

D. Donald Trump

Answers

Chapter 37 – Holidays At The White House

1. D – Barack Obama family

2. C – Benjamin Harrison

3. B – Grover Cleveland

4. C – John F Kennedy Jr

5. B – Fanny Hayes

6. A – Andrew Jackson

The snowballs were specially fashioned cotton balls.

7. C – Caroline Kennedy

8. B – Tad Lincoln

The turkey was named Jack and roamed freely on the White House grounds.

9. D – Children of John F Kennedy

They might have been able to pull it off if it weren't for all the Secret Service agents with them.

10. A - Franklin D Roosevelt

38

Traveling With The First Family

Answers are given on page 364.

1. Which presidential daughter was presented to King George III, the king responsible for the colonies fighting for their independence?

   A. Eliza Madison   *C. Nabby Adams*

   B. Louisa Catherine Adams   *D. Maria Jefferson*

2. Which president's children, during their White House days, traveled abroad more than any other presidential children?

   A. Herbert Hoover's children   *C. John F Kennedy's children*

   B. Donald Trump's children   *D. Barack Obama's children*

3. Which president and son explored the Amazon?

   A. T. Roosevelt & son Kermit   *C. F. Pierce & son Benjamin*

   B. Z. Taylor & son Dick   *D. H. Hoover & son Herbert Jr*

4. What future president's son was thought to be lost at sea for five months and presumed dead?

A. Allan Hoover   C. Charles Adams

B. Barron Trump   D. Chester Alan Chester Jr

5. Who was the first president, who along with the first lady and two sons, was the first sitting president to travel to the West Coast?

A. Herbert Hoover   C. Theodore Roosevelt

B. Rutherford B Hayes   D. William H. Harrison

6. Which 2 presidential sons while on an expedition to Asia confirmed the existence of the giant panda – the first men from the west to do so?

A. Ted Jr & Kermit Roosevelt   C. Abraham & John Van Buren

B.Richard & Francis Cleveland   D. Don Jr & Eric Trump

7. In 1905, the president sent his daughter along on a diplomatic delegation as a goodwill ambassador, the *first* First Daughter to ever serve in this role, on a four month voyage to Asia. Who was she?

A. Caroline Kennedy   C. Maureen Reagan

B. Martha Jefferson   D. Alice Roosevelt

8. While traveling with the president and first lady to Africa to launch the President's emergency Plan for AIDS relief, which First Daughter later described the trip as life-changing? She became founder and CEO of Global Health Corps as a result.

A. Barbara Bush   C. Tricia Nixon

B. Chelsea Clinton   D. Caroline Kennedy

9. Which First Daughter traveled with her father, the sitting president, for a secret meeting with Churchill and Stalin at Yalta?

A. Margaret Truman   C. Luci Johnson

B. Anna Roosevelt   D. Ivanka Trump

10. Which president's son while part of a group sponsored by the National Outdoor Leadership Course in Africa had to evade a charging rhinocerous and got lost in the snake-infested African bush and a search party of Masai warriors were sent out to search for them. Who was this son of a president?

A. Steve Ford   C. Eric Trump

B. Jeb Bush   D. John F Kennedy, Jr

Answers

Chapter 38 – Traveling With The First Family

1. C – Nabby Adams

2. D - Barack Obama's children

3. A – Theodore Roosevelt & son Kermit

4. C – Charles Adams

* *His father was sending his eleven-year old son Charles from England back to America. Originally he had an escort, but the ship had to divert to Spain for repairs where his escort left him alone in a strange country where he didn't speak the language. Eventually he made it home, but by then his family had feared him dead and lost at sea.*

5. B – Rutherford B Hayes

6. A- Ted Jr & Kermit Roosevelt

7. D – Alice Roosevelt

8. A – Barbara Bush

9. B – Anna Roosevelt

10. D – John F Kennedy, Jr

39

Romance & Weddings

Answers are given on page 368.

1. Who was the *first* First Daughter to be married at the White House?

    A. Maria Jefferson   *C. Alice Tyler*

    B. Maria Monroe   *D. Martha Johnson*

2. Which president-elect's daughter married the grandson of a former president?

    A. Caroline Kennedy   *C. Knoxie Taylor*

    B. Margaret Truman   *D. Julie Nixon*

3. Which sitting president's daughter once dated a future president, but they did not hit it off?

    A. Luci Johnson   *C. Mollie Garfield*

    B. Tricia Nixon   *D. Nellie Grant*

4. Which First Son married the first girl he ever dated, a girl from Mexico who spoke no English?

A. *Eric Trump*   C. *Dick Taylor*

B. *Elliott Roosevelt*   D. *Jeb Bush*

5. Which president is the only one to have 2 daughters get married at the White House?

A. *Lyndon B Johnson*   C. *George W Bush*

B. *Woodrow Wilson*   D. *Richard Nixon*

6. Which First Daughter is the only one to have her wedding take place at Camp David?

A. *Lynda Johnson*   C. *Doro Bush*

B. *Caroline Kennedy*   D. *Chelsea Clinton*

7. Who is the only First Daughter to have her wedding take place in the Rose Garden at the White House?

A. *Alice Roosevelt*   C. *Lynda Johnson*

B. *Nellie Grant*   D. *Tricia Nixon*

8. Who was the *first* First Daughter to be married in a church while her father was president?

A. *Maria Monroe*   C. *Margaret Truman*

B. *Luci Johnson*   D. *Nellie Grant*

9. Which First Daughter was the first to cut her wedding cake with the sword of a White House aide?

A. Alice Roosevelt   C. Caroline Kennedy

B. Luci Johnson   D. Mollie Garfield

10. Which president's daughter married Jefferson Davis who would one day be president of the Confederate States?

A. Mollie Garfield   C. Pearl Tyler

B. Knoxie Taylor   D. Abbie Fillmore

11. Which president is the only president to have a son who married in the White House?

A. John Quincy Adams   C. Franklin Pierce

B. James Buchanan   D. Woodrow Wilson

12. Who was the *last* First Daughter to be married at the White House?

A. Anna Roosevelt   C. Lynda Johnson

B. Margaret Truman   D. Jenna Bush

Answers

Chapter 39 – Romance & Weddings

1. B – Maria Monroe

2. D – Julie Nixon

3. B- Tricia Nixon

Tricia Nixon once went on a date with George W Bush when he was in the National Guard. The date had been set up by his father, also a future president who at the time was working in the Nixon administration. The date did not go well and immediately after dinner Tricia asked George to take her home.

4. D – Jeb Bush

5. B – Woodrow Wilson

Lyndon B Johnson also had two daughters marry during his administration, but only one of his daughters had her wedding at the White House.

6. C – Doro Bush

7. D – Tricia Nixon

8. B – Luci Johnson

9. A – Alice Roosevelt

10. B – Knoxie Taylor

11. A – John Quincy Adams

12. C – Lynda Johnson

40

Do You Know...

Answers are given on page 372.

1. Which First Son's life was saved by the brother of the man who would later assassinate his father during his presidency?

    A. Michael Reagan   *C. Quentin Cleveland*

    B. Robert Lincoln   *D. Harry Garfield*

2. Which president had the most children? (He had 15 children.)

    A. George H W Bush   *C. John Tyler*

    B. Jimmy Carter   *D. Zachary Taylor*

3. Who is currently the oldest living First Family member (as of the year 2017)?

    A. Caroline Kennedy   *C. John Eisenhower*

    B. Lynda Johnson   *D. Ron Reagan*

4. Which presidential daughter and husband, as of the year 2017, are worth over $700 million?

A. Ivanka Trump   C. Caroline Kennedy

B. Chelsea Clinton   D. None of the above

5. Which president's son tracked grizzly bears while working for the National Geographic Society?

A. Dick Taylor   C. Charles Taft

B. Kermit Roosevelt   D. Steve Ford

6. Which president's daughter while working as an assistant teacher came to school dressed as Dr. Seuss' *'The Cat In The Hat'*?

A. Julie Nixon   C. Margaret Truman

B. Jenna Bush   D. Doro Bush

7. Which two president's children's mother was the famous actress Jane Wyman?

A. Maureen & Michael Reagan   C. Eleanor & Jessie Wilson

B. Susan & Jack Ford   D. Don Jr & Eric Trump

8. Which president's son after graduating from college moved out west and lived out of the back of his truck for about a year and a half?

A. Steve Ford   C. Jeb Bush

B. Don Trump, Jr   D. Allan Hoover

9. Which First Daughter was charged by a 6,000 lb pet runaway elephant at a pet show and was saved by a Secret Service agent?

A. Sasha Obama   *C. Amy Carter*

B. Jenna Bush   *D. Tricia Nixon*

10. Which First Son did not move into the White House immediately after his father became president so he could finish his school year without having to change schools?

A. Smith Van Buren   *C. John Eisenhower*

B. Cal Coolidge, Jr   *D. Barron Trump*

Answers

Chapter 40 – Do You Know...

1. B – Robert Lincoln

2. C – John Tyler

3. B – Lynda Johnson
*From the book **'Children of the Presidents'** by Cheryl Pryor - Lynda Johnson is the oldest of the presidential children still living, but remarkably two of John Tyler's grandsons are still living as of the writing of this book in the year 2017. John Tyler was born in the 18th century during the administration of George Washington and Tyler, a pre-Civil War president, was the 10th president.*

4. A – Ivanka Trump

Caroline Kennedy and her immediate family come in a close second with a net worth of over $500 million.

5. D – Steve Ford

6. B – Jenna Bush

7. A – Maureen & Michael Reagan

8. B - Don Trump, Jr

9. C – Amy Carter

10. D - Barron Trump

41

Achievements Of The First Family

Answers are given on page 377.

1. Which president's son served in the newly created Fuel Administration during WWI, for which by the end of the war he received the Distinguished Service Medal for his work?

A. Herbert Hoover, Jr

C. Russell Harrison

B. Harry Garfield

D. Robert Lincoln

2. Which president's daughter has her own jewelry and fashion line designed for young professionals?

A. Ivanka Trump

C. Barbara Bush

B. Doro Bush

D. Caroline Kennedy

3. Which president's daughter was a concert soprano?

A. Amy Carter

C. Margaret Truman

B. Sasha Obama

D. Julie Nixon

4. Which First Son was given the title "the radio genius of the industry," by an aviation trade magazine?

A. *Hal Garfield*   C. *Russell Benjamin*

B. *John Eisenhower*   D. *Herbert Hoover, Jr*

5. Which president's daughter was a successful model?

A. *Patti Davis Reagan*   C. *Tricia Nixon*

B. *Ivanka Trump*   D. *Caroline Kennedy*

6. Which First Son was an actor and worked on a soap opera and several movies with big name stars?

A. *Ron Reagan*   C. *John Kennedy, Jr*

B. *Don Trump, Jr*   D. *Steve Ford*

7. Which First Daughter became U.S. ambassador to Japan?

A. *Lynda Johnson*   C. *Chelsea Clinton*

B. *Caroline Kennedy*   D. *Julie Eisenhower*

8. Two First Sons have received the Medal of Honor. Name one of them.

A. *Webb Hayes*   C. *John Eisenhower*

B. *Ted Roosevelt, Jr*   D. *Hal Garfield*

9. Do you know which president's daughter Oprah Winfrey called 'a role model' for the 21st century woman?

A. *Chelsea Clinton*   C. *Malia Obama*

B. *Jenna Bush*   D. *Ivanka Trump*

10. Which First Daughter was Dean of Bryn Mawr?

    A. Helen Taft   *C. Chelsea Clinton*

    B. Jessie Wilson   *D. Ivanka Trump*

11. Which First Son while in England serving as U.S. minister of Great Britain negotiated with the King of England to keep England out of the Civil War, perhaps changing the outcome of the war?

    A. Robert Lincoln   *C. Charles Adams*

    B. Dick Taylor   *D. Payne Madison*

12. At the age of 25, which president's daughter became the youngest director of a publicly traded company?

    A. Caroline Kennedy   *C. Lynda Johnson*

    B. Chelsea Clinton   *D. Ivanka Trump*

13. Who was the 2nd First Son to follow in his father's footsteps to the Oval Office, also becoming president?

    A. John Quincy Adams   *C. George W Bush*

    B. Benjamin Harrison   *D. John Kennedy, Jr*

14. Which president's son worked for Herbert Hoover in the Food Administration finding a way to feed the people in Europe at the conclusion of WWI?

    A. Robert Taft   *C. Charles Adams*

    B. Dick Taylor   *D. Robert Lincoln*

15. Which two First Sons, already executive vice presidents of the company, were put in charge of their father's business worth billions once their father made his new office in the Oval Office?

A. Sons of Franklin D Roosevelt

C. Sons of George H W Bush

B. Sons of Gerald Ford

D. Sons of Donald Trump

Answers

Chapter 41 – Achievements Of The First Family

1. B – Harry Garfield

2. A – Ivanka Trump

3. C – Margaret Truman

4. D – Herbert Hoover, Jr

5. B – Ivanka Trump

6. D – Steve Ford

7. B – Caroline Kennedy

8. Either answer A – Webb Hayes or B – Ted Roosevelt, Jr would be correct.

9. D – Ivanka Trump

10. A – Helen Taft

11. C – Charles Adams
This was the son of John Quincy Adams a high-achiever, not to be confused with Charles the son of John Adams.

12. D – Ivanka Trump

13. C – George W Bush

14. A – Robert Taft

15. D – Sons of Donald Trump

42

History In The Making

Answers are given on page 381.

1. Which president's son was there to witness the signing of the Treaty of Paris which officially ended the Revolutionary War and recognized America's independence?

    A. John Quincy Adams   *C. Peter Jefferson*

    B. Jacky Washington   *D. Payne Madison*

2. Name one of the two presidential sons who were at the Appomattox Court House during the surrender of Robert E Lee?

    A. Fred Grant   *C. Robert Lincoln*

    B. Gardi Tyler   *D. None of the above*

3. The son of which president was sent to England as a representative of the U.S. for the coronation of Queen Victoria?

    A. James Madison   *C. James Polk*

    B. Martin Van Buren   *D. Millard Fillmore*

4. Which First Daughter was one of only five American women

permitted to witness the historic signing of the Versailles Treaty?

A. *Martha Jefferson*   C. *Anna Roosevelt*

B. *Eliza Monroe*   D. *Margaret Wilson*

5. Which president's son witnessed the signing of the Treaty of Ghent that ended the War of 1812?

A. *Peter Jefferson*   C. *John Quincy Adams*

B. *Andrew Jackson, Jr*   D. *Payne Madison*

6. Which president's son was in China during the Boxer Rebellion as part of the relief force that rescued trapped Westerners in Peking, including a future president and first lady?

A. *Robert Lincoln*   C. *John Eisenhower*

B. *Fred Grant*   D. *Webb Hayes*

7. Which president was in large part responsible for the Trail of Tears, even though he had an adopted Indian son?

A. *Andrew Jackson*   C. *John Tyler*

B. *William Henry Harrison*   D. *Zachary Taylor*

8. Which First Daughter's father ordered the use of atomic bombs on Hiroshima and Nagasaki?

A. *Anna Roosevelt*   C. *Caroline Kennedy*

B. *Margaret Truman*   D. *Jessie Wilson*

9. Which president's son's signature appeared on Confederate dollars?

    A. Smith Van Buren   *C. Robert Tyler*

    B. Robert Lincoln   *D. Dick Taylor*

10. What young presidential son traveled with the troops during the Civil War witnessing battles and life as a soldier?

    A. Dick Taylor   *C. Quentin Roosevelt*

    B. Fred Grant   *D. Herbert Hoover, Jr*

Answers

Chapter 42 – History In The Making

1. A – John Quincy Adams

2. Either B – Gardi Tyler or C – Robert Lincoln would be a correct answer as they were both on site.

3. B – Martin Van Buren

4. D – Margaret Wilson

The first lady was also there to witness the signing of the Versailles Treaty. She was the 1st First Lady to attend foreign diplomatic talks.

5. C – John Quincy Adams

6. D – Webb Hayes

The future president and first lady rescued during the Boxer Rebellion was Herbert Hoover and his wife.

7. A – Andrew Jackson

8. B – Margret Truman

9. C – Robert Tyler

Robert Tyler served as Register of the Treasury of the Confederacy and it was due to his position that his signature was on Confederate dollars.

10. B – Fred Grant

43

Wars During Their Lifetime

Answers are given on pages 385 - 386.

1. Which First Son, a general, volunteered to lead the assault in the first wave of attacks at Normandy on D-Day?

A. John Eisenhower

C. Ted Roosevelt, Jr

B. John Coolidge

D. Richard Cleveland

2. Which First Son at the age of seven witnessed the Battle of Bunker Hill from a hilltop near his home?

A. Jacky Washington

C. Alan Arthur

B. Charles Johnson

D. John Quincy Adams

3. General Patton described which First Son as "one of the bravest men I've ever known"?

A. Ted Roosevelt, Jr

C. George W Bush

B. Webb Hayes

D. Ron Reagan

4. Which president's two daughters lived at the White House while their husbands were in Vietnam and had to listen to protestors outside the White House?

A. George W Bush   C. Richard Nixon

B. Ronald Reagan   D. Lyndon B Johnson

5. Which First Daughter traveled to Europe during WWI singing and putting on concerts to entertain the troops?

A. Margaret Wilson   C. Mollie Garfield

B. Alice Roosevelt   D. Margaret Truman

6. Which president's son was shot down by a German fighter pilot?

A. John Kennedy, Jr   C. Charles Taft

B. Quentin Roosevelt   D. John Coolidge

7. Which presidential son helped negotiate the end of the War of 1812?

A. John Quincy Adams   C. Peter Jefferson

B. Payne Madison   D. Don Trump, Jr

8. Which president's son was General Omar Bradley referring to when he said his fighting and leadership during D-Day was "the single bravest act" he witnessed during the entire war?

A. Ron Reagan   C. John Eisenhower

B. Robert Lincoln   D. Ted Roosevelt, Jr

9. Which sitting president's son joined the army during the Civil War?

A. Robert Lincoln   C. Fred Grant

B. Andrew Johnson, Jr   D. John Tyler, Jr

10. Which president, in his pre-presidential days, took his eleven-year old son with him while fighting in the Civil War?

A. Zachary Taylor   C. Ulysses S Grant

B. Abraham Lincoln   D. William H Harrison

11. During what war did George Washington's stepson die after suffering from camp fever which is a form of dysentery soldiers in camp suffered with?

A. Revolutionary War   C. Civil War

B. French & Indian War   D. War of 1812

12. Which presidential son flew in Eddie Rickenbacker's squadron during WWI?

A. John Eisenhower   C. Robert Taft

B. Quentin Roosevelt   D. Herbert Hoover, Jr

Answers

Chapter 43 – Wars During Their Lifetime

1. C – Ted Roosevelt, Jr

*From **'Children of the Presidents'** by Cheryl Pryor: Ted served during WWII as a brigadier general. When he learned of the attack that was to take place on Utah Beach he put in a request to lead the assault. His request was denied more than once and was told there would be no generals taking part in the assault. Ted continued the fight to be a part of the invasion stating that to have a general land in the first wave of attacks at Normandy would boost morale for the men who would most certainly be on a suicide mission. Eventually it was agreed he could take part, but only after it was made very clear that his chances of survival were practically nonexistent.*

It wasn't just the fact that he was a general or the son of a president, but he was 56 years old and suffering from battle wounds from the last world war and couldn't walk without the aid of a walking stick. But, he did indeed lead the assault standing on the beach with bullets flying around his head directing his troops to their positions. He was a courageous and inspirational leader for the troops he led that day; and yes, he did survive.

2. D – John Quincy Adams

3. A – Ted Roosevelt, Jr

4. D – Lyndon B Johnson

5. A – Margaret Wilson

6. B – Quentin Roosevelt

7. A – John Quincy Adams

8. D – Ted Roosevelt, Jr

9. A – Robert Lincoln

10. C – Ulysses S Grant

11. A – Revolutionary War

12. B – Quentin Roosevelt

44

Scandals Involving The First Family

Answers are given on pages 391 - 392.

1. Which president's son was accused of being involved in an assassination plot?

    A. Chip Carter   C. Chester Arthur, Jr

    B. Herbert Hoover, Jr   D. Elliott Roosevelt

2. Which president's son had his mother committed to an insane asylum?

    A. Payne Madison   C. Russell Harrison

    B. Robert Lincoln   D. George W Bush

3. Which president's son was arrested for DUI?

    A. Payne Madison   C. George W Bush

    B. John Eisenhower   D. Don Trump Jr

4. Which First Daughter posed nude for Playboy magazine?

    A. Ivanka Trump   C. Susan Ford

    B. Tricia Nixon   D. Patti Davis Reagan

5. Which two First Daughters caught the media's attention with using a fake ID and being caught in underage drinking?

   A. Ivanka & Tiffany Trump   C. Barbara & Jenna Bush

   B. Malia & Sasha Obama   D. Maureen & Patti Reagan

6. Which president had two children whose ex-spouses committed suicide and another attempted suicide?

   A. John Quincy Adams   C. Zachary Taylor

   B. Franklin D Roosevelt   D. James Garfield

7. Which First Sons smoked dope in the White House leaving bongs laying about?

   A. Sons of Jimmy Carter   C. Sons of Gerald Ford

   B. Sons of George H W Bush   D. Sons of Herbert Hoover

8. Which First Daughter is being sued for copyright infringement where an author claims her feminist children's book is an unauthorized reproduction of his work?

   A. Tiffany Trump   C. Chelsea Clinton

   B. Patti Davis Reagan   D. Jenna Bush

9. Which First Daughter was abused by her first husband?

   A. Doro Bush   C. Caroline Kennedy

   B. Maureen Reagan   D. Ethel Roosevelt

10. Which First Daughter was hired as a special correspondent at NBC due to her family name, was paid $600,000 (which averaged out to be $27,000 a minute) for a part-time job? Not only did she have no experience, but she had always been 'hands-off' to the press and now she was a member of the press and was *still* hands-off.

A. Chelsea Clinton

C. Amy Carter

B. Luci Johnson

D. Caroline Kennedy

11. Which 2 First Daughters had to face the humiliation of their father being the only president in U.S. history to resign?

A. L. B. Johnson's daughters

C. R. Nixon's daughters

B. W. Wilson's daughters

D. G. W Bush's daughters

12. Which First Daughter had a daughter not of her husbands, but fathered by a senator she was having an affair with?

A. Patti Davis Reagan

C. Fanny Hayes

B. Ruth Cleveland

D. Alice Roosevelt

13. Which First Daughter claimed her mother, the First Lady, mentally and physically abused her?

A. Chelsea Clinton

C. Amy Carter

B. Patti Davis Reagan

D. Caroline Kennedy

14. Which president's five children had 19 marriages between them?

A. Franklin D Roosevelt

C. George H W Bush

B. Jimmy Carter

D. Gerald Ford

15. Which First Daughter is involved in her family's foundation that during her mother's 2nd run for the presidency it was *"strongly"* suggested that foreign governments 'paid to play'?

A. Ivanka Trump

C. Jenna Bush

B. Chelsea Clinton

D. Lynda Johnson

Answers

Chapter 44 – Scandals Involving The First Family

1. D - Elliott Roosevelt

*From the book **'Children of the Presidents'** by Cheryl Pryor: Elliott Roosevelt was accused of being involved in an assassination plot on the Bahamanian Prime Minister. He offered $100,000 to an alleged mobster front man to assassinate the prime minister paying him $10,000 up front. The check with his signature was produced along with taped conversations. Elliott maintained up until his death that it wasn't true. He was investigated by the Senate in 1973 of his ties to organized crime.*

2. B – Robert Lincoln

3. C – George W Bush

4. D – Patti Davis Reagan

5. C – Barbara & Jenna Bush

6. B – Franklin D Roosevelt

7. A – Sons of Jimmy Carter

8. C – Chelsea Clinton

9. B – Maureen Reagan

10. A – Chelsea Clinton

11. C – Richard Nixon's daughters

12. D – Alice Roosevelt

13. B – Patti Davis Reagan

14. A – Franklin D Roosevelt

15. B – Chelsea Clinton

45

Grandchildren of the Presidents

Answers are given on page 396.

1. The grandson of which president built Arlington House which later became part of Arlington Cemetery?

    A. George Washington   *C. James Madison*

    B. Thomas Jefferson   *D. Abraham Lincoln*

2. Which pre-Civil War president who was born during George Washington's administration has two grandsons still living today (as of the year 2017)?

    A. Zachary Taylor   *C. Abraham Lincoln*

    B. Thomas Jefferson   *D. John Tyler*

3. Which president's grandson also became a president?

    A. John Adams   *C. Andrew Johnson*

    B. William H Harrison   *D. Theodore Roosevelt*

4. Which president's grandson had Camp David named after him? *Hint: He married a president-elect's daughter.*

A. *Grover Cleveland*   C. *Dwight D Eisenhower*

B. *Franklin D Roosevelt*   D. *William McKinley*

5. *True or False.* After Washington's stepson Jacky died, George and Martha raised two of Jacky's children.

   True   *False*

6. During which president's administration did his grandson live at the White House and became "the most famous baby in the world," according to the press?

A. *Millard Fillmore*   C. *Ulysses S Grant*

B. *Franklin Roosevelt*   D. *Benjamin Harrison*

7. Which president had a grandchild that was deaf?

A. *Cal Coolidge*   C. *Abraham Lincoln*

B. *James Monroe*   D. *Jimmy Carter*

8. The granddaughter of which president married a prince in Russia making her a 'bona fide' princess?

A. *Ulysses S Grant*   C. *Herbert Hoover*

B. *James Garfield*   D. *William H Taft*

9. Which president's young grandchildren, children of his daughter, speak Mandarin Chinese?

A. Zachary Taylor   C. Herbert Hoover

B. Donald Trump   D. George H.W. Bush

10. The great-granddaughter of which president was married to Civil War General Robert E. Lee?

A Ulysses S Grant   C. George Washington

B. Zachary Taylor   D. Abraham Lincoln

Answers

Chapter 45 – Grandchildren Of The Presidents

1. A – George Washington

2. D – John Tyler

3. B William H Harrison

4. C – Dwight D Eisenhower

5. True

6. D – Benjamin Harrison

* The baby was known as Baby McKee

7. B – James Monroe

8. A – Ulysses S Grant

President Grant's granddaughter Julia, the daughter of his son Fred, became a Russian princess. The prince she married came from one of the oldest and richest in the Russian empire. She and her family had to flee Russia during the Russian Revolution with her jewels sewn into her clothing. They moved to the U.S. and settled in Florida. She wrote of her tales of fleeing from the Russian Revolution. The book is titled **'Revolutionary Days' by Princess Julia Cantacuzene.*

9. B – Donald Trump

10. C – George Washington

46

First Family Pets

Answers are given on pages 400 - 401.

1. Which Presidential family had Siam, the first Siamese kitten to come to America?

A. *Family of Rutherford B. Hayes*   C. *Family of Jimmy Carter*

B. *Family of Calvin Coolidge*   D. *Family of Gerald Ford*

2. Which First Family had a Golden Retriever named Liberty that had puppies while living in the White House?

A *Reagan family*   C. *Garfield family*

B. *Franklin D Roosevelt family*   D. *Ford family*

3. Which Presidential family had an alligator given to them by the Marquis de Lafayette?

A. *Washington's family*   C. *J.Q. Adam's family*

B. *Jefferson's family*   D. *Madison's family*

4. Which First Family had 2 Portuguese water dogs, one named Bo and the other named Sunny?

A Lyndon B Johnson family

C. Coolidge family

B. Obama family

D. Carter family

5. Which Presidential family had sheep that grazed on the White House lawn?

A. Family of Woodrow Wilson

C. Family of F.D. Roosevelt

B. Family of Theodore Roosevelt

D. Family of William H. Taft

6. Which president kept a goat named Old Whiskers who pulled his grandchildren around in a cart?

A. Abraham Lincoln

C. John Tyler

B. Benjamin Harrison

D. George Washington

7. Which First Daughter had a pet green garter snake named Emily Spinach she often wore draped around her neck?

A. Margaret Truman

C. Alice Roosevelt

B. Ivanka Trump

D. Malia Trump

8. Which First Son had a pet kangaroo rat that would hop across the table to the president to be fed a lump of sugar?

A. John F Kennedy, Jr

C. Allan Hoover

B. Kermit Roosevelt

D. Cal Coolidge, Jr

9. Abraham Lincoln promised his young sons ponies if he won the presidency, which presidential hopeful promised his daughters a dog if

he won; and he did?

A. Richard Nixon   C. Barack Obama

B. Lyndon B Johnson   D. George W Bush

10. Which First Son took his pony Algonquin up in the White House elevator and into the private quarters to cheer up his sick brother when he was recovering from the measles?

A. Fred Grant   C. Russell Harrison

B. Harry Garfield   D. Quentin Roosevelt

11. Which Presidential family was given the gift of two tiger cubs from the Sultan of Oman?

A. Family of M. Van Buren   C. Family of T. Jefferson

B. Family of Z. Taylor   D. Family of A. Johnson

12. Which President's daughter had a pony named Macaroni and she could be seen riding him on the White House lawn?

A. Amy Carter   C. Caroline Kennedy

B. Nellie Grant   D. Mollie Garfield

Answers

Chapter 46– First Family Pets

1. A – Family of Rutherford B. Hayes

The Siamese cat was originally sent to First Lady Lucy Hayes but was a beloved pet of First Daughter Fanny Hayes. Previous to the cat arriving at the White House Siamese cats were regal pets living in the palaces of royalty in Siam (now Thailand) and served as guardians of Buddhist temples. The cat was named Siam by the Hayes family. Other Siamese cats that made their homes in the White House were pets of Amy Carter and Susan Ford.

2. D – Ford family

3. C – John Quincy Adams' family

The alligator lived in a White House bathroom terrorizing many guests.

4. B – Obama family

5. A – Family of Woodrow Wilson

6. B - Benjamin Harrison

* One day the goat while pulling the president's grandson in the cart on the grounds of the White House escaped with the president running down Pennsylvania Avenue chasing the goat and his grandson.*

7. C – Alice Roosevelt

8. B – Kermit Roosevelt

9. C – Barack Obama

10. D – Quentin Roosevelt

11. A – family of Martin Van Buren

* Congress made the president send the tiger cubs to the zoo.*

12. C – Caroline Kennedy

Their daughter, Caroline, rode the pony around the grounds of the White House and was a favorite photographic opportunity of the press.

47

After The White House

Answers are given on page 405.

1. Which First Daughter volunteered for the Red Cross for sixty years?

    A. Ethel Roosevelt   *C. Patsy Washington*

    B. Margaret Wilson   *D. Jenna Bush*

2. Which First Daughter in her old age lived in a shelter for poor women?

    A. Ivanka Trump   *C. Lynda Johnson*

    B. Letty Tyler   *D. Caroline Kennedy*

3. Which First Son took up oil painting after his retirement from the presidency?

    A. George Washington   *C. John Eisenhower*

    B. Thomas Jefferson   *D. George W Bush*

4. Which First Daughter was arrested four times for protesting?

A. *Amy Carter*   C. *Malia Obama*

B. *Chelsea Clinton*   D. *Tiffany Trump*

5. Which First Daughter went to live in India in an ashram and changed her name to Nishta?

A. *Margaret Truman*   C. *Amy Carter*

B. *Margaret Wilson*   D. *Doro Bush*

6. Which First Daughter or First Son lived the longest – to the age of 96?

A. *Eliza Monroe*   C. *Alice Roosevelt*

B. *Caroline Kennedy*   D. *Lynda Johnson*

7. Which First Daughter traveled giving speeches on the topic of women's right to vote?

A. *Eliza Monroe*   C. *Barbara Bush*

B. *Pearl Tyler*   D. *Helen Taft*

8. Which president's children with his second wife were all born, all seven of them, after leaving the White House?

A. *Thomas Jefferson*   C. *John Tyler*

B. *Franklin D Roosevelt*   D. *Grover Cleveland*

9. After his days of the presidency, which president and his son went to Africa to hunt big game and to collect specimens for the Smithsonian?

A. *Theodore Roosevelt & son Kermit*   C. *George H W Bush & son Jeb*

B. *Donald Trump & son Don, Jr*   D. *Abe Lincoln & son Tad*

10. Which First Daughter at the age of fifty graduated from college, finally losing the label of being the only woman in her family in the last three generations without a college degree?

A. *Amy Carter*   C. *Doro Bush*

B. *Jessie Wilson*   D. *Luci Johnson*

11. After the death of this president's illegitimate daughter it was proven by DNA that she was indeed the daughter of the president. Who was the president?

A. *Bill Clinton*   C. *Lyndon B Johnson*

B. *Warren Harding*   D. *John F Kennedy*

12. Which First Daughter was alive during the administrations of Benjamin Harrison through Jimmy Carter?

A. *Ruth Cleveland*   C. *Alice Roosevelt*

B. *Mollie Garfield*   D. *Caroline Kennedy*

Answers

Chapter 47 — After The White House

1. A – Ethel Roosevelt

2. B – Letty Tyler

3. D – George W Bush

4. A – Amy Carter

5. B – Margaret Wilson

6. C – Alice Roosevelt

7. D – Helen Taft

8. C – John Tyler

9. A. Theodore Roosevelt & son Kermit

10. D – Luci Johnson

11. B – Warren Harding

12. C – Alice Roosevelt

48

Sickness & Death

Answers are given on page 409.

1. Which president's son was close to three presidential assassinations?

   A. Robert Lincoln   C. Elliott Roosevelt

   B. Hal Garfield   D. Charles Roosevelt

2. Which First Daughter was in a gym exercising when she went into sudden cardiac arrest with no previous knowledge of heart problems at the age of fifty-three? Her life was saved by a surgeon who was at the gym who was able to shock her back with an automated external defibrillator.

   A. Luci Johnson   C. Caroline Kennedy

   B. Doro Bush   D. Susan Ford

3. Who was the 1ˢᵗ First Daughter to die of breast cancer?

   A. Knoxie Taylor   C. Nabby Adams

   B. Eliza Monroe   D. Susan Ford

4. Which First Son developed a blister after a day on the tennis courts at the White House and died from blood poisioning?

    A. Cal Coolidge, Jr   *C. Robert Taft*

    B. Willie Lincoln   *D. Kermit Roosevelt*

5. Which First Son was diagnosed with tuberculosis and had to convalesce in a sanatorium for a year?

    A. George Adams   *C. Lachian Tyler*

    B. Herbert Hoover, Jr   *D. Benjamin Pierce*

6. Which president's son died in a plane crash, a plane he himself was piloting?

    A. Michael Reagan   *C. Marvin Bush*

    B. Steve Ford   *D. John Kennedy, Jr*

7. Two of which president's sons were with him when he was assassinated?

    A. Abraham Lincoln   *C. James Garfield*

    B. William McKinley   *D. Gerald Ford*

8. Which First Son shot himself committing suicide?

    A. Kermit Roosevelt   *C. Jeff Carter*

    B. Franklin Roosevelt, Jr   *D. Payne Madison*

9. Which president-elect's son was killed in a train accident two months

before his father's inauguration?

A. *Willie Lincoln*

C. *Charles Adams*

B. *Benjamin Pierce*

D. *Andrew Johnson, Jr*

10. Which First Son was the 1st First Family member to die in the White House?

A. *Willie Lincoln*

C. *Patrick Kennedy*

B. *Peter Jefferson*

D. *Cal Coolidge, Jr*

Answers

Chapter 48 – Sickness & Death

1. A – Robert Lincoln

2. D – Susan Ford

3. C – Nabby Adams

4. A – Cal Coolidge, Jr

5. B – Herbert Hoover, Jr

6. D – John Kennedy, Jr

7. C - James Garfield

8. A – Kermit Roosevelt

9. B – Benjamin Pierce

10. A – Willie Lincoln

Thank you for choosing 'The Presidents, First Ladies, & First Family Trivia.' I hope you enjoyed testing your trivia knowledge and maybe even learned something about the Presidents, First Ladies , and First Family and the history of the times during their administrations.

I would appreciate it if you would take the time to leave feedback to let other readers know what you thought about the book.

If you are interested in learning more about the First Family members, or children of the presidents, read the fascinating stories of their lives in 'Children of the Presidents.'

Thank you,

Cheryl Pryor

www.ingramcontent.com/pod-product-compliance
Lightning Source LLC
Chambersburg PA
CBHW071402090426
42737CB00011B/1321